THE GREATEST MOVIES OF ALL TIME

2ND EDITION

CONTENTS

PREFACE

Congratulations. You have in your hands a comprehensive guide to the greatest movies made from 1915 to 1990.

This new, expanded Second Edition features over 825 movies – 180 more than our previous edition. The Greatest Movies of All Time is published to help you select and enjoy great movies from the past as well as recent hits.

Your guidebook also spotlights Academy Award winners and nominees. The first Oscars were awarded in overlapping periods beginning in the late 1920's, which coincides with the release of the first talking picture, THE JAZZ SINGER. Starting in 1934, Oscars have been awarded every year, so your book provides listings for each year from 1934 to 1990.

In addition, you'll find many other great movies in these pages – classics, comedy, drama, mystery, adventure, westerns, musicals, science fiction and more. So, go ahead, browse through your book. Discover great movies you enjoyed as a child which you'll want to re-enjoy now. Or great movies you've always wanted to see but haven't.

Your book features a huge selection. We have indicated movies not yet available on video as we went to press. But please check with us regularly. Because your BLOCKBUSTER Video® store brings you many movie classics as soon as they are released on video.

That's just one of many differences you'll discover at your neighborhood BLOCKBUSTER Video store.

HOW TO GET THE MOST FROM YOUR GUIDE

The Greatest Movies of All Time, Second Edition, is a bigger, better, easy to use guide to selecting movies you'll enjoy.

It is organized chronologically by year. Each year lists Academy Award nominees and major winners – Best Picture, Best Actor, Actress, Director and Screenplay as well as other categories. For every movie listed, your guide provides at a glance:

- Titles
- BLOCKBUSTER movie categories
- Major stars
- Directors
- Thorough but brief summaries
- Oscar nominees and winners

See you soon at BLOCKBUSTER Video, America's Family Video Store.™

1915
The Birth of a Nation
BLOCKBUSTER CATEGORY: Silent
STARRING: Lillian Gish, Mae Marsh, Henry B. Walthall
DIRECTED BY: D.W. Griffith

This sprawling Civil War melodrama, made by the greatest director of the silent era, is the first true epic in movie history. The saga of the war and its devastating aftermath is related through the experiences of two families. Memorable images abound: Battle scenes employing thousands of extras, the poignant homecoming of a broken Confederate colonel, a frightening raid by the Ku Klux Klan. The movie stirred controversy in its day because Griffith, a Southerner, did not depict the Klan as harshly as audiences expected.

1916
Intolerance
BLOCKBUSTER CATEGORY: Silent
STARRING: Lillian Gish, Robert Harron, Mae Marsh
DIRECTED BY: D.W. Griffith

Griffith, director of THE BIRTH OF A NATION - the GONE WITH THE WIND of its day - followed it up with this multi-part historical epic on the theme of "man's inhumanity to man." The four storylines range from a modern soap opera to the movie's centerpiece, an eye-popping Biblical spectacle climaxed by the fall of Babylon. That battle sequence alone, with its swordfights, flamethrowing catapults, and exotic tortures, set the standard by which all such films would be measured.

1922
Nosferatu
BLOCKBUSTER CATEGORY: Silent
STARRING: Max Schreck, Alexander Granach, Greta Schroeder
DIRECTED BY: F. W. Murnau

This frightening German film is the screen's first adaptation of DRACULA, and it still packs a wallop. When a young realtor is sent to Transylvania to arrange the sale of some property in Bremen, he finds that the prospective buyer, Count Dracula, is a vampire intent on spreading his scourge through central Europe. In contrast to the suave Draculas enacted by Bela Lugosi and Christopher Lee, this film's count - portrayed by cadaverously thin stage actor Max Schreck - is a hideous embodiment of pestilence, who is followed to Bremen by hordes of rats and an outbreak of plague. The film's title is a Slavic word meaning "undead."

1926
Metropolis
BLOCKBUSTER CATEGORY: Silent
STARRING: Brigitte Helm, Alfred Abel,
Rudolph Klein-Rogge
DIRECTED BY: Fritz Lang

The greatest science fiction movie of the silent era, this classic German film centers on the growing strife between an oppressed working class and the idle rich who exploit them in a futuristic society. The movie's hero is the son of the leader of the ruling class, its villain a mad scientist who creates a breathtaking female robot in a frightening sequence that foreshadows FRANKENSTEIN. The film's special effects and depictions of the future are still impressive.

The Crowd

BLOCKBUSTER CATEGORY: Silent
STARRING: James Murray, Eleanor Boardman,
Bert Roach, Estelle Clark
DIRECTED BY: King Vidor

In this abstract silent film, a must-see, a man becomes lost in the crush of daily living. Vidor excelled as the film's director and received an Oscar nomination. Murray, Boardman, Roach and Clark all gave attention-getting performances worthy of special recognition. Oscar-nominated for Best Artistic Quality of Production and Director. Registered as a national treasure with the Library of Congress.

The General

BLOCKBUSTER CATEGORY: Silent
STARRING: Buster Keaton, Marion Mack, Jim Farley
DIRECTED BY: Buster Keaton

Keaton's incomparable comic genius and one of Hollywood's greatest chase scenes combine to make this a true masterpiece of the silent film era. Yankees steal the grand locomotive, "The General," with Mack aboard. Her boyfriend, Confederate army engineer Keaton, will not give up his chase until he wins back his girl *and* his train - even though it means chasing both right through Union lines. Hilarious sight gags abound, backdropped by remarkable location photography reminiscent of Matthew Brady's work. Registered as a national treasure with the Library of Congress.

The Jazz Singer

BLOCKBUSTER CATEGORY: Classics
STARRING: Al Jolson, Warner Oland, May McAvoy
DIRECTED BY: Alan Crosland

In the film that brought movies into the age of sound, Jolson offers a forceful performance as a cantor's son. Much to his father's chagrin, he forfeits a career as cantor to become a star on the stage. Remade with Danny Thomas in 1953 and again with Neil Diamond in 1980. For a comic look at Hollywood's reaction to this pioneering sound achievement, see SINGIN' IN THE RAIN (1952). Only partial sound.
OSCAR WIN: *Special award for its innovative use of sound*

The Last Command

BLOCKBUSTER CATEGORY: Silent
STARRING: Emil Jannings, Evelyn Brent, William Powell
DIRECTED BY: Josef von Sternberg

An arrogant Russian general (Jannings) finds his way to Hollywood after the great revolution, and is cast as (what else?) an arrogant Russian general. Hailed for its plot, the silent film won Jannings the first Oscar for Best Actor. Director Josef von Sternberg was also lauded for his excellence. Two years later, Jannings again played a likely victim for humiliation in THE BLUE ANGEL. Oscar-nominated for Best Production.
OSCAR WIN: *Best Actor (Jannings)*

1927-1928

==

Pandora's Box
BLOCKBUSTER CATEGORY: Foreign
STARRING: Louise Brooks, Franz (Francis) Lederer, Fritz Kortner
DIRECTED BY: G.W. Pabst
American actress Brooks lights up this fatalistic story with the radiance only a star can deliver as a girl with frail standards who slides from promiscuity into prostitution, eventually attracting the attention of Jack the Ripper. Silent on screen; explosive to watch. In recent years, Brooks has been deservedly rediscovered as the ultimate 20's vamp. Pabst also deserved adulation for his incisive directing.

The Passion of Joan of Arc
BLOCKBUSTER CATEGORY: Not available on video
STARRING: Falconetti, Eugene Sylvain, Andre Berley,
Michael Simon
DIRECTED BY: Carl Theodor Dreyer
The last days of St. Joan's life, including her trial, are depicted by French film great Falconetti. Using actual transcripts from the trial for a script, as well as dramatic close-ups, the director was able to realistically recreate Joan's suffering and her devotion to her beliefs. Church interrogations and her punishment at the stake are vividly portrayed.

Seventh Heaven
BLOCKBUSTER CATEGORY: Not available on video
STARRING: Janet Gaynor, Charles Farrell, David Butler,
Ben Bard
DIRECTED BY: Frank Borzage
The place: Paris. The time: Prior to and during World War I. A Parisian waif (Gaynor) is victimized by her unscrupulous lover, but redeemed by the love of Chico, an honest sanitation worker. As screen romances go, this one is about the most famous. Gaynor received the Best Actress Oscar for her collective work in 1927-1928, including her stand-out performance in SEVENTH HEAVEN, plus STREET ANGEL and SUNRISE. Oscar-nominated for Best Production.
OSCAR WINS: *Best Director (Borzage), Actress (Gaynor), Best Writing-adapted (Benjamin Glazer), Interior Decoration*

Sunrise
BLOCKBUSTER CATEGORY: Not available on video
STARRING: George O'Brien, Janet Gaynor, Bodil Rosing,
Margaret Livingston
DIRECTED BY: F.W. Murnau
Dynamic photography floods the screen, imbuing this classic with a magical quality. Desire and redemption are explored in the poignant tale about a farmer who strays from his true love when a city-wise seductress wants him to get rid of his wife. The ending is happily-ever-after. Great German director Murnau constructed mammoth settings and used expressionistic lighting techniques to enhance the deceptively simple story. Registered as a national treasure with the Library of Congress. Oscar-nominated for Best Interior Decoration.
OSCAR WINS: *Best Artistic Quality of Production, Actress (Gaynor, also cited in 1927-1928 Awards for SEVENTH HEAVEN and STREET ANGEL), Cinematography.*

==

Two Arabian Nights

BLOCKBUSTER CATEGORY: Not available on video
STARRING: William Boyd, Mary Astor, Louis Wolheim,
                    Michael Vavitch
DIRECTED BY: Lewis Milestone

Two fighting American soldiers, comedically portrayed by Boyd and Wolheim, escape from the Germans during World War I by posing as unlikely Arabs. Their destination is Jaffe, where they become rivals for an Arabian girl (Astor). Milestone's award for Comedy Direction was the only such award given.
OSCAR WIN: *Best Comedy Direction (Milestone)*

The Way of All Flesh

BLOCKBUSTER CATEGORY: Not available on video
STARRING: Emil Jannings, Belle Bennett, Phyllis Haver,
                    Donald Keith
DIRECTED BY: Victor Fleming

Jannings' first American feature is also one of the two films for which he won an Oscar (THE LAST COMMAND was the other). It shows him as an aging German-American bank cashier who becomes a vagrant after an unexpected run-in with a seductress on a train. She steals the bank bonds he is carrying for his employer, triggering his downfall. Oscar-nominated for Best Production.
OSCAR WIN: *Best Actor (Jannings)*

Wings

BLOCKBUSTER CATEGORY: Silent
STARRING: Clara Bow, Charles "Buddy" Rogers, Richard Arlen,
                    Gary Cooper
DIRECTED BY: William A. Wellman

Actions speak louder than words in the first Oscar-winner for Best Production. Two American pilots (Rogers and Arlen) compete for the affections of a small-town girl, played to the hilt by Bow. Wellman's riveting action sequences, both in the air and on the ground, and some of the best aerial photography turn this World War I aviation story into one of the most exciting silent adventure dramas. Cooper makes a brief appearance, but a lasting impression; Bow goes to Europe as a driver to be close to her boyfriend. In addition to being the first Oscar winner, the film was the only non-speaking picture to win the award.
OSCAR WINS: *Best Production, Best Engineering Effects*

Alibi

BLOCKBUSTER CATEGORY: Not available on video
STARRING: Chester Morris, Eleanor Griffith,
Regis Toomey, Mae Busch
DIRECTED BY: Roland West

An ex-con woos an wins a policeman's daughter, drawing her into his convoluted murder scheme. New and imaginative filmmaking techniques are evidenced in this forerunner talkie. Morris, Griffith, Toomey and Busch all provide viewers with quality performances hard to match. Oscar-nominated for Best Production and Best Actor (Morris).

Broadway Melody

BLOCKBUSTER CATEGORY: Musicals
STARRING: Bessie Love, Anita Page, Charles King, Jed Prouty,
Kenneth Thompson
DIRECTED BY: Harry Beaumont

The first full-length musical that had it all - talking, singing and dancing! This MGM smash hit included such memorable songs as "Give My Regards to Broadway," "You Were Meant For Me" and a big two-color Technicolor production number, "Wedding Of The Painted Doll." King plays the amorous songwriter who spoils the show biz act of Love and Page. They learn, however, to put their personal problems behind them when the curtain goes up. Oscar-nominated for Best Actress (Love).
OSCAR WIN: *Best Production*

The Cocoanuts

BLOCKBUSTER CATEGORY: Comedy
STARRING: The Marx Brothers, Kay Francis
DIRECTED BY: Joseph Santley and Robert Florey

The Marx Brothers take over a Florida resort hotel and total chaos results. This early talkie is more polished than most - it's based on a stage success by the Marx boys, and they had each routine perfected long before the cameras rolled.

Coquette

BLOCKBUSTER CATEGORY: Not available on video
STARRING: Mary Pickford
DIRECTED BY: Sam Taylor

The love affair between a cold-hearted Southern belle and a rough-hewn mountain man ends in tragedy. Pickford's inspired acting won her an Oscar. The title song, "Coquette," was provided by composer Irving Berlin.
OSCAR WIN: *Best Actress (Pickford)*

The Divine Lady

BLOCKBUSTER CATEGORY: Not available on video
STARRING: Corinne Griffith, Victor Varconi, H.B. Warner,
Ian Keith
DIRECTED BY: Frank Lloyd

How does a lower-class woman achieve a higher station in life? One easy path is by marrying the British Ambassador at the Court of Naples. How does this same

woman become notorious? By also loving Horatio Nelson, Britan's greatest hero. Corinne Griffith is Emma Hamilton, the lady with a fickle fancy. Victor Varconi is Nelson and Warner is Sir William Hamilton. Oscar-nominated for Best Cinematography.
OSCAR WIN: *Best Director (Lloyd)*

The Hollywood Revue of 1929
BLOCKBUSTER CATEGORY: Not available on video
STARRING: Jack Benny, Conrad Nagel, Joan Crawford,
                  Buster Keaton, John Gilbert, Norma Shearer,
                  Marion Davies, Laurel & Hardy
DIRECTED BY: Charles Riesner
This all-star review features some of the greatest names in Hollywood. Charles Riesner directs 130 minutes of first-rate entertainment - a cavalcade of legendary talent. Oscar-nominated for Best Production and Interior Decoration.

In Old Arizona
BLOCKBUSTER CATEGORY: Not available on video
STARRING: Edmund Lowe, Warner Baxter, Dorothy Burgess,
                  J. Farrell MacDonald
DIRECTED BY: Raoul Walsh and Irving Cummings
Another incarnation of the notorious Cisco Kid, brought to life by Baxter in an Academy Award-winning performance. The bandit manages to stay one step ahead of the law as he robs Wells Fargo, but moves dangerously close to death as he becomes infatuated with a double-dealing Mexican girl (Burgess). Oscar-nominated for Best Production.
OSCAR WIN: *Best Actor (Baxter)*

Madame X
BLOCKBUSTER CATEGORY: Not available on video
STARRING: Ruth Chatterton, Raymond Hackett, Sidney Taylor
DIRECTED BY: Lionel Barrymore
Filmed several times as a silent picture, this early talkie delivers compelling drama. It's about a woman whose personal mistakes force her to sacrifice herself to shield her husband and child. It's Chatterton's show as she falls into a pattern of sexual escape and heavy drinking after her mother-in-law stages her "death" to avoid a scandal. Oscar-nominated for Best Actress (Chatterton) and Director (Barrymore).

Our Dancing Daughters
BLOCKBUSTER CATEGORY: Not available on video
STARRING: Joan Crawford, Johnny Mack Brown,
                  Dorothy Sebastian, Anita Page
DIRECTED BY: Harry Beaumont
A wild young socialite ultimately succeeds because she's in control, but her friend isn't and falls to her death while drunk. Joan Crawford's notorious dance in her underwear in this film grabbed the viewing public's attention and swept her into stardom. Critics consider Beaumont's work of art an explosive portrait of its time. Oscar-nominated for Best Screenplay (Lovett) and Cinematography.

The Patriot

BLOCKBUSTER CATEGORY: Not available on video
STARRING: Emil Jannings, Florence Vidor, Lewis Stone, Vera Voronina
DIRECTED BY: Ernst Lubitsch

Deadly plots to oust Czar Paul the First from power end in the downfall of the 18th century Russian dictator. Jannings drew deserved praise as the ruler who finally meets an untimely death. Oscar-nominated for Best Production, Actor (Stone) and Interior Decoration.

OSCAR WINS: *Best Writing Achievement (Hans Kraly), Director (Lubitsch)*

White Shadows in the South Seas

BLOCKBUSTER CATEGORY: Not available on video
STARRING: Monte Blue, Raquel Torres, Robert Anderson
DIRECTED BY: W.S. Van Dyke II

The first MGM sound film (with synchronized sound effects and music) portrays an alcoholic doctor (Blue) who attempts to protect a tribe of natives in the South Seas from the chicanery of an unprincipled trader (Anderson). Torres convincingly co-stars as a native girl. The movie was magnificently filmed entirely on location in the Marquesas Islands.

OSCAR WIN: *Best Cinematography*

All Quiet on the Western Front
BLOCKBUSTER CATEGORY: Classics
STARRING: Lew Ayres, Louis Wolheim, John Wray,
　　　　　　Raymond Griffith
DIRECTED BY: Lewis Milestone
The experiences of a group of German schoolboys are revealed in this
stunning anti-war movie, based on Erich Maria Remarque's novel. During World
War I, they volunteer to serve their country, only to find their illusions of glory
bitterly shattered at the front. Oscar-nominated for Best Writing Achievement
(George Abbott, Maxwell Anderson and Dell Andrews) and Cinematography.
OSCAR WINS: Best Production, Director (Milestone)

Anna Christie
BLOCKBUSTER CATEGORY: Classics
STARRING: Greta Garbo, Charles Bickford, Marie Dressler
DIRECTED BY: Clarence Brown
Garbo's "Gif me a viskey, baby" line marked her first spoken words on film and is
almost as well-remembered as the chanted phrase, "that old debbil sea," in the film
adaptation of Eugene O'Neill's play. Garbo and the rest of the legendary cast
defined screen acting at that time. Oscar-nominated for Best Actress (Garbo),
Director (Brown) and Cinematography.

The Big House
BLOCKBUSTER CATEGORY: Not available on video
STARRING: Chester Morris, Wallace Beery, Lewis Stone,
　　　　　　Robert Montgomery
DIRECTED BY: George Hill
Beery is enthralling as a condemned convict in one of the most searing and realistic
of the early prison pictures. Montgomery is equally superb as a scared informer.
Oscar-nominated for Best Production.
OSCAR WINS: *Best Writing Achievement (Frances Marion), Sound Recording (the
first time this category was recognized)*

Bulldog Drummond
BLOCKBUSTER CATEGORY: Mystery/Suspense
STARRING: Ronald Colman, Joan Bennett, Lilyan Tashman
DIRECTED BY: F. Richard Jones
Colman's smooth, mesmerizing voice and urbane manner bring sound and
animation to the Bulldog Drummond of the printed page. The actor made the role
all his own on screen and became a star. Bulldog comes to the rescue of a lady
whose uncle has been kidnapped by phony psychiatrists. Followed by several
sequels. Oscar-nominated for Best Actor (Colman) and Interior Decoration.

The Devil's Holiday
BLOCKBUSTER CATEGORY: Not available on video
STARRING: Nancy Carroll, Phillips Homes, Morgan Farley,
　　　　　　Paul Lukas, Zasu Pitts, Morton Downey, Sr.
DIRECTED BY: Edmund Goulding

1929-1930

Carroll won her first starring role when Jeanne Eagels, the film's original star, died of a drug overdose. Hallie Hobert is a manipulative manicurist who schemes to marry David Stone (Holmes) for a ticket to easy street. When her conscience begins to take over, the movie becomes a thought-provoking endeavor. Oscar-nominated for Best Actress (Carroll).

Disraeli
BLOCKBUSTER CATEGORY: Not available on video
STARRING: George Arliss, Joan Bennett
DIRECTED BY: Alfred E. Green
Prime Minister Benjamin Disraeli (Arliss) hampers a group of Russian agents and, at the same time, raises money to purchase the Suez Canal. For his first performance in a movie with sound (at 61 years old), he recreates the role he played silently nine years earlier. Another first: he became the first British actor in an American film to win a Best Actor Oscar. The movie was Oscar-nominated for Best Production.
OSCAR WIN: *Best Actor (Arliss)*

The Divorcee
BLOCKBUSTER CATEGORY: Classics
STARRING: Norma Shearer, Chester Morris, Robert Montgomery
DIRECTED BY: Robert Z. Leonard
Shearer had a talent for playing on-screen wayward wives. In this film, she discards her philandering husband and decides to give the adventurous "single" life a whirl. Oscar-nominated for Best Production and Writing Achievement (Julian Josephson).
OSCAR WIN: *Best Actress (Shearer)*

The King of Jazz
BLOCKBUSTER CATEGORY: Musicals
STARRING: Bing Crosby, Paul Whiteman
DIRECTED BY: John Murray Anderson
A splashy Bing Crosby musical, notable for its early two-color Technicolor photography. There are plenty of sight gags and vaudeville-type scenarios, highlighted by Gershwin's "Rhapsody in Blue," and plenty of lavish production numbers. You'll also enjoy a short animation interlude, tossed in as a special bonus. They just don't make them like this anymore.
OSCAR WIN: *Best Interior Decoration (Herman Rosse)*

The Love Parade
BLOCKBUSTER CATEGORY: Not available on video
STARRING: Maurice Chevalier, Jeanette MacDonald, Lillian Roth
DIRECTED BY: Ernst Lubitsch
The stars toy with each other before falling in step with their "love parade" in this effervescent musical. Lubitsch charms audiences with his skillful direction; Chevalier puts his best foot forward, with the same style and charm of his role in GIGI. Oscar-nominated for Best Production, Actor (Chevalier), Director (Lubitsch), Cinematography, Interior Decoration and Sound Recording.

Raffles

BLOCKBUSTER CATEGORY: Not available on video
STARRING: Ronald Colman, George Fitzmaurice, Kay Francis,
Bramwell Fletcher
DIRECTED BY: Harry D'Arrast

A lighthearted comedy that promises fun for all! Follow the adventures of the wily
gentleman thief who constantly evades capture by Scotland Yard. Colman is perfect
as the amateur cracksman and a hard act to follow for David Niven who portrays the
same character in the 1940 remake. Excellent screenplay based on the novel by E.W.
Hornung. Oscar-nominated for Best Actor (Colman), Sound Recording and Interior
Decoration.

The Big Trail

BLOCKBUSTER CATEGORY: Westerns
STARRING: John Wayne, Marguerite Churchill, Tully Marshall
DIRECTED BY: Raoul Walsh
Pioneers on the first great wagon train face countless perils as they blaze a trail westward. Remarkably ambitious early western, shot entirely on location, retains much of its original power. John Wayne's first starring role.

The Blue Angel

BLOCKBUSTER CATEGORY: Foreign
STARRING: Marlene Dietrich, Emil Jannings
DIRECTED BY: Josef von Sternberg
An aura of decadence is created on-screen with the help of von Sternberg and Dietrich. Jannings is the professor who wants to protect his students from nightclub singer Dietrich and ends up needing protection himself from her charms. The professor is so emotionally unstable, however, that his first sexual encounter with her results in total destruction. Dietrich's performance led to her European stardom and a legendary invitation to Hollywood. In German and English.

Cimarron

BLOCKBUSTER CATEGORY: Westerns
STARRING: Richard Dix, Irene Dunne, Estelle Taylor
DIRECTED BY: Wesley Ruggles
Meet a wild product of the Old West (Dix) and his more genteel wife (Dunne) - the Cravat family - as they face the Oklahoma prairie and home on the range with all its challenges. Based on Edna Ferber's novel. This is the only western that won a Best Film Academy Award. Oscar-nominated for Best Actress (Dunne), Actor (Dix), Director (Ruggles) and Cinematography. This is the better known re-make.
OSCAR WINS: *Best Picture, Writing - adaptation (Howard Estabrook), Interior Decoration.*

City Lights

BLOCKBUSTER CATEGORY: Classics
STARRING: Charlie Chaplin, Virginia Cherrill, Florence Lee
DIRECTED BY: Charles Chaplin
Truly one of the most notable works in the history of filmmaking by one of the film's greatest comedians and the last of Chaplin's totally silent films. In this moving and marvelously funny movie, the "Little Tramp" falls in love with a blind flower girl and raises money for the operation needed to restore her vision. Chaplin wears three hats, as writer, director and star.

The Dawn Patrol

BLOCKBUSTER CATEGORY: Classics
STARRING: Richard Barthelmess, Douglas Fairbanks, Jr., Neil
Hamilton, William Hanney
DIRECTED BY: Howard Hawks
In France during World War I, flying officers wait their turn to leave on missions

from which they may not return. An exceptional cast of characters and gripping
dialogue made this early talkie effective for its day. Much of the aerial footage was
re-used in other films to follow.
OSCAR WIN: *Best Original Story (Saunders)*

A Free Soul

BLOCKBUSTER CATEGORY: Classics
STARRING: Norma Shearer, Clark Gable, Lionel Barrymore,
         Leslie Howard, James Gleason
DIRECTED BY: Clarence Brown
What could be more enjoyable and entertaining than watching Gable in an early
performance, play a mobster with sexual affections for the daughter of a boozing
attorney. This frank courtroom drama, considered shocking in the 30's, is based on
the memoirs of Adela Rogers St. John. A tamer remake can be seen in THE GIRL
WHO HAD EVERYTHING (1953). Oscar-nominated for Best Director (Brown) and
Actress (Shearer).
OSCAR WIN: *Best Actor (Barrymore)*

The Front Page

BLOCKBUSTER CATEGORY: Classics
STARRING: Pat O'Brien, Adolphe Menjou, Frank McHugh,
         Edward Everett Horton, Mary Brian
DIRECTED BY: Lewis Milestone
Stop the presses! This film's a hit! The Chicago newspaper world comes to life in an
upbeat way. Fast and funny is the action, and animated is the dialogue between
warring reporter O'Brien and editor Menjou as they battle journalistic ethics in this
masterpiece. Fantastic filmmaking and enhanced by a cast of pros. Remade, with a
sex change, as HIS GIRL FRIDAY (1940), as THE FRONT PAGE (1974), and again
as SWITCHING CHANNELS (1988). Oscar-nominated for Best Picture, Actor
(Menjou) and Director (Milestone).

Min and Bill

BLOCKBUSTER CATEGORY: Classics
STARRING: Marie Dressler, Wallace Beery
DIRECTED BY: George Hill
High impact is the perfect term to describe this early sound film. Dressler and
Beery team up to play determined, rough-and-tumble waterfront locals who try to
stop authorities from taking Marie's daughter away to a "proper" home.
OSCAR WIN: *Best Actress (Dressler)*

Public Enemy

BLOCKBUSTER CATEGORY: Classics
STARRING: James Cagney, Jean Harlow, Joan Blondell,
         Beryl Mercer, Mae Clarke
DIRECTED BY: William A. Wellman
Cagney dominates the screen in a larger-than-life portrayal of an Irish gangster. In
addition to a first-rate cast that includes such heavies as Harlow and Blondell,
Cagney and Clarke's legendary "grapefruit scene" will continue to make this film
memorable. Wellman also makes this picture worth watching. Oscar-nominated for
Best Original Story (John Bright and Kubec Glasman).

1930-1931

Skippy

BLOCKBUSTER CATEGORY: Not available on video
STARRING: Jackie Cooper, Robert Coogan, Mitzi Green
DIRECTED BY: Norman Taurog

Taurog demonstrates his directorial expertise in this film about the mischievous young son (Cooper, whose role made him a star) of a local health official who goes "slumming" for friends. Great family entertainment is guaranteed. Oscar-nominated for Best Picture, Actor (Cooper) and Writing - adapted (Joseph L. Mankiewicz and Sam Mintz).
OSCAR WIN: *Best Director (Taurog)*

Tabu

BLOCKBUSTER CATEGORY: Not available on video
STARRING: Matahi and Bill Banbridge
DIRECTED BY: F.W. Murnau and Robert Flaherty

There's trouble in paradise! A romantic story of young Polynesian lovers who challenge an age-old tabu of their tribe in a visually exotic movie made by two very different talents - German director F.W. Murnau (who financed and directed the major part of the picture) and Robert J. Flaherty, the documentary filmmaker responsible for such greats as NANOOK OF THE NORTH (1922) and MOANA (1925). Filmed in Tahiti and Bora Bora with a local, non-professional cast.
OSCAR WIN: *Best Cinematography (Floyd Crosby)*

13

Arrowsmith

BLOCKBUSTER CATEGORY: Classics
STARRING: Ronald Colman, Helen Hayes, Myrna Loy
DIRECTED BY: John Ford

Colman's first bid for serious-actor status was this solid winner based on Sinclair Lewis' novel. Colman plays an idealistic researcher who tries to remain true to his ethics as a doctor, despite personal tribulations and temptations. Loy essays an early role as a vampish rich girl and Hayes is the pure wife. Ford's direction is sensitive and compelling. Oscar-nominated for Best Picture.

Bad Girl

BLOCKBUSTER CATEGORY: Not available on video
STARRING: Sally Eilers, James Dunn
DIRECTED BY: Frank Borzage

A simple story, the hardships of a young couple when the wife unexpectedly gets pregnant, gets an extremely sensitive treatment from director Borzage, a pioneering filmmaker of realistic themes. Oscar-nominated for Best Picture.
OSCAR WIN: *Best Director (Borzage) and Writing - adapted (Edwin Burke)*

Blonde Venus

BLOCKBUSTER CATEGORY: Classics
STARRING: Marlene Dietrich, Cary Grant, Herbert Marshall,
　　　　　　　Dickie Moore
DIRECTED BY: Joseph von Sternberg

Dietrich singing "Hot Voodoo" in a gorilla suit is only one of the supreme oddities in director von Sternberg's sumptuous camp classic. Dietrich is a loving mother who sells herself to nightclub owner Grant in order to pay for her scientist husband's medical bills. The emphasis is on decor, fancy camera work, glamour, and - most of all - Dietrich's seductive star power. She and von Sternberg had teamed up the same year on the equally bizarre SCARLET EMPRESS, the earlier THE BLUE ANGEL (1930) and MOROCCO (1930), among others.

The Champ

BLOCKBUSTER CATEGORY: Classics
STARRING: Wallace Beery, Jackie Cooper, Irene Rich
DIRECTED BY: King Vidor

A master director does it again, this time with the tearjerking story of a down-and-out boxer and his sensitive son, who are threatened with separation when the wife (Rich) who abandoned them returns for the boy. The film continued the success of child actor Cooper and won Beery an Oscar (in a tie with Fredric March for DR. JEKYLL AND MR. HYDE). Remade as the THE CLOWN in 1953 with Red Skelton and THE CHAMP in 1979 with Jon Voight and Faye Dunaway. Oscar-nominated for Best Picture and Director.
OSCAR WINS: *Best Actor (Beery), Original Story (Frances Marion)*

Dracula

BLOCKBUSTER CATEGORY: Horror
STARRING: Bela Lugosi, David Manners, Helen Chandler
DIRECTED BY: Tod Browning

This first great horror movie of the sound era, with Bela Lugosi recreating his stage role as Transylvania's most famous nobleman, set the standard for decades of vampire movies. Count Dracula migrates from his crumbling castle to fogbound London, where he bleeds the city dry until he runs afoul of vampire-hunter Van Helsing. The opening sequences in Castle Dracula, and on the ship bound for London, are among the creepiest ever filmed.

Dr. Jekyll and Mr. Hyde

BLOCKBUSTER CATEGORY: Classics
STARRING: Fredric March, Miriam Hopkins, Rose Hobart
DIRECTED BY: Rouben Mamoulian

The first and best sound remake of Robert Louis Stevenson's classic story about the doctor whose serum causes him to develop a monstrous split personality. March handles his dual role superbly, and Hopkins is perfect as the victim of the sinister Mr. Hyde. Mamoulian's inventive use of photographic and editing effects greatly enhances the terror. Oscar-nominated for Best Writing - adapted (Percy Hoffenstein and Samuel Heath)and Cinematography.
OSCAR WIN: *Best Actor (March, in a tie with THE CHAMP's Wallace Beery)*

Frankenstein

BLOCKBUSTER CATEGORY: Classics
STARRING: Boris Karloff, Colin Clive, Mae Clarke
DIRECTED BY: James Whale

Young Elizabeth cannot understand why her fiance, Henry Frankenstein, is too busy to help with their pre-nuptial arrangements. If only she knew: Henry and his deformed assistant are busy stitching a man together from parts of dead bodies. When the brain of a homicidal criminal is implanted into the creature's skull, it turns into Boris Karloff and goes on the most famous rampage in monster movie history. Director James Whale leavens the horror with sardonic humor. This home video version also restores some long-missing footage, including the monster's accidental killing of a village child.

Grand Hotel

BLOCKBUSTER CATEGORY: Classics
STARRING: John Barrymore, Greta Garbo, Lionel Barrymore,
Joan Crawford,Jean Hersholt, Lewis Stone
DIRECTED BY: Edmund Goulding

MGM registered some of its major actors in this adaptation of Vicki Baum's novel and the all-star formula worked so well, it has been used again and again ever since. The great cast (John Barrymore as a thief, Garbo as a ballerina and Crawford as a secretary) perform each of their scenarios to perfection. An appealing, grand-scale production guaranteed to entertain for years to come.
OSCAR WIN: *Best Picture*

Monkey Business

BLOCKBUSTER CATEGORY: Classics
STARRING: The Marx Brothers
DIRECTED BY: Norman Z. McLeod

The four Marx Brothers are stowaways on an ocean liner - attempting, with minimal success, to pass themselves off as members of Parisian society. Somehow, the ship reaches New York harbor with our heros still on board, whereupon they head straight for Long Island and turn upper class society into a shambles. This is the first Marx Brothers vehicle that was written for the screen, and isn't an adaptation of a stage revue. Thelma Todd, an accomplished comic actress in her own series of short films, makes a sexy comic adversary for Groucho.

One Hour with You

BLOCKBUSTER CATEGORY: Not available on video
STARRING: Maurice Chevalier, Jeanette MacDonald, Roland Young
DIRECTED BY: Ernst Lubitsch and George Cukor

Philandering Parisian doctor Chevalier's affairs become public in this light-as-a-souffle musical. Director Lubitsch's famous style, along with Cukor's exceptional direction of the actors, rank this film with the best of early sound musicals. Oscar-nominated for Best Picture.

Red Dust

BLOCKBUSTER CATEGORY: Classics
STARRING: Clark Gable, Jean Harlow, Mary Astor, Gene Raymond
DIRECTED BY: Victor Fleming

Rubber plantation owner Gable's lusty relationship with wisecracking Harlow is put to the test when Astor (the wife of Raymond) comes to visit. Director Fleming's film has an unusually erotic tone, particularly in a love scene between Gable and the virginal (but married) Astor, set in a jungle during a rainstorm. Harlow proves her star power with her looks and ability to direct a sarcastic one-liner at Gable. Remade with Gable by director John Ford as MOGAMBO (1953).

Scarface, the Shame of the Nation

BLOCKBUSTER CATEGORY: Classics
STARRING: Paul Muni, Ann Dvorak, Boris Karloff, George Raft
DIRECTED BY: Howard Hawks

The rise and fall of gangster Tony Camonte (an excellent Muni performance) is detailed in this violent, lightning-paced film, loosely based on Al Capone. Hawks' work placed him in the top of the echelon of crime film directors, and the hints of incest between Tony and his sister gave the movie trouble with censors. A landmark melodrama. Remade with Al Pacino in 1983.

The Sin of Madelon Claudet

BLOCKBUSTER CATEGORY: Classics
STARRING: Helen Hayes, Robert Young, Neil Hamilton, Lewis Stone
DIRECTED BY: Edgar Selwyn

Hayes is the mother of an illegitimate child who is forced to give him up and lose her social standing. This early MADAME X-type soap opera won the queen of the American stage her first Oscar.

OSCAR WIN: *Best Actress (Hayes)*

Cavalcade

BLOCKBUSTER CATEGORY: Not available on video
STARRING: Diana Wynyard, Clive Brook, Una O'Connor
DIRECTED BY: Frank Lloyd
A big budget adaptation of Noel Coward's stage play about the hardships suffered by the Marryot family after World War I and during the Depression. The film is praised for its cynical anti-war attitude, excellent acting and brilliant production design, as well as Lloyd's terse direction. Oscar-nominated for Best Actress (Wynyard).
OSCAR WINS: *Best Picture, Director (Lloyd), Interior Decoration*

A Farewell to Arms

BLOCKBUSTER CATEGORY: Classics
STARRING: Helen Hayes, Gary Cooper
DIRECTED BY: Frank Borzage
Stage and screen great Helen Hayes soars as an English nurse in this magnificent adaptation of Ernest Hemingway's tragic romance. Cooper is the soldier she falls in love with during World War I combat, complete with spectacular scenery and locales. Oscar-nominated for Best Picture.
OSCAR WINS: *Best Cinematography, Sound Recording*

Flying Down to Rio

BLOCKBUSTER CATEGORY: Musicals
STARRING: Dolores Del Rio, Gene Raymond, Raul Roulien
DIRECTED BY: Thornton Freeland
This enduring charmer, a Latin American revue constructed as a series of picture postcards come to life, is packed with such visually stunning set-pieces as a line of chorus girls dancing on the wings of a plane cruising over exotic Rio de Janeiro . But the movie is notable chiefly as the debut vehicle as the dancing team of Fred Astaire and Ginger Rogers, who perform the elaborate number, "The Carioca". Oscar-nominated for Best Song ("The Carioca").

Forty-Second Street

BLOCKBUSTER CATEGORY: Musicals
STARRING: Dick Powell, Ruby Keeler, Warner Baxter,
Una Merkel, Ginger Rogers
DIRECTED BY: Lloyd Bacon
The best and most influential of all 30's backstage musicals. The now-famous plot - a big Broadway musical's leading lady breaks her leg right before opening night and an inexperienced chorus girl has to take her place - and unforgettable music, crackerjack characterizations and Busby Berkeley's inspired choreography make this a walloping treat. This film added a touch of Depression-era realism to its characters, giving them the right amount of desperation for "hoofing it" so hard. This became a big musical on Broadway five decades later. Oscar-nominated for Best Picture and Sound Recording.

I Am a Fugitive from a Chain Gang
BLOCKBUSTER CATEGORY: Classics
STARRING: Paul Muni
DIRECTED BY: Mervyn LeRoy

A searing classic that actually helped to change the prison situations it depicted. Paul Muni is the title character, trapped on a treacherous Southern chain gang where the hellish conditions could, and do, kill many of the imprisoned. Muni is exceptional in the lead and the film so shocked the public that legislation was enacted to clean up the corrupt prison systems shown. The realism in the film set the tone for all expose-style films to follow. Oscar-nominated for Best Picture, Actor (Muni) and Sound Recording.

King Kong
BLOCKBUSTER CATEGORY: Science Fiction
STARRING: Fay Wray, Robert Armstrong, Bruce Cabot
DIRECTED BY: Merian C. Cooper and Ernest B. Schoedsack

Filmmaker Carl Denham (Armstrong) needs a "love interest" for his next nature documentary, so he finds waif Wray and charters a ship to a mysterious island where it's not only the natives who are restless. Willis O'Brien's stop-motion animation brings the giant gorilla Kong and his world vividly to life. The Empire State Building scene is the stuff of legends. Wray is still the standard by which all scream queens are measured, and her "relationship" with Kong has been scrutinized by Freudian scholars for years. A landmark film unequaled since its first appearance.

Little Women
BLOCKBUSTER CATEGORY: Classics
STARRING: Katharine Hepburn, Joan Bennett, Spring Byington, Frances Dee
DIRECTED BY: George Cukor

A perfect Hepburn vehicle and a perfect family film. Louisa May Alcott's story of the March sisters, whose father has gone off to fight in the Civil War, gets a superb screen adaptation. Each of the sisters finds independence and strength, and some find romance. Cukor's incisive direction brings a classic to life. This is considered the very best of the four adaptations (at least) of this story. Oscar-nominated for Best Picture.
OSCAR WIN: *Best Writing - adapted (Victor Heerman and Sarah Y. Mason)*

Love Me Tonight
BLOCKBUSTER CATEGORY: Not available on video
STARRING: Maurice Chevalier, Jeanette MacDonald
DIRECTED BY: Rouben Mamoulian

A lighter-than-air, charming adaptation of Rodgers and Hart's Broadway musical. Chevalier is a Parisian tailor who tries to win the heart of a princess (MacDonald). Mamoulian's effervescent direction and flashy editing techniques were considered innovative in their day and still work wonders for contemporary audiences.

Mata Hari

BLOCKBUSTER CATEGORY: Classics
STARRING: Greta Garbo, Ramon Navarro, Lionel Barrymore
DIRECTED BY: George Fitzmaurice

Greta Garbo portrays the sultry World War I double agent as a woman torn between love and duty. Plenty of suspense as well as the expected, glossy MGM production values, with Garbo's sexy dance sequence a standout.

Morning Glory

BLOCKBUSTER CATEGORY: Classics
STARRING: Katharine Hepburn, Douglas Fairbanks, Jr.,
　　　　　　　Adolphe Menjou
DIRECTED BY: Lowell Sherman

Hepburn's first Oscar was earned for her performance as a headstrong, small-town girl yearning to be an actress in the big city. The story, based on Zoe Atkins' play, is enjoyable, and Hepburn steals the show.
OSCAR WIN: *Best Actress (Hepburn)*

The Mummy

BLOCKBUSTER CATEGORY: Horror
STARRING: Boris Karloff, Zita Johann, David Manners
DIRECTED BY: Karl Freund

The original MUMMY is a shocker totally unlike all the others that followed (in which a bandaged monster stalks his prey). The title creature - a triumph of makeup by Jack Pierce, who created FRANKENSTEIN two years earlier - is seen in full makeup only in the opening. Then, he's reincarnated as sinister high priest Ardeth Bey (Boris Karloff), who prowls modern-day Cairo searching for the young woman who unknowingly resembles his lost love from 3,000 years earlier. A flashback sequence, re-used in several sequels and showing how the Mummy came to be entombed alive, is one of the scariest scenes in horror movie history.

The Mystery of the Wax Museum

BLOCKBUSTER CATEGORY: Horror
STARRING: Lionel Atwill, Fay Wray, Glenda Farrell
DIRECTED BY: Michael Curtiz

Long considered a "lost" film, this macabre gem from the golden age of screen horror has been fully restored in its original Technicolor. Lionel Atwill plays the sinister proprietor of a New York wax museum; he seeks revenge against the partner who caused him to be hideously disfigured in a fire years earlier. He also has his sights set on lovely Fay Wray, who has the bad luck to be a dead ringer for Marie Antoinette, and is thus a prime candidate for Atwill's new display. Plenty of foggy, waterfront atmosphere, and a corker of a climax. The film was later remade with Vincent Price as HOUSE OF WAX.

The Private Life of Henry VIII
BLOCKBUSTER CATEGORY: Classics
STARRING: Charles Laughton, Wendy Barrie, Elsa Lanchester
DIRECTED BY: Alexander Korda
Laughton is perfectly cast as the spoiled and despotic King Henry VIII. The film centers on his many wives and his battle with Sir Thomas More over the creation of the Church of England. Terrific performances by all, including Lanchester (Laughton's real-life wife) as Anne of Cleves. Oscar-nominated for Best Picture.
OSCAR WIN: *Best Actor (Laughton)*

She Done Him Wrong
BLOCKBUSTER CATEGORY: Classics
STARRING: Mae West, Cary Grant, Gilbert Roland
DIRECTED BY: Lowell Sherman
"Come up and see me." West plays Diamond Lil, a saloon owner and madame with designs on pretty-boy Salvation Army officer Grant. West's racy dialogue (the film was based on her play), the film's detailed settings, and an early glimpse of the hilariously corruptible Grant add up to a remarkable comedy that, even today, is surprisingly frank in its intentions. Oscar-nominated for Best Picture.

The Barretts of Wimpole Street

BLOCKBUSTER CATEGORY: Not available on video
STARRING: Norma Shearer, Fredric March, Charles Laughton
DIRECTED BY: Sidney Franklin

Elizabeth Barrett (Shearer) and Robert Browning (March) can't avoid their romantic attraction, even though her father (Laughton) is totally against it. Director Franklin spins a heartfelt slice-of-life tale as Shearer, March and Laughton turn in wonderful performances. If you like romantic movies, you'll love this one.

Cleopatra

BLOCKBUSTER CATEGORY: Classics
STARRING: Claudette Colbert, Warren William, Henry Wilcoxon
DIRECTED BY: Cecil B. DeMille

Colbert is superb as the Queen of the Nile, whose affairs and Roman lovers are lavishly displayed on screen. The actress plays Cleopatra flirtatiously, adding spice to the plot. After Julius Caesar's death, Cleopatra focuses on Mark Antony, and Colbert focuses on a winning performance. The supporting cast is also captivating. A lavish DeMille production. Oscar-nominated for Best Picture, Film Editing and Sound Recording.
OSCAR WIN: *Best Cinematography*

The Gay Divorcee

BLOCKBUSTER CATEGORY: Classics
STARRING: Ginger Rogers, Fred Astaire, Edward Everett Horton, Alice Brady
DIRECTED BY: Mark Sandrich

The first movie tailored specifically to Ginger Rogers and Fred Astaire, this is a sparkling musical about a lovesick dancer pursuing his heart's desire. The legendary leads entertain to the hilt. Director Sandrich extracts excellent performances from the cast of pros. Oscar-nominated for Best Picture and Musical Adaptation.
OSCAR WIN: *Best Song ("The Continental," the first time this award was given)*

Imitation of Life

BLOCKBUSTER CATEGORY: Not available on video
STARRING: Claudette Colbert, Louise Beavers, Fredi Washington
DIRECTED BY: John M. Stahl

Handkerchiefs are required for this sentimental soap opera about a working girl (Colbert), her maid (Beavers), her maid's daughter (Washington), and their dealings with racial confusion. Stahl's master-piece is as visually enticing as his other 30's triumphs, BACK STREET and MAGNIFICENT OBSESSION, and all three were remade in the 1950's. Oscar-nominated for Best Picture.

It Happened One Night
BLOCKBUSTER CATEGORY: Classics
STARRING: Clark Gable, Claudette Colbert, Walter Connolly
DIRECTED BY: Frank Capra
When a flighty girl from the social set escapes from her father, she falls for a
reporter traveling by bus. The granddaddy of sophisticated comedy romances
features a four-star cast in a charming Capra production. The film's sweep of all
major Academy Award categories was not equaled until 1975 with ONE FLEW
OVER THE CUCKOO'S NEST.
OSCAR SWEEP: *Best Picture, Director (Capra), Actor (Gable), Actress (Colbert),
Writing - adapted (Robert Riskin)*

Manhattan Melodrama
BLOCKBUSTER CATEGORY: Classics
STARRING: Clark Gable, William Powell, Myrna Loy
DIRECTED BY: W.S. Van Dyke II
Prior to being killed by the FBI, bank robber John Dillinger was actually watching
this film, based on his own life. Gable and Powell are wonderful as friends who
choose opposite sides of the law. Loy is also superb as the charming woman caught
between opposing forces.
OSCAR WIN: *Best Original Story (Arthur Caesar)*

The Merry Widow
BLOCKBUSTER CATEGORY: Musicals
STARRING: Maurice Chevalier, Jeanette MacDonald, Edward
Everett Horton, Una Merkel
DIRECTED BY: Ernst Lubitsch
A remake of the 1925 silent film detailing the downfall of the Hapsburg Empire.
Lubitsch's version, a parody of Franz Lehar's operetta, is a delight. A prince is forced
into marrying the widow of his well-to-do subject; that way, he can keep the wealth
in the kingdom. Chevalier, MacDonald, Horton and Merkel brilliantly play essential
roles. Lubitsch takes an operetta without music and makes it a winner.
OSCAR WIN: *Best Interior Decoration*

One Night of Love
BLOCKBUSTER CATEGORY: Not available on video
STARRING: Grace Moore, Lyle Talbot, Tullio Carminati
DIRECTED BY: Victor Schertzinger
Here is a tuneful musical spotlighting an American girl's trip to Italy, where she
hopes to achieve stardom in the opera. While trying, the maestro captures her heart.
Moore and Talbot turn in mesmerizing performances, and the wonderful score
makes this a delightful treat. Oscar-nominated for Best Picture, Actress (Moore)
and Director.
OSCAR WINS: *Best Sound Recording, Musical Score (the first time this award was
given)*

The Thin Man

BLOCKBUSTER CATEGORY: Mystery/Suspense
STARRING: William Powell, Myrna Loy, Maureen O'Sullivan, Nat Pendleton
DIRECTED BY: W.S. Van Dyke II

The characters of Nick and Nora Charles made their film debut in this superb mystery. The plot revolves around the quest for a "thin man" who killed an inventor. Powell and Loy apply plenty of their charisma to an already intriguing plot. Created by Dashiell Hammett. Five sequels followed. Oscar-nominated for Best Picture, Screenplay, Director (Van Dyke II) and Actor (Powell).

Viva Villa!

BLOCKBUSTER CATEGORY: Not available on video
STARRING: Wallace Beery, Stuart Erwin, Fay Wray, Leo Carrillo
DIRECTED BY: Jack Conway

A fast-moving, historical account with a crisp screenplay and plenty of action, this film focuses on the Mexican revolution. Beery's depiction of the calculating Villa is riveting. Oscar-nominated for Best Picture.
OSCAR WIN: *Best Assistant Director*

Alice Adams

BLOCKBUSTER CATEGORY: Classics
STARRING: Katharine Hepburn, Fred MacMurray, Fred Stone,
          Evelyn Venable
DIRECTED BY: George Stevens

This social dilemma is as old as mankind, but the performances are as fresh as ever.
The story of a girl from the wrong side of the tracks straining against her social
limitations is gloriously adapted from Booth Tarkington's novel to the big screen.
The small town atmosphere is effectively captured under the direction of Stevens.
Hepburn's mannerisms and angular beauty etch forever the character of Alice
Adams. Oscar-nominated for Best Picture and Actress (Hepburn).

Bride of Frankenstein

BLOCKBUSTER CATEGORY: Classics
STARRING: Boris Karloff, Colin Clive, Elsa Lanchester,
          Ernest Thesiger
DIRECTED BY: James Whale

The most "gothic" Universal Studios horror film ever is also one of the few sequels
that is better than its original. Evil Dr. Praetorious (Thesiger) befriends the monster
(Karloff) and forces Dr. Frankenstein (Clive) to build a female creature
(Lanchester). Her "birth" scene is even wilder than the preceding film's, thanks to
James Whale's impressionistic direction. Karloff's reaction to his bride's rejection
displays a pathos rarely seen in horror movies. Oscar-nominated for Best Sound
Recording.

Captain Blood

BLOCKBUSTER CATEGORY: Classics
STARRING: Errol Flynn, Olivia de Havilland, Lionel Atwill,
          Basil Rathbone
DIRECTED BY: Michael Curtiz

Critics applauded and fans cheered Errol Flynn in his first major starring role. He
was supported by a first-rate cast in the thrilling transformation of the Sabatini pirate
swashbuckler into the motion picture. Expertly directed by Curtiz, Flynn - in his
usual debonair fashion - commands the screen. Oscar-nominated for Best Picture
and Sound Recording.

Dangerous

BLOCKBUSTER CATEGORY: Classics
STARRING: Bette Davis, Franchot Tone
DIRECTED BY: Alfred E. Green

Davis is magnificent in the story about an aspiring architect who tries to save a great
actress from the depths of despair and loses his heart to her. It is a thrill to watch
Davis in action in this sentimental tale. Tone enhances Davis' role; director Green
brings out the finest in both.
OSCAR WIN: *Best Actress (Davis)*

1935

David Copperfield

BLOCKBUSTER CATEGORY: Classics
STARRING: W.C. Fields, Lionel Barrymore, Edna May Oliver,
Basil Rathbone, Roland Young, Freddie Bartholomew
DIRECTED BY: George Cukor

The first and possibly the most memorable screen adaptation of this classic Charles Dickens novel offers sensational performances from a distinguished cast. Disliked by his mean stepfather and helped by his eccentric aunt, orphan David grows up to become an author and eventually marry his childhood sweetheart. Director Cukor breathes fire and life into Dickens' characters. The film overflows with remarkable characterizations. W.C. Fields steals the show with an amusing portrayal of Mr. Micawber. Oscar-nominated for Best Picture, Assistant Director and Film Editing.

The Informer

BLOCKBUSTER CATEGORY: Classics
STARRING: Victor McLaglen, Preston Foster
DIRECTED BY: John Ford

A true classic that has withstood the test of time and taste! McLaglen and Foster star in this important, heartfelt movie that takes place during the Irish rebellion. The story embraces a slow-minded traitor who reveals the identity of a compatriot and then feels the pains of his conscience. For almost two hours, Ford brings viewers a taste of Ireland and the emotions stirred by a rebellion. Oscar-nominated for Best Picture.
OSCAR SWEEP: *Best Director (Ford), Actor (McLaglen), Screenplay (Dudley Nichols), Musical Score, Film Editing*

The Lives of a Bengal Lancer

BLOCKBUSTER CATEGORY: Classics
STARRING: Gary Cooper, Franchot Tone, Richard Cromwell,
C. Aubrey Smith
DIRECTED BY: Henry Hathaway

Here's a glorified schoolboy's adventure - a tribute to the proud heroics with which the British Empire defends its colonial holdings. This escapist film is action in its finest hour. Cooper and Tone are excellent as seasoned soldiers who help a raw recruit. Oscar-nominated for Best Picture, Director (Hathaway), Screenplay, Interior Decoration and Sound Recording.
OSCAR WIN: *Best Assistant Director*

Mutiny on the Bounty

BLOCKBUSTER CATEGORY: Classics
STARRING: Clark Gable, Charles Laughton, Franchot Tone
DIRECTED BY: Frank Lloyd

Lloyd directed one of the greatest films of all times and brought out the talents of his all-star cast in never-to-be forgotten roles. Laughton's Oscar-nominated reenactment of the infamous Captain Bligh is riveting. Gable and Tone also get the chance to display their epic talents. Remade as MUTINY ON THE BOUNTY (1962) and THE BOUNTY (1984) Oscar-nominated for Best Actor (Laughton, Gable and Tone), Director (Lloyd), Screenplay (Jules Furthman, Talbot Jennings and Carey Wilson) and Musical Score.
OSCAR WIN: *Best Picture*

Naughty Marietta

BLOCKBUSTER CATEGORY: Musicals
STARRING: Jeanette MacDonald, Nelson Eddy, Frank Morgan, Elsa Lanchester
DIRECTED BY: W.S. Van Dyke II

The legendary duo, Eddy and MacDonald, were paired for the very first time as an Indian and princess in Victor Herbert's operetta. The new team, forever linked in the viewing public's mind, went on to thrill audiences for years to come. Van Dyke's direction is splendid. Oscar-nominated for Best Picture.
OSCAR WIN: *Best Sound Recording*

A Night at the Opera

BLOCKBUSTER CATEGORY: Classics
STARRING: The Marx Brothers, Margaret Dumont, Sig Ruman, Kitty Carlisle, Allan Jones, Walter King, Edward Keane
DIRECTED BY: Sam Wood

Music and romance intermingle with gags as Groucho, Chico and Harpo mix it up with Margaret Dumont, a patron of the opera, and Sig Ruman, director of the New York Opera Company. Memorable moments: scores of people entering and then leaving a tiny ship's cabin, and a madcap climax during a performance of grand opera. This was the first of the five Marx Brothers' films at MGM and included all but Zeppo, who had become their agent.

The Scoundrel

BLOCKBUSTER CATEGORY: Not available on video
STARRING: Noel Coward, Stanley Ridges, Julie Haydon, Martha Sleeper, Eduardo Ciannelli, Alexander Woollcott, Lionel Stander
DIRECTED BY: Ben Hecht and Charles MacArthur

After a writer who survives by using others dies, his spirit comes back to atone for his actions. A sophisticated melodrama, distinguished by the acting genius of Coward and a strong cast of players. Hecht and MacArthur capture the pathos in this melodrama.
OSCAR WIN: *Best Original Story (Hecht and MacArthur)*

A Tale of Two Cities

BLOCKBUSTER CATEGORY: Classics
STARRING: Ronald Colman, Elizabeth Allen, Basil Rathbone, Blanche Yurka
DIRECTED BY: Jack Conway

MGM production qualities are at their zenith in this adaptation of Charles Dickens' monumental novel. This movie contains many unforgettable sequences, not to mention the main story of Sydney Carton (Colman), who sacrifices himself to the guillotine in order to save another life, and the epic storming of the Bastille. Madame Defarge (Yurka) is especially memorable. Oscar-nominated for Best Picture and Film Editing.

Anthony Adverse

BLOCKBUSTER CATEGORY: Classics
STARRING: Fredric March, Olivia de Havilland, Claude Rains, Gale Sondergaard
DIRECTED BY: Mervyn LeRoy

Grandscale cinema. A naive and ambitious young man travels through early 19th-century America and learns to grow up from his experiences. This film further strengthened March's reputation as a multifaceted actor. Oscar-nominated for Best Picture.

OSCAR WINS: Best Supporting Actress (Sondergaard), Cinematography, Film Editing, Musical Score, Interior Decoration

Camille

BLOCKBUSTER CATEGORY: Classics
STARRING: Greta Garbo, Robert Taylor, Lionel Barrymore
DIRECTED BY: George Cukor

Get out your handkerchiefs for this "women's film" par excellence! Garbo stars as a lovely courtesan who tragically sacrifices herself for her true love (Taylor). Cukor's sensitive direction brings out the fullest in Garbo's most legendary performance, which received an Oscar nomination for Best Actress.

Dodsworth

BLOCKBUSTER CATEGORY: Classics
STARRING: Walter Huston, Mary Astor, David Niven, Mary Ouspenskaya
DIRECTED BY: William Wyler

A whirlwind emotional drama. American businessman Dodsworth (Huston) takes his wife on a tour of Europe and their values and relationship are irrevocably altered. This extremely adult Samuel Goldwyn production was based on the Sinclair Lewis novel and was Oscar-nominated for Best Picture, Screenplay (Sidney Howard), Director (Wyler), Actor (Houston) and Supporting Actress (Ouspenskaya) and Sound Recording.

OSCAR WIN: Best Interior Decoration

Follow the Fleet

BLOCKBUSTER CATEGORY: Musicals
STARRING: Fred Astaire, Ginger Rogers, Randolph Scott
DIRECTED BY: Mark Sandrich

A song and dance favorite. Astaire decides to join the Navy when his girl turns him down for marriage. He meets, romances and dances with (who else?) Rogers. Plenty of hummable Irving Berlin tunes to carry along the frothy storyline, including "Let's Face the Music and Dance," and "Let Go of Yourself." One of the very best of the Rogers-Astaire teamings also includes Betty Grable and Lucille Ball in bit parts.

Fury

BLOCKBUSTER CATEGORY: Not available on video
STARRING: Spencer Tracy, Sylvia Sidney, Bruce Cabot
DIRECTED BY: Fritz Lang

1936

The first American film by great German director Lang is a powerful study of justice and revenge when innocent Tracy is lynched by an angry mob who mistake him for a cold-blooded murderer. The only catch is that Tracy survives and comes back to get even. Director Lang applied his famous use of expressionistic effects to build the suspense and paranoia in this precursor to the famous *film noir* movies of the 40's and 50's. Oscar-nominated for Best Story (Norman Krasna).

The Great Ziegfeld
BLOCKBUSTER CATEGORY: Musicals
STARRING: William Powell, Myrna Loy, Luise Rainer, Fanny Brice, Virginia Bruce
DIRECTED BY: Robert Z. Leonard
Grandiose, almost epic, fictionalized biography of the great showman, Florenz Ziegfeld, and the relationships he shared with his wives and co-workers. Powell is perfect in the title role, as are Bruce, Loy and Rainer (who won an Oscar). The most famous scene in this entertaining film is the "A Pretty Girl is Like a Melody" number, so enormous that it looks as if it were filmed in an aircraft hanger instead of on a Broadway stage. Oscar-nominated for Best Screenplay (William Anthony McGuire), Director (Leonard), Interior Decoration and Film Editing.
OSCAR WINS: *Best Picture, Actress (Rainer), Dance Direction*

Libeled Lady
BLOCKBUSTER CATEGORY: Classics
STARRING: Jean Harlow, William Powell, Myrna Loy
DIRECTED BY: Jack Conway
Peerless MGM comedy, from the 30's heyday of newspaper spoofs, when every studio was influenced by the stage and screen success of THE FRONT PAGE. Newspaper editor Spencer Tracy will stoop to anything to get a story on heiress Myrna Loy - even pitting his fiancee (Jean Harlow) and ex-boss (William Powell) against each other, to see who delivers the scoop first. Remade as EASY TO WED (1946). Oscar-nominated for Best Picture.

Modern Times
BLOCKBUSTER CATEGORY: Classics
STARRING: Charlie Chaplin, Paulette Goddard, Chester Conklin
DIRECTED BY: Charles Chaplin
Although classified as a silent film, this tender comedy has music (by Chaplin), sound effects, and even limited dialogue. In this, the final appearance of the Little Tramp, an engaging factory worker (Chaplin) deals with uncooperative machinery, a labor strike, and other perils of modern times. Along the way, he falls in love with an orphan waif (Goddard, then Chaplin's real-life wife). No one but the great Chaplin could have so successfully combined classic, hilarious slapstick with such a touching and poignant love tale. Like fine wine, MODERN TIMES improves year after year. Registered as a national treasure with the Library of Congress.

Mr. Deeds Goes to Town
BLOCKBUSTER CATEGORY: Classics
STARRING: Charlie Chaplin, Jean Arthur
DIRECTED BY: Frank Capra

Another Capra classic. Small town, philosophical Longfellow Deeds (Cooper) inherits a fortune from his uncle and tries to give it all away to needier people. Arthur is a cynical reporter who tries to find out how Deeds could be so generous and ends up falling in love with him as his relatives try to commit him for insanity. Capra pulls out all the sentimental stops in this comedy-drama that celebrates the virtues of "the little people."Oscar-nominated for Best Picture, Actor (Cooper) and Screenplay (Robert Riskin).
OSCAR WIN: *Best Director (Capra)*

My Man Godfrey
BLOCKBUSTER CATEGORY: Classics
STARRING: Carole Lombard, William Powell, Alice Brady, Mischa Auer
DIRECTED BY: Gregory La Cava
A group of extremely rich New Yorkers holds a scavenger hunt and ditzy Lombard's list includes finding a "forgotten man." She brings home a bum, Godfrey (Powell), and gives him a job as the family butler. He ends up teaching the rich a few lessons in life in this screwball comedy classic. Lombard and Powell are at the height of their acting powers and the dialogue contains some of the best comedy writing of the decade. Oscar-nominated for Best Picture, Director (La Cava), Screenplay (Eric Hatch and Morris Ryskind), Actress (Lombard), Actor (Powell), Supporting Actress (Brady)and Supporting Actor (Auer).

San Francisco
BLOCKBUSTER CATEGORY: Classics
STARRING: Spencer Tracy, Clark Gable, Jeanette MacDonald
DIRECTED BY: W.S. Van Dyke II
The first big budget disaster spectacular is set right before the infamous 1906 San Francisco earthquake. Gable is a saloon owner who tries to seduce innocent singer MacDonald while being warned to mend his ways by the saintly Tracy. A special effects landmark, with climactic earthquake footage that still amazes, even in light of modern cinema's technology. Oscar-nominated for Best Picture, Story (Robert Hopkins) and Assistant Director.
OSCAR WIN: *Best Sound Recording*

The Story of Louis Pasteur
BLOCKBUSTER CATEGORY: Not available on video
STARRING: Paul Muni, Josephine Hutchinson, Anita Louise
DIRECTED BY: William Dieterle
The story of the scientist who found cures for many diseases and revolutionized medicine comes to the screen, Hollywood-style. Muni plays Pasteur as the driven, dedicated man who cured rabies and invented the pasteurization process. Notable as the first of many 30's screen biographies and still one of the best. Oscar nominated for Best Picture.
OSCAR WINS: *Best Actor (Muni), Screenplay (Pierre Collings and Sheridan Gibney), Original Story (Collings and Gibney)*

The Awful Truth

BLOCKBUSTER CATEGORY: Classics
STARRING: Cary Grant, Irene Dunne, Ralph Bellamy
DIRECTED BY: Leo McCarey

A hilarious screwball comedy about a divorced couple who discover the awful truth: they still love each other! Grant and Dunne are the epitome of wit and sophistication as they try their best to break up each other's new romances, bicker over who gets custody of the dog and trade insults in delightful 30's repartee. Oscar-nominated for Best Picture and Screenplay, Actress (Dunne), and Supporting Actor (Bellamy).
OSCAR WIN: *Best Director (McCarey)*

Captains Courageous

BLOCKBUSTER CATEGORY: Classics
STARRING: Spencer Tracy, Freddie Bartholomew,
 Lionel Barrymore
DIRECTED BY: Victor Fleming

Kipling's classic comes to life with an impressive cast and fine performances. Young child star (Bartholomew) is a spoiled heir who falls overboard from an ocean liner and gets rescued by a gruff, Portuguese fisherman (Tracy). The young boy comes to share the fisherman's love of the sea while learning important lessons about trust, courage and love. This excellent adaptation received an Oscar nomination for Best Picture, while writers Marc Connolly, John Lee Mahin and Dale Van Every shared the nomination for Best Screenplay.
OSCAR WIN: *Best Actor (Tracy)*

Dead End

BLOCKBUSTER CATEGORY: Classics
STARRING: Joel McCrea, Sylvia Sidney, Humphrey Bogart,
 Claire Trevor
DIRECTED BY: William Wyler

A well-directed, engrossing film that examines the harsh reality of poverty in New York slums. Lillian Hellman wrote the script, blending comedy and drama in a series of vignettes adapted from Sidney Kingsley's powerful Broadway play. The film is also famous for introducing the Dead End Kids, who later went on to star in ANGELS WITH DIRTY FACES (1938) and the Bowery Boys series. Oscar-nominated for Best Picture, Actress (Trevor) and Cinematography.

The Good Earth

BLOCKBUSTER CATEGORY: Classics
STARRING: Paul Muni, Luise Rainer
DIRECTED BY: Sidney Franklin

Outstanding special effects and brilliant cinematography by Karl Freund highlight this beautiful production of Pearl Buck's novel. The tale of love and corruption includes splendid performances by Muni and Rainer as the poor, Chinese peasants who survive drought, locusts and poverty, only to lose to Muni's eventual wealth and consuming greed. The film earned Oscar nominations for Best Picture and Director (Franklin).
OSCAR WINS: *Best Actress (Rainer), Cinematography*

The Life of Emile Zola

BLOCKBUSTER CATEGORY: Classics
STARRING: Paul Muni, Joseph Schildkraut, Gail Sondergaard
DIRECTED BY: William Dieterle

An effective and honest biography, notable for its strong performances, memorable vignettes and lavish production. France's famed 19th-century author Zola (Muni) springs to the defense of Jewish officer Dreyfus (Schildkraut) who is unjustly accused of treason. Dieterle and Muni both received Oscar nominations for their fine efforts.
OSCAR WINS: *Best Picture, Supporting Actor (Schildkraut), Screenplay (Heinz Herald, Geza Herczeg and Norman Reilly Raine)*

Lost Horizon

BLOCKBUSTER CATEGORY: Classics
STARRING: Ronald Colman, Jane Wyatt, Sam Jaffe, H.B. Warner
DIRECTED BY: Frank Capra

In Shangri-La, people live forever, peace reigns and the only law is "Be kind." Escapees from a revolution find several types of refuge after their plane is forced down in this magical paradise. Adapted from James Hilton's Utopian novel, this unusual movie is a must-see classic, replete with excellent acting, great sets and a haunting finale. The film received Oscar nominations for Best Picture, Supporting Actor (Warner) and Score.

Snow White and the Seven Dwarfs

BLOCKBUSTER CATEGORY: Not available on video
STARRING: Voices of Adriana Caselotti, Harry Stockwell, others
DIRECTED BY: David Hand

Disney's first full-length animated feature brings to life the Grimm fairy tale of fair Snow White, the seven lovable dwarfs and the wicked, jealous queen. Wonderful songs (by Larry Morey and Frank Churchill), superb animation, plus the collaboration of eight Disney writers have succeeded in creating a timeless classic. Registered as a national treasure with the Library of Congress .

Stage Door

BLOCKBUSTER CATEGORY: Classics
STARRING: Katharine Hepburn, Ginger Rogers, Adolphe Menjou,
Lucille Ball, Eve Arden, Ann Miller, Andrea Leeds
DIRECTED BY: Gregory La Cava

A dynamite cast and unbeatable dialogue mark this wonderful film, based on the famous Edna Ferber/George S. Kaufman play. An all-girl theatrical boarding house brings together a diverse ensemble of young actresses struggling to make it in the theater. Menjou plays a leering producer with relish, Hepburn stars as a rich girl trying to succeed on her own, and many soon-to-be-famous actresses turn out memorable performances in this behind-the-scenes comedy/drama. Oscar-nominated for Best Picture, Director (La Cava, Supporting Actress (Leeds), and Screenplay (Morris Ryskind and Anthony Veiller).

1937

A Star is Born

BLOCKBUSTER CATEGORY: Classics
STARRING: Janet Gaynor, Fredric March, Adolphe Menjou,
Lionel Stander, Andy Devine
DIRECTED BY: William Wellman

The original version of the now-classic story about a self-destructive superstar whose acting career declines while his young wife enjoys a meteoric rise to stardom. Good early color cinematography is an unexpected bonus. The moving screenplay by writers Alan Campbell, Robert Carson and the famed Dorothy Parker received an Oscar nomination, as did Wellman for Best Director, March for Actor and Gaynor for Actress.
OSCAR WIN: Best Original Story (Wellman and Carson), Special Award for Color Photography

Stella Dallas

BLOCKBUSTER CATEGORY: Classics
STARRING: Barbara Stanwyck, John Boles, Anne Shirley,
Alan Hale
DIRECTED BY: King Vidor

In this classic tear-jerker, Stanwyck made millions of theater-goers weep with her touching portrayal of an upwardly mobile, selfless mother who sacrifices all for her daughter's happiness. Stanwyck received an Oscar nomination as the vulgar, yet sensitive, misfit mother. A Best Supporting Actress nomination went to Shirley for her role as the stalwart, loyal daughter. Remade as STELLA (1990) Bette Midler.

Topper

BLOCKBUSTER CATEGORY: Classics
STARRING: Cary Grant, Constance Bennett, Roland Young,
Arthur Lake
DIRECTED BY: Norman Z. McLeod

Grant and Bennett are a free-spirited couple killed in an auto accident. Before they can get to heaven, however, they must perform a good deed: to teach mild-mannered and proper banker Topper (Young) to relax and enjoy life. They appear at will, but only to Topper - leading to a steady stream of hilarious high jinks. Young earned an Oscar nomination as Best Supporting Actor in this delightful comic fantasy that spawned several sequels, a remake and a long-running television series.

The Adventures of Robin Hood
BLOCKBUSTER CATEGORY: Classics
STARRING: Errol Flynn, Olivia de Havilland, Basil Rathbone,
Claude Rains
DIRECTED BY: Michael Curtiz and William Keighley

The greatest adventure movie of all time! Flynn is perfectly cast as the quintessential swashbuckling rogue who robs from the rich, gives to the poor, thwarts the villains and wins his lady-love with ease. The Oscar-winning musical score, breathtaking cinematography and exciting story all work to make this film unequaled entertainment. Oscar-nominated for Best Picture. Remade in 1991 with Kevin Costner
OSCAR WINS: *Best Score (Erich Wolfgang Korngold), Editing, Art Direction*

Alexander Nevsky
BLOCKBUSTER CATEGORY: Foreign
STARRING: Nikolai Cherkassov, Nikolai Okhlopkov
DIRECTED BY: Sergei Eisenstein

A Russian masterpiece. Prince Nevsky leads the Russian army against German invaders during the 13th century, an ironic parallel to pre-World War II conditions at the time of filming. Edward Tisse's photography adds visual splendor to this grand epic, further heightened by the majesty of Sergei Prokofiev's original score. The breathtaking battle on the ice is one of the most exciting and influential in cinema.

Alexander's Ragtime Band
BLOCKBUSTER CATEGORY: Not available on video
STARRING: Tyrone Power, Alice Faye, Don Ameche,
Ethel Merman
DIRECTED BY: Henry King

Step back in time to the golden years of vaudeville, when song and dance men and beautiful girls tripped the light fantastic on ol' Broadway. This nostalgic musical comedy follows the ups and downs of a family of performers in the early 1900's, with a rousing score of 26 Irving Berlin hits to keep everyone's toes tapping.

Algiers
BLOCKBUSTER CATEGORY: Classics
STARRING: Charles Boyer, Sigrid Gurie, Hedy Lamarr,
Joseph Calleia, Gene Lockhart
DIRECTED BY: John Cromwell

"Come, let me take you to the Casbah." Crafty Pepe Le Moko (Boyer) flees from the North African police to the Casbah and charms his way into the arms of a sultry new love (Lamarr in her American film debut). Boyer received an Oscar nomination as Best Actor for what is probably his most famous role, with Gene Lockhart nominated as Best Supporting Actor for his role as the informer. James Wong Howe's masterful cinematography was also nominated for an Academy Award.

Boys Town
BLOCKBUSTER CATEGORY: Classics
STARRING: Spencer Tracy, Mickey Rooney, Henry Hull
DIRECTED BY: Norman Taurog

1938

Tracy gives an unforgettable performance as real-life Father Flanagan whose credo, "There's no such thing as a bad boy," is put soundly to the test. As the latest arrival to Flanagan's school for juvenile delinquents, Rooney pulls out all the stops as the irrepressible, yet lovable, bad boy. Ultimately, he reforms, thanks to wise and wily guidance. Oscar nominations for Best Picture, Director (Taurog) and Screenplay (John Meehan, Dore Schary).

OSCAR WINS: *Best Actor (Tracy), Original Story (Eleanor Griffin and Schary)*

Bringing up Baby
BLOCKBUSTER CATEGORY: Classics
STARRING: Cary Grant, Katharine Hepburn, Charlie Ruggles
DIRECTED BY: Howard Hawks

Hollywood's screwiest screwball comedy. Grant is a shy, absent-minded paleontologist in search of a missing dinosaur bone. Hepburn plays a kooky, fast-talking heiress with Asta the dog and pet leopard, Baby, in tow. Ruggles, the explorer, is adept at imitating the cry of the loon. In fact, looniness reigns supreme in this laugh-a-minute comedy which has gained growing acclaim since its original release, fueled by unparalleled direction and terrific comic performances. Remade as WHAT'S UP, DOC? (1972) with Ryan O'Neal and Barbra Streisand.

The Citadel
BLOCKBUSTER CATEGORY: Classics
STARRING: Robert Donat, Rosalind Russell, Ralph Richardson, Rex Harrison
DIRECTED BY: King Vidor

Brilliant acting contributes to this compelling film about a young, dedicated Scottish physician (Donat) who gives up his poor Welsh practice to make his fortune treating rich hypochondriacs. Neglecting his faithful wife (Russell) and friends, he's close to losing everything that matters - until tragedy delivers an unexpected twist. Based on A.J. Cronin's successful novel, this fine British import received four Oscar nominations: Best Picture, Actor (Donat), Director (Vidor) and Screenplay (Ian Dalrymple, Elizabeth Hill and Frank Wead).

Grand Illusion
BLOCKBUSTER CATEGORY: Foreign
STARRING: Erich von Stroheim, Pierre Fresnay, Jean Gabin
DIRECTED BY: Jean Renoir

A classic anti-war movie. Faultlessly directed by French master Renoir, the story explores the bonds that men share and how war tests those bonds. It centers around a group of French prisoners during World War I, focusing on an aristocratic P.O.W. (Fresnay) who is befriended by his cultured German captor (von Stroheim), technically "the enemy," but of similar social class. Fresnay's decision to help fellow inmates escape ultimately affects them all. Inspired screenplay and equally impressive acting. The first foreign film to be Oscar-nominated for Best Picture.

Jezebel

BLOCKBUSTER CATEGORY: Classics
STARRING: Bette Davis, Henry Fonda, George Brent, Fay Bainter
DIRECTED BY: William Wyler
A high-spirited Southern belle (Davis) loses her fiance (Fonda) when she defies convention and wears a "scandalous" red dress to the ball. The magnificent performance by Davis is augmented by a superb script, artful direction, a strong supporting cast and wonderful cinematography. The film earned Oscar nominations for Best Picture, Cinematography and Score.
OSCAR WINS: *Best Actress (Davis), Supporting Actress (Bainter)*

Pygmalion

BLOCKBUSTER CATEGORY: Classics
STARRING: Leslie Howard, Wendy Hiller, Wilfrid Lawson
DIRECTED BY: Anthony Asquith and Leslie Howard
George Bernard Shaw wrote both the original play and the screenplay for this delightful romantic comedy about the ambitious cockney flower girl (Hiller) who is transformed into a captivating English lady by stuffy phonetics Professor Henry Higgins (Howard). Howard received an Oscar nomination for Best Actor and also as co-director. Also Oscar-nominated for Best Picture and Actress (Hiller). This was later remade, musically, and with a different ending as MY FAIR LADY (1964).
OSCAR WINS: *Best Adaptation (Ian Dalrymple, Cecil Lewis and W.P. Lipscomb), Screenplay (Shaw)*

You Can't Take It with You

BLOCKBUSTER CATEGORY: Classics
STARRING: James Stewart, Jean Arthur, Edward Arnold,
Ann Miller, Lionel Barrymore, Spring Byington
DIRECTED BY: Frank Capra
When the daughter (Arthur) of an eccentric, poor family becomes engaged to the son (Stewart) of a rich, conservative family, hilarious fireworks erupt! Barrymore has a field day as the poorer relations' philosophical patriarch while a great supporting cast adds to the fun. Based on the Pulitzer Prize-winning play by Moss Hart and George S. Kaufman, the screen version pulled in seven Oscar nominations, including Best Supporting Actress (Byington), Screenplay (Robert Riskin), Cinematography, Sound Recording and Film Editing.
OSCAR WINS: *Best Picture, Director (Capra)*

Dark Victory

BLOCKBUSTER CATEGORY: Classics
STARRING: Bette Davis, George Brent, Humphrey Bogart, Geraldine Fitzgerald
DIRECTED BY: Edmund Goudling

Powerful, dramatic tearjerker nominated for Best Picture and one of Bette Davis' (who earned an Oscar nomination) most memorable roles. A high-living Long Island socialite discovers she has a brain tumor - and is going blind on her way to certain death. Transformed by the sudden realization of her own mortality, she sets out to add meaning and substance to her final days and die with dignity. The film offers an extraordinary depth of emotion. Also Oscar-nominated for Original Score.

Destry Rides Again

BLOCKBUSTER CATEGORY: Westerns
STARRING: James Stewart, Marlene Dietrich
DIRECTED BY: George Marshall

This is the rollicking story of a wild, wide-open Western town and the gunless sheriff who tames it. When word gets out that the son of a famous lawman is returning to town, law-abiding citizens rejoice - until they learn that the junior Destry is a milk-drinking peace lover who refuses to carry a gun. Nevertheless, between bouts of resisting the determined charms of saloon singer Dietrich, Destry's unorthodox approach to peace-keeping wins out in the end. A highlight is Dietrich's marvelous vocal rendition of "See What the Boys in the Back Room Will Have."

Drums Along the Mohawk

BLOCKBUSTER CATEGORY: Classics
STARRING: Claudette Colbert, Henry Fonda, Edna May Oliver
DIRECTED BY: John Ford

Flawless direction and a magnificent performance by Oliver, who received a Supporting Actress Oscar nomination for her powerful portrayal of a frontier matriarch place this movie among the finest Revolutionary War tales ever made. Colbert is a young, frightened bride from the East; husband Fonda goes off to battle. Colonists cope with Indian attacks, harsh environment and the realities of the War for Independence in this heartwarming tribute to the human spirit. Also Oscar-nominated for Cinematography.

The Four Feathers

BLOCKBUSTER CATEGORY: Classics
STARRING: Ralph Richardson, John Clements, June Duprez, Jack Allen
DIRECTED BY: Zoltan Korda

The year is 1898. It is the eve of a dangerous British military expedition to the Sudan, when young officer Clements, deciding the military life is not for him, resigns his commission. He is branded a coward by his associates and his fiancee and presented with feathers as a badge of shame. To prove his courage and redeem his name, he makes his own way to the Sudan and, disguised as a native warrior, wins honor on the field of battle - surreptitiously returning the feathers one by one. Rousing adventure and exquisite photography make this film a classic. Oscar-nominated for Cinematography.

＝＝

1939

＝＝

Gone With the Wind

BLOCKBUSTER CATEGORY: Classics
STARRING: Clark Gable, Vivien Leigh, Olivia de Havilland,
Leslie Howard, Hattie McDaniel
DIRECTED BY: Victor Fleming

A stunning Civil War panorama of the Siege of Atlanta, as seen through the lives of a leading family of the crumbling Southern aristocracy. From pampered beauty Scarlett O'Hara (Leigh) to gallant, cavalier Rhett Butler (Gable), to Mammy, the loyal and beloved slave (McDaniel, the first black Oscar winner), this landmark film is considered by some the consummate work of epic cinematography. Flawless production by David O. Selznick. Oscar-nominated for Best Actor (Gable), Supporting Actress (de Havilland), Special Effects, Sound Recording and Score. Registered as a national treasure in the Library of Congress.
OSCAR SWEEP: Best Picture, Director, Actress (Leigh), Supporting Actress (McDaniel), Screenplay (Sidney Howard), Cinematography, Editing, Interior Decoration and two special awards (for use of color and use of coordinated equipment in production)

Goodbye, Mr. Chips

BLOCKBUSTER CATEGORY: Classics
STARRING: Robert Donat, Greer Garson
DIRECTED BY: Sam Wood

Mr. Chips (Donat) is a caring but painfully shy and proper British schoolmaster until the day he encounters the vacationing Garson, the only individual capable of penetrating his shell. Under her gentle (and sometimes not-so-gentle) hand, he comes to understand his true nature, overcome his shyness and become an inspiration to his students. The movie, based on the novel by James Hilton, was nominated for Best Picture as well as Director (Wood), Actress (Garson), Screenplay (Eric Maschwitz, R.C. Sherriff and Claudine West) and Sound Recording. Remade as a musical with Peter O'Toole.
OSCAR WIN: *Best Actor (Donat)*

Gunga Din

BLOCKBUSTER CATEGORY: Classics
STARRING: Cary Grant, Douglas Fairbanks Jr., Victor McLaglen,
Sam Jaffe, Joan Fontaine
DIRECTED BY: George Stevens

Grant, Fairbanks and McLaglen shine as a trio of sergeants in Her Majesty's Indian Regiment, faced with a native rebellion. Loosely based on the famous Kipling poem, the film boasts lavish battle scenes, riveting action and colorful spectacle, blended with just the right touch of comic relief. Jaffe is particularly appealing as Gunga Din, the loyal native water boy with soldierly ambitions. This lavish spectacle has been hailed as one of Hollywood's all-time greatest military adventures. Restored to original two-hour lehgth for home video.

The Hunchback of Notre Dame
BLOCKBUSTER CATEGORY: Classics
STARRING: Charles Laughton, Maureen O'Hara,
Edmund O'Brien, Sir Cedric Hardwicke
DIRECTED BY: William Dieterle

Laughton's haunting portrayal of Quasimodo, the deformed bell-ringer at Notre Dame Cathedral, is a cinematic experience not to be missed. Quasimodo, whose grotesque appearance belies a deep and vulnerable sensitivity, saves gypsy girl Esmeralda (O'Hara), who had once shown him a small kindness, from an angry mob. Marked for retaliation by church officials, the hunchback maintains an indomitable human dignity far beyond that of his cruel and self-righteous tormentors. Setting and mood are a fascinating and reasonably accurate recreation of medieval Paris. Oscar-nominated for Best Sound Recording and Score. Remade as HUNCHBACK with Anthony Hopkins and Lesley Anne-Downe.

Mr. Smith Goes to Washington
BLOCKBUSTER CATEGORY: Classics
STARRING: James Stewart, Claude Rains, Jean Arthur,
Harry Carey
DIRECTED BY: Frank Capra

Scoutmaster Smith (Stewart), seen by "the machine" as a controllable dark horse, is drafted against his will to run for Senate. Railroaded into office, he maintains his inherent goodness through myriad trials and tribulations. As he discovers the true intent of his supporters, his innocence gives way to a stubborn determination to do what's right in the face of overwhelming forces of greed around him. Audiences have stood up and cheered at the rousing final moments of victory. Oscar nominations for Best Picture, Actor (Stewart), Director (Capra), Screenplay (Sidney Buchman), Supporting Actor (Carey and Rains), Interior Decoration, Sound Recording, Score and Film Editing. Registered as a national treasure with the Library of Congress.
OSCAR WIN: *Best Original Story (Lewis R. Foster)*

Ninotchka
BLOCKBUSTER CATEGORY: Classics
STARRING: Greta Garbo, Melvyn Douglas, Bela Lugosi
DIRECTED BY: Ernst Lubitsch

Garbo earned a Best Actress Oscar nomination for her first comedic role: Ninotchka, a hard-line Russian agent sent to Paris to bring a cadre of over-indulgent comrades to heel. She meets Douglas, a devil-may-care playboy who puts his talent to the task of seducing the beautiful ice queen. The delightful interplay between the two, as Garbo reluctantly succumbs to the romantic charms of both Douglas and the City of Lights, makes for a truly enjoyable romantic comedy. Other Oscar nominations for this sparkling comedy include Best Picture, Original Story (Melchior Lengyel), and Billy Wilder, Walter Reisch and Charles Brackett's delightful Screenplay.

1939

Rules of the Game

BLOCKBUSTER CATEGORY: Foreign
STARRING: Marcel Dalio, Nora Gregor, Gaston Modet, Jean Renoir, Roland Toutain
DIRECTED BY: Jean Renoir

Shortly after its opening, the master print of this delicious French comedy of affairs was damaged; it was not until 1961 that it was completely restored. Filled with humor, insight and deep emotion, this wonderful film takes place on a single weekend in a French country house, where flirtations and indiscretions between the upper-crust vacationers and the servant class abound, leading to a tragic end. Superb performances and masterful direction make this a true film classic.

Son of Frankenstein

BLOCKBUSTER CATEGORY: Horror
STARRING: Boris Karloff, Basil Rathbone, Bela Lugosi
DIRECTED BY: Rowland V. Lee

Boris Karloff's third and last outing as Frankenstein's monster is a horror masterpiece. Wolf von Frankenstein (Basil Rathbone) returns to his ancestral home with his wife and young son, and discovers that the dreaded monster lies in a coma in the abandoned laboratory. He revives the creature and it goes on a rampage. Bela Lugosi delivers his best performance since DRACULA as the twisted servant, Ygor. The surrealist castle set is spooky beyond description, and the excitement is further enhanced by Frank Skinner's full-blooded music.

Stagecoach

BLOCKBUSTER CATEGORY: Westerns
STARRING: John Wayne, Claire Trevor, Thomas Mitchell, George Bancroft
DIRECTED BY: John Ford

Oscar-nominated for Best Picture, Director (Ford), Cinematography, Interior Decoration and Film Editing, Ford's first "talkie" Western set the stage for the genre for generations to come. In his first major role, Wayne, as the outlaw Ringo Kid, joins a group of stagecoach passengers - a dance hall girl, a prissy Easterner, a drunken doctor - on a perilous journey through Apache country. He is soon arrested by Bancroft, but is released to help defend against a fierce Apache attack. Only the outlaw's reckless courage saves the group from certain death - or worse. A wonderful example of "ensemble" scripting, directing and acting. Remade in 1966 and 1986.
OSCAR WIN: *Best Supporting Actor (Mitchell)*

The Wizard of Oz

BLOCKBUSTER CATEGORY: Family
STARRING: Judy Garland, Ray Bolger, Bert Lahr, Jack Haley, Margaret Hamilton
DIRECTED BY: Victor Fleming

A wonderful story based on the novel by Frank Baum, along with stunning special effects and a marvelous soundtrack, make this the definitive fantasy film. A farm girl in Kansas (in black & white) gets blown to the Magical Kingdom of Oz (in

Technicolor), where she sets off to seek the Wizard's help to get home. She encounters a plethora of fantastic friends and foes before ultimately succeeding on her quest. "Over the Rainbow" would be Garland's trademark the rest of her career. Oscar-nominated for Best Picture, Cinematography, Interior Decoration and Special Effects. Registered as a national treasure with the Library of Congress .

OSCAR WINS: *Best Song ("Over the Rainbow"), and a special award for Garland as Best Screen Juvenile*

The Women

BLOCKBUSTER CATEGORY: Classics
STARRING: Mary Boland, Joan Crawford, Norma Shearer, Rosalind Russell, Joan Fontaine, Paulette Goddard, Hedda Hopper, Margaret Dumont
DIRECTED BY: George Cukor

With an all-star, all-woman cast of more than 125, this acerbic comedy of cat-fighting, husband-stealing and back-stabbing delves into the lives of pending divorcees. The complex plot is full of devious twists and turns; the dialogue is fast, sly and cutting and the superb performances are flawless and extremely entertaining. Includes one sequence in color. Remade as THE OPPOSITE SEX.

Wuthering Heights

BLOCKBUSTER CATEGORY: Classics
STARRING: Laurence Olivier, Merle Oberon, David Niven
DIRECTED BY: William Wyler

In what may be his finest non-Shakespearean performance, Olivier, as the dark and moody Heathcliff, helps bring this rich Victorian classic to life. An orphan, Heathcliff, is taken in by a well-to-do family and falls in love with the spoiled daughter, Cathy. Cathy is forced by circumstances to marry within her station, but the intense romance between Heathcliff (now grown wealthy through his driving ambition) and the passionate Cathy continues unabated. The film was nominated for seven Academy Awards including Best Picture, Director (Wyler), Actor (Olivier), Screenplay (Ben Hecht and Charles MacArthur), Supporting Actress (Fitzgerald), Interior Decoration and Score.

OSCAR WIN: *Best Cinematography - b&w*

Young Mr. Lincoln

BLOCKBUSTER CATEGORY: Classics
STARRING: Henry Fonda, Alice Brady, Donald Meek, Marjorie Weaver
DIRECTED BY: John Ford

Lamar Trotti earned an Academy Award nomination for the original story of this affectionate, insightful glimpse at the early years of one of America's greatest presidents. In a flawless performance, Fonda develops Abraham Lincoln from a rough-hewn woodsman into a savvy, unperturbable wit. Uncompromising attention to period detail add to the believable and utterly entertaining quality of this enjoyable American classic.

1940

The Bank Dick

BLOCKBUSTER CATEGORY: Comedy
STARRING: W.C. Fields, Franklin Pangborn, Grady Sutton
DIRECTED BY: Eddie Cline

The town ne'er-do-well inadvertently foils a bank holdup, and is promptly placed in charge of bank security. W.C. Fields himself wrote the script for this farce (using the pseudonym "Mahatma Kane Jeeves"), and he cast the film with some of his favorite comic actors, including Franklin Pangborn as the prissy bank manager and sad-eyed Grady Sutton as the hapless teller in love with Fields' daughter.

Boom Town

BLOCKBUSTER CATEGORY: Drama
STARRING: Clark Gable, Spencer Tracy, Claudette Colbert
DIRECTED BY: Jack Conway

Clark Gable and Spencer Tracy are high stakes oil speculators in a fever-pitch race to see whose drilling operation strikes the black gold first. Claudette Colbert and Hedy Lamarr throw a little romance into the already tense rivalry. A solid MGM action melodrama. Oscar-nominated for Cinematography, Special Effects.

Fantasia

BLOCKBUSTER CATEGORY: Not available on video
DIRECTED BY: Ben Sharpsteen, Edward H. Plumb

Walt Disney's famous classic animated feature combines classical music with cartoons. Extraordinary animation makes an exciting counterpoint to the music of Beethoven, Bach, Tchaikovsky and others. Mickey Mouse lends his unique charm to The Sorcerer's Apprentice, while other Disney characters romp through the film's remaining sequences. Leopold Stokowski conducts.
OSCAR WINS: *Special Awards for new form of "visualized music" and advanced use of sound.*

The Grapes of Wrath

BLOCKBUSTER CATEGORY: Classics
STARRING: Henry Fonda, Jane Darwell, John Carradine, Dorris Bowden
DIRECTED BY: John Ford

A must-see masterpiece, based on John Steinbeck's novel. Fonda, in the role of his life, is magnificent as Tom Joad, who migrates with his family from the Oklahoma Dust Bowl to California, seeking farm work during the Depression. The movie is a panorama of unforgettable characters, struggling against heartbreaking odds for survival. Oscar nominations include Best Picture, Screenplay (Nunnally Johnson), Actor (Fonda), Sound Recording and Film Editing. Trivia note: John Ford never even read the Book! Registered as a national treasure with the Library of Congress.
OSCAR WINS: *Best Director (Ford), Best Supporting Actress (Darwell)*

The Great Dictator

BLOCKBUSTER CATEGORY: Classics
STARRING: Charlie Chaplin, Paulette Goddard, Jack Oakie
DIRECTED BY: Charlie Chaplin

The results are hilarious when Chaplin brings his slapstick genius to his first all-talking picture. Chaplin's dual roles as a poor Jewish ghetto barber and look-alike dictator Adenoid Hynkel of Tomania heighten the pointed anti-Hitler satire. Jack Oakie is splendid as his rival, Benzino Napaloni of Bacteria. It's only a matter of time before the barber and the dictator are involved in a case of mistaken identities, which is played to the hilt to the delight of all. Chaplin dances with the globe in this one. Oscar nominations were received for Best Picture, Actor (Chaplin), Supporting Actor (Oakie) and Original Screenplay (Chaplin).

The Great McGinty

BLOCKBUSTER CATEGORY: Classics
STARRING: Brian Donlevy, Muriel Angelus, Akim Tamiroff, Allyn Joslyn
DIRECTED BY: Preston Sturges

A dumb bum (Donlevy) rises from obscurity to the governor's mansion as the result of a crooked election, then loses it all when he tries to go straight. Sturges made his debut with this film, as director and writer of the smart and snappy screenplay that won an Oscar for its unforgettable characters and memorable scenes. His multi-viewpoint script pre-dated CITIZEN KANE's structure by a year.
OSCAR WIN: *Best Screenplay (Sturges)*

His Girl Friday

BLOCKBUSTER CATEGORY: Classics
STARRING: Cary Grant, Rosalind Russell, Ralph Bellamy, Gene Lockhart
DIRECTED BY: Howard Hawks

Director Howard Hawks breathed new life into this hilarious remake of THE FRONT PAGE (1931), changing the lead character Hildy Johnson into a woman and setting a fast and furious pace with rapid-fire dialogue. Grant is a scheming newspaper editor. Russell plays Hildy, Grant's star reporter and ex-wife, who wants to marry a mama's boy insurance agent (Bellamy), but is staying on the job to cover one last hot murder scoop. A brilliant cast and sharp script make this movie non-stop fun.

Kitty Foyle

BLOCKBUSTER CATEGORY: Classics
STARRING: Ginger Rogers, Dennis Morgan, James Craig, Eduardo Ciannelli
DIRECTED BY: Sam Wood

Ambitious Kitty Foyle must choose between her love for a noble doctor and a proposal from a wealthy suitor. Rogers won acting kudos as the working-girl heroine in this touching love story. Other outstanding performances from a strong supporting cast contributed to the film's being nominated for an Oscar as Best Picture. Also nominated for Screenplay (Dalton Trumbo), Director (Wood) and Sound Recording.
OSCAR WIN: *Best Actress (Rogers)*

The Letter

BLOCKBUSTER CATEGORY: Drama
STARRING: Bette Davis, Herbert Marshall, James Stephenson
DIRECTED BY: William Wyler

In the plantation house of a sweltering tropical estate, a gunshot rings out. A man staggers out the front door and slumps to the ground. . . followed by Bette Davis, a pistol clutched tight in her hand. That's just the opening to this top-drawer melodrama of infidelity, blackmail and murder, written by W. Somerset Maugham and directed for maximum tension by the man who would later give us THE BEST YEARS OF OUR LIVES and BEN-HUR. Davis gives a *tour-de-force* performance as a woman claiming self-defense for what everyone else believes is cold-blooded murder. Oscar-nominations for Best Picture, Director (Wyler),Best Actress (Davis), Supporting Actor (Stephenson), Cinematography, Film Editing, Score.

The Philadelphia Story

BLOCKBUSTER CATEGORY: Classics
STARRING: Cary Grant, Katharine Hepburn, James Stewart
DIRECTED BY: George Cukor

The dialogue sparkles in this witty adaptation of Phillip Barry's Broadway hit. An heiress (Hepburn) is preparing to get married for the second time when her first husband (Grant) and an inquisitive reporter (Stewart) arrive on the scene. An Oscar nomination went to Cukor for his expert direction. Also nominated for Best Picture, Actress (Hepburn) and Supporting Actress (Hussey).
OSCAR WINS: *Best Actor (Stewart), Screenplay - adapted (Donald Ogden Stewart)*

Pinocchio

BLOCKBUSTER CATEGORY: Kids
STARRING: Voices of Dickie Jones, Cliff Edwards, others
SUPERVISED BY: Ben Sharpsteen and Hamilton Luske

Released the same year as Disney's FANTASIA, this is regarded by many as the studio's highest achievement. The magical fantasy is based on the Collodi story about a poor, lonely woodcutter who makes a puppet that comes to life and wants more than anything to be a real boy. The animation is astonishing, the songs delightful and the characters unforgettable. Humor alternates with downright scary situations, and there are few moments in film as poignant as when Jiminy Cricket sings "When You Wish Upon A Star."
OSCAR WINS: *Best Song ("When You Wish Upon a Star"), Original Score*

Pride and Prejudice

BLOCKBUSTER CATEGORY: Classics
STARRING: Laurence Olivier, Greer Garson
DIRECTED BY: Robert Z. Leonard

Jane Austen's sparkling, deliciously witty comedy of manners is enhanced by an excellent cast and polished scripting by Aldous Huxley (author of *Brave New World*) and Jane Murfin. Early 19th-century English parents are looking to marry off their five eligible daughters. Especially entertaining are contrary lovers Olivier and Garson, trading sophisticated barbs all the way to the alter.
OSCAR WIN: *Best Interior Decoration - b&w*

Rebecca

BLOCKBUSTER CATEGORY: Alfred Hitchcock
STARRING: Laurence Olivier, Joan Fontaine, George Sanders, Judith Anderson
DIRECTED BY: Alfred Hitchcock

Hitchcock's first and only Best Picture Oscar winner was for this compelling romance mystery. Following a whirlwind courtship, a shy young woman (Fontaine) becomes the second wife of a dashing nobleman (Olivier). She soon realizes she is living in the shadow of his first wife, Rebecca. Hitchcock's masterful direction and Franz Waxman's mesmerizing music underscore this wonderful Gothic classic, based on the popular Daphne du Maurier novel. Oscar nominations for Best Director (Hitchcock), Actor (Olivier), Actress (Fontaine), Supporting Actress (Anderson), Screenplay (Robert E. Sherwood and Joan Harrison), Score, Film Editing and Special Effects.
OSCAR WINS: *Best Picture, Cinematography - b&w*

Santa Fe Trail

BLOCKBUSTER CATEGORY: Westerns
STARRING: Errol Flynn, Olivia de Havilland, Raymond Massey
DIRECTED BY: Michael Curtiz

Episodic, multi-levelled Civil War historical epic that would be fascinating if only for its casting: Tasmanian Errol Flynn as Jeb Stuart, Britain's Raymond Massey as abolitionist John Brown, and Ronald Reagan as George Armstrong Custer! Action veteran Michael Curtiz (who directed Flynn as Robin Hood two years earlier) staged this sweeping outdoor drama with verve and confidence. Flynn played Custer one year later in THEY DIED WITH THEIR BOOTS ON.

The Sea Hawk

BLOCKBUSTER CATEGORY: Classics
STARRING: Errol Flynn, Brenda Marshall, Claude Rains
DIRECTED BY: Michael Curtiz

One of Errol Flynn's finest swashbucklers, this masterpiece has been restored to its full length - for the first time in 50 years - for home video. Flynn is at his most handsome and athletic as a British privateer who almost singlehandedly wages war against the Spanish, in a thoroughly satisfying adaptation of Rafael Sabatini's novel. Oscar-nominated for Sound Recording and Special Effects.

The Sea Wolf

BLOCKBUSTER CATEGORY: Classics
STARRING: John Garfield, Ida Lupino, Edward G. Robinson
DIRECTED BY: Michael Curtiz

Although it's set on a ship at sea and based on a novel by adventure specialist Jack London, this classic is actually stark suspense at its best. Two stowaways (Garfield, Lupino) match wits with a sharp-tongued sea captain who is, they soon discover, quite insane. This period melodrama contains enough storms and conventional shipboard action to satisfy the undemanding, but there's much more just below the surface. All of the actors - and Robinson in particular - are outstanding. Oscar-nominated for Special Effects.

The Shop Around the Corner

BLOCKBUSTER CATEGORY: Classics
STARRING: James Stewart, Margaret Sullavan, Frank Morgan
DIRECTED BY: Ernst Lubitsch

A young man and woman work in a small shop in Budapest, and can't stand each other. What they don't realize is that, as correspondents in a lonely hearts club, they have secretly fallen in love by mail. One of the most enduringly popular romantic comedies of the 1940's, briskly directed by the man who gave us NINOTCHKA and TO BE OR NOT TO BE.

The Thief of Bagdad

BLOCKBUSTER CATEGORY: Classics
STARRING: Sabu, Conrad Veidt, John Justin, Rex Ingram
DIRECTED BY: Michael Powell, Ludwig Berger, Tim Whelan

An enchanting Arabian fantasy, made all the more wonderful with incredible photography, special effects and a vivid musical score. A mischievous young thief helps a prince save his kingdom from an evil magician with the help of a genie and a magic flying carpet. Exceptional acting by a magnificent cast. Oscar-nominated for Best Score.
OSCAR WINS: *Best Special Effects, Cinematography - color, Interior Decoration - color*

Ball of Fire
BLOCKBUSTER CATEGORY: Classics
STARRING: Barbara Stanwyck, Gary Cooper,
Oscar Homolka
DIRECTED BY: Howard Hawks

A stripper (Stanwyck), on the lam from gangsters, seeks refuge among a group of college professors. It's a perfect matchup: They're assembling a dictionary of American slang, and she speaks like she stepped right out of a Jimmy Cagney movie. Gary Cooper plays the youngest (and shyest) of the academics, and he's soon smitten with Stanwyck. A raucous, breezy comedy that was one of the first scripting jobs for Billy Wilder, later the director of SOME LIKE IT HOT. Oscar-nominated for Best Actress (Stanwyck), Original Story (Wilder and Thomas Monroe), Sound, Music (Alfred Newman).

Citizen Kane
BLOCKBUSTER CATEGORY: Classics
STARRING: Orson Welles, Joseph Cotton,
Everett Sloane
DIRECTED BY: Orson Welles

CITIZEN KANE set Hollywood on its ear when the movie was released in 1941. Welles, just 25 years old at the time, co-wrote, directed and starred in his first film effort. Loosely based on the life of William Randolph Hearst, the story revolves around the scandalous public and private life of a newspaper publisher. The picture is famous for its breakthrough cinematic inventiveness, multi-viewpoint script, and all-around entertainment value. Many call it the greatest American film ever made. Oscar-nominated for Best Picture, Director, Actor (Welles), Cinematography, Film Editing, Scoring, Sound Recording and Interior Decoration. Registered as a national treasure with the Library of Congress.
OSCAR WIN: *Best Original Screenplay (Herman J. Mankiewicz and Welles)*

Dumbo
BLOCKBUSTER CATEGORY: Kids
STARRING: Voices of Sterling Holloway, Verna Felton, others
DIRECTED BY: Ben Sharpsteen

Disney adds a delightful twist to the classic ugly-duckling tale with this charming story of the shy little circus elephant who is ridiculed for his huge ears. What a surprise when he discovers he can use them as wings and fly! Memorable scenes like the crows' song and the pink elephants' dream sequence are boosted by the Oscar-winning score. "Baby Mine" was also Oscar-nominated for Best Song.
OSCAR WIN: *Best Musical Score*

Here Comes Mr. Jordan
BLOCKBUSTER CATEGORY: Classics
STARRING: Robert Montgomery, Evelyn Keyes, Claude Rains,
James Gleason
DIRECTED BY: Alexander Hall

The entertaining comedy-fantasy is about a prizefighter who dies before his time in a plane crash and is sent back to earth to live in another body. A first-rate story and enthusiastic performances by an outstanding cast. The movie was remade in 1978 as

HEAVEN CAN WAIT. Oscar nominations include Best Picture, Director (Hall), Cinematography, Actor (Montgomery) and Supporting Actor (Gleason).
OSCAR WINS: *Best Story (Harry Segall), Screenplay (Sidney Buchman and Seton I. Miller)*

High Sierra

BLOCKBUSTER CATEGORY: Classics
STARRING: Humphrey Bogart, Ida Lupino, Arthur Kennedy
DIRECTED BY: Raoul Walsh
Humphrey Bogart, an ex-con newly released from prison, wants to go straight but soon finds himself mixed up in an elaborate bank robbery that seems doomed from the start. Bogart accepted the part after George Raft turned it down, and the movie's success made Bogie a superstar. Gangster movie veteran Raoul Walsh (THE ROARING TWENTIES) directs the tough-as-nails screenplay by the up-and-coming John Huston.

How Green Was My Valley

BLOCKBUSTER CATEGORY: Not available on video
STARRING: Walter Pidgeon, Maureen O'Hara, Roddy McDowall, Donald Crisp, Sara Allgood
DIRECTED BY: John Ford
Life in a Welsh coal mining town is seen through the eyes of a small boy, whose close-knit family becomes divided by a labor dispute. The film is an exquisite labor of love. Endowed with beautiful photography, sensitive direction, a well-written screenplay and magnificent performances, the picture received ten Oscar nominations, including Best Screenplay, (Philip Dune), Supporting Actress (Allgood), Scoring and Film Editing.
OSCAR SWEEP: *Best Picture, Director (Ford), Supporting Actor (Crisp), Original Story (Harry Segall), Cinematography-b&w, Interior Decoration - b&w*

Johnny Eager

BLOCKBUSTER CATEGORY: Classics
STARRING: Robert Taylor, Lana Turner, Van Heflin
DIRECTED BY: Mervyn LeRoy
Charming gangster Robert Taylor is romancing college student Lana Turner, and her district attorney father, Edward Arnold, doesn't like that one bit. This is an ambitious production which is enriched by Van Heflin's Oscar-winning portrayal of Taylor's alcoholic best friend.
OSCAR WIN: *Best Supporting Actor (Heflin)*

The Lady Eve

BLOCKBUSTER CATEGORY: Classics
STARRING: Barbara Stanwyck, Henry Fonda, Charles Coburn
DIRECTED BY: Preston Sturges
A beautiful, sexy con artist (Stanwyck) sets out to bilk a gullible millionaire (Fonda) who has a passion for snakes. The chemistry's hot between Stanwyck and Fonda, and the supporting cast is terrific. Lending his genius to this delicious romantic farce is 1940's top comedy director Sturges, with his witty, sophisticated script and trademark fast-paced dialogue and visuals. Oscar-nominated for Best Original Story (Monckton Hoffe).

The Little Foxes

BLOCKBUSTER CATEGORY: Classics
STARRING: Bette Davis, Herbert Marshall, Teresa Wright,
Patricia Collinge
DIRECTED BY: William Wyler

A greedy Southern family double deals among themselves to build a factory on what was once a beautiful plantation. Davis outdoes herself as Regina, the ruthless conniver who heads the clan and is willing to risk everything, even her husband's life, to succeed. The excellent cast features many actors recreating their original roles from the hit play by Lillian Hellman, who also wrote the screenplay. Oscar nominations were received for Best Picture, Director (Wyler), Actress (Davis), Supporting Actress (Collinge and Wright), Original Story, Screenplay (Hellman), Interior Decoration, Scoring and Film Editing.

The Maltese Falcon

BLOCKBUSTER CATEGORY: Classics
STARRING: Humphrey Bogart, Mary Astor, Sydney Greenstreet,
Peter Lorre, Elisha Cook, Jr.
DIRECTED BY: John Huston

Huston debuted as a director and also wrote the screenplay for this trendsetting detective drama. And what a cast! Bogart landed his first major, heroic role as hard-boiled Sam Spade. His character, along with those created by Greenstreet, Lorre, Astor and Cook became archetypes for the genre. But it is Huston who instilled the breakneck pace, moody images and sinister atmosphere that became the forerunner of the *film noir* style that would later dominate detective films. Oscar nominations for Best Picture, Supporting Actor (Greenstreet) and Screenplay (Huston). Registered as a national treasure with the Library of Congress. Also see SATAN MET A LADY, an earlier version with Bette Davis.

Meet John Doe

BLOCKBUSTER CATEGORY: Classics
STARRING: Gary Cooper, Barbara Stanwyck, Edward Arnold
DIRECTED BY: Frank Capra

One of the first of director Frank Capra's populist fables, this classic of Americana stars Gary Cooper as a charismatic idealist placed in charge of a promotional campaign by a politician. Trouble is, the politician (played to slimy perfection by Edward Arnold) is an absolute crook who's just using our hero. Worldly-wise Barbara Stanwyck is caught in the middle.
Oscar-nominated for Original Story (Richard Connell & Robert Presnell).

Never Give A Sucker an Even Break

BLOCKBUSTER CATEGORY: Classics
STARRING: W.C. Fields, Gloria Jean, Leon Errol,
Margaret Dumont
DIRECTED BY: Edward Cline

A wild and wacky farce in which Fields plays himself in his last starring role. Fields tries to get backing from a skeptical producer for a movie about one of his bizarre and highly improbable romantic adventures. No real plot, but plenty of hilarious scenes, especially a classic car chase that Abbott and Costello reused for their movie IN SOCIETY (1944).

Sergeant York

BLOCKBUSTER CATEGORY: Classics
STARRING: Gary Cooper, Walter Brennan, Joan Leslie,
Margaret Wycherly
DIRECTED BY: Howard Hawks

The true story of the backwoods pacifist soldier who single-handedly captured 137 Germans during World War I. A fast-paced, poignant film with sensitive and intelligent direction by Hawks and a sincere, touching performance by Cooper. Oscar nominations for just about everything, including Best Picture, Director (Hawks), Supporting Actor (Brennan), Supporting Actress (Wycherly), Original Screenplay (Harry Chandlee, Abem Finkel, John Huston and Howard Koch), Cinematography, Interior Decoration, Sound Recording and Scoring.
OSCAR WINS: *Best Actor (Cooper), Film Editing*

Sullivan's Travels

BLOCKBUSTER CATEGORY: Comedy
STARRING: Joel McCrea, Veronica Lake, William Demarest
DIRECTED BY: Preston Sturges

Joel McCrea plays a fabulously successful director of hit movies, the Steven Spielberg of his day, who yearns to stop making fluff like HEY,HEY IN THE HAYLOFT and SO LONG, SARONG and direct a serious sociological study. His producers are in a panic when McCrea disguises himself as a hobo and - with Veronica Lake in tow - sets off to ride the rails and "discover the true America". A peerless romantic comedy, decades ahead of its time, directed by the greatest comedy filmmaker of the early 40's, Preston Sturges.

Suspicion

BLOCKBUSTER CATEGORY: Alfred Hitchcock
STARRING: Joan Fontaine, Cary Grant, Nigel Bruce
DIRECTED BY: Alfred Hitchcock

An intriguing Hitchcock thriller about a wealthy wallflower (Fontaine) who marries an irresponsible playboy (Grant) with a disreputable past. After her spendthrift husband squanders their finances, the wife starts to fear that he's plotting to murder her for the insurance money. When his best friend dies, tension mounts and her suspicions flare higher. Oscar-nominated for Best Picture and Scoring.
OSCAR WIN: *Best Actress (Fontaine)*

That Hamilton Woman

BLOCKBUSTER CATEGORY: Classics
STARRING: Laurence Olivier, Vivien Leigh
DIRECTED BY: Alexander Korda

The real-life chemistry of married couple Olivier and Leigh lends added realism to their portrayals of England's famous naval hero Lord Admiral Nelson and Emma Hamilton, making the ill-fated romance of this historical couple seem all the more poignant. Excellent acting and many memorable scenes heighten this touchingly beautiful, heartbreakingly sad costume drama. Oscar-nominated for Cinematography, Interior Decoration and Special Effects.
OSCAR WIN: *Best Sound Recording*

1941

They Died With Their Boots On
BLOCKBUSTER CATEGORY: Westerns
STARRING: Errol Flynn, Olivia de Havilland, Arthur Kennedy
DIRECTED BY: Raoul Walsh

This action epic is an episodic western saga chronicling the events leading up to Gen. George Armstrong Custer's bloody battle at Little Big Horn. Errol Flynn is suitably dashing and swaggering as the legendary, mysterious cavalry officer. He's teamed with Olivia de Havilland (his co-star since 1935's CAPTAIN BLOOD) in their last movie together. The climactic sequence is one of the most spectacular western finales ever filmed.

Bambi

BLOCKBUSTER CATEGORY: Kids
STARRING: Voices of Bobby Stewart, Peter Behn, others
DIRECTED BY: David Hand

One of Disney's best and most popular full-length animated features, based on Felix Salten's book about a baby fawn who grows up to be the prince of the forest. As the story unfolds, the phases of the deer's life parallel the cycle of seasons. Also, we meet Bambi's wonderful forest friends, including the hilarious and unforgettable rabbit, Thumper. A charming and funny children's classic. Oscar-nominated for Best Sound Recording, Scoring and Song ("Love Is A Song").

Casablanca

BLOCKBUSTER CATEGORY: Classics
STARRING: Humphrey Bogart, Ingrid Bergman, Claude Rains, Paul Henreid
DIRECTED BY: Michael Curtiz

One of the best-loved films of all time. An old flame just happens to walk into Rick's gin joint in World War II Casablanca, where she and her underground leader husband are trying to arrange their escape from the Nazis. The film is a rich mixture of romance and intrigue, assisted by clever, well-paced dialogue and a first-rate cast of memorable characters. You'll want to play it again...and again. Oscar nominations include Best Actor (Bogart), Supporting Actor (Rains), Cinematography, Scoring and Film Editing. Registered as a national treasure with the Library of Congress.
OSCAR SWEEP: Best Picture, Director (Curtiz), Screenplay (Julius G. Epstein, Philip G. Epstein and Howard Koch)

Cat People

BLOCKBUSTER CATEGORY: Classics
STARRING: Simone Simon, Kent Smith
DIRECTED BY: Jacques Tourneur

The first of producer Val Lewton's intelligently written and directed horror films. A man marries a mysterious young woman who fears she may have inherited the family tendency to turn into a killer panther. Horror is subtly yet effectively achieved with provocative camera angles, eerie sound effects and sinister atmosphere. The swimming pool sequence is one of the most terrifying in cinema. Remade in 1982.

Holiday Inn

BLOCKBUSTER CATEGORY: Musicals
STARRING: Bing Crosby, Fred Astaire, Marjorie Reynolds
DIRECTED BY: Mark Sandrich

The quintessential holiday musical, whose threadbare plot – two pals are in love with the same girl, as they plan to open a winter resort – provides an excuse for some marvelous Irving Berlin tunes. The pace is fast, and there are some delightful contributions from such vintage character actors as Walter Abel and Louise Beavers. Oscar-nominated for Best Original Story (Irving Berlin), Scoring of a Musical Picture.
OSCAR WIN: Best Song ("White Christmas")

King's Row
BLOCKBUSTER CATEGORY: Classics
STARRING: Ann Sheridan, Robert Cummings, Ronald Reagan
DIRECTED BY: Sam Wood

This small-town (and big-budget, all-star) soap opera made a star of Ronald Reagan. Anyone who has ever seen this movie eagerly awaits the scene in which Reagan, awaking from an operation performed by an unscrupulous surgeon, looks down at the empty space where his legs used to be and screams, "Where's the rest of me?!" The bulk of the movie, happily, is nowhere near so gruesome; in fact, its portrait of the lives and loves of the residents of a pre-World War I American village has seldom, if ever, been topped. Look for Judith Anderson, Claude Rains and Charles Coburn in the stellar supporting cast. Oscar-nominated for Best Picture, Best Director (Wood), Cinematography.

The Magnificent Ambersons
BLOCKBUSTER CATEGORY: Classics
STARRING: Joseph Cotten, Dolores Costello, Agnes Moorehead, Tim Holt
DIRECTED BY: Orson Welles

Welles both directed and wrote the screenplay (based on Booth Tarkington's novel) about a prideful, rich Midwestern family who refuses to change with the times. Welles, fresh from CITIZEN KANE (1941), was at his creative height, employing innovative deep-focus photography, a moving camera and sharp contrasts of light and dark. The studio reshot much of Welles' footage, cut 60 minutes and added a happy ending. The film is full of Welles' genius, fine acting and great camerawork of Stanley Cortez. Oscar-nominated for Best Picture, Supporting Actress (Moorehead), Cinematography and Interior Decoration.

Mrs. Miniver
BLOCKBUSTER CATEGORY: Classics
STARRING: Greer Garson, Walter Pidgeon, Teresa Wright, Henry Travers, Dame May Whitty
DIRECTED BY: William Wyler

Seven Academy Awards went to this moving film about the courage of an English middle-class family who struggles to cope with the hardships and plight of World War II at home. The film not only strengthened our ties with our British allies, but was an effective morale booster for all during those troubled times. Oscar-nominated for Best Actor (Pidgeon), Supporting Actor (Travers), Supporting Actress (Whitty), Sound Recording, Film Editing and Special Effects.
OSCAR SWEEP: *Best Picture, Director (Wyler), Actress (Garson), Supporting Actress (Wright), Screenplay (George Froeschel, James Hilton, Claudine West, Arthur Wimperis), Cinematography - b&w*

Now, Voyager
BLOCKBUSTER CATEGORY: Classics
STARRING: Bette Davis, Claude Rains, Paul Henreid, Gladys Cooper
DIRECTED BY: Irving Rapper

Davis, in her most powerful film, stars as a shy spinster who blooms under the help of her psychiatrist, who sends her on a cruise to an ill-fated romance. Max Steiner's haunting score, a talented cast and a heavy dose of romance (like the classic scene when Henreid lights two cigarettes at once) make this the ultimate cinematic romance. Oscar nominations for Best Actress (Davis) and Supporting Actress (Cooper).
OSCAR WIN: *Best Scoring*

The Palm Beach Story

BLOCKBUSTER CATEGORY: Classics
STARRING: Claudette Colbert, Joel McCrea, Rudy Vallee, Mary Astor
DIRECTED BY: Preston Sturges

A zany, screwball comedy with more nutty characters than a fruitcake. The frustrated, ambitious wife of a ne'er-do-well engineer flees to posh Palm Beach where she encounters an eccentric millionaire suitor, his wacky sister, the wealthy Wienie King, the looney Ale and Quail Club, and even her husband! Sturges adds his trademark fast-paced madness.

The Pride of the Yankees

BLOCKBUSTER CATEGORY: Classics
STARRING: Gary Cooper, Teresa Wright, Babe Ruth, Walter Brennan
DIRECTED BY: Sam Wood

The excellent biography of Yankees' baseball great Lou Gherig, who died of the crippling muscle disease that now bears his name. Cooper is perfect as the sincere, dedicated ball player. His emotional farewell address at Yankee Stadium is a classic, guaranteed to have you reaching for your handkerchief. The film received eleven Oscar nominations, including Best Picture, Actor (Cooper), Actress (Wright), Original Story (Paul Gallico), Screenplay (Herman J. Mankiewicz and Jo Swerling), Cinematography, Interior Decoration, Sound Recording, Scoring and Special Effects.
OSCAR WIN: *Best Editing*

Random Harvest

BLOCKBUSTER CATEGORY: Classics
STARRING: Ronald Colman, Greer Garson, Philip Dorn
DIRECTED BY: Mervyn LeRoy

Ronald Colman, who was perfectly cast as the idealist hero of LOST HORIZON (1937), is equally appealing in an adaptation of yet another James Hilton novel. This time, he's a shell-shocked World War I veteran plagued with amnesia. He marries dancer Greer Garson and settles down to a simple life. . . only to have a car accident jog him back to his original identity. Garson, who won an Oscar that same year for starring in MRS. MINIVER, plays some of the best scenes of her career opposite Colman in this movie. Oscar-nominated for Best Picture, Actor (Colman), Supporting Actress (Susan Peters), Director (LeRoy), Screenplay Adaptation, Interior Decoration.

This Gun for Hire
BLOCKBUSTER CATEGORY: Classics
STARRING: Alan Ladd, Veronica Lake, Brian Donlevy
DIRECTED BY: Frank Tuttle

Trendsetting crime movie, from a Graham Greene novel (*A Gun For Sale*), in which a hired killer (Alan Ladd, in the role that made him a star) is, for the first time, the leading character in a film, not just its stock villain. There's another first in this film, an attempt to probe the psychology of the killer. W.R. Burnett, author of *Little Caeser* and *Asphalt Jungle*, was one of the scriptwriters.

To Be or Not To Be
BLOCKBUSTER CATEGORY: Classics
STARRING: Jack Benny, Carole Lombard, Robert Stack
DIRECTED BY: Ernst Lubitsch

Classic black comedy. Benny is hilarious as "that great, great actor" who leads a Polish Shakespearean troupe and outwits the Nazis during World War II. His imitations of Hamlet and Hitler are priceless. Lombard, in her last role, adds pizzazz as his flirtatious wife. Subtle, skillfull direction makes the most of the outrageous situations and darkly funny dialogue. Oscar-nominated for Best Scoring. Remade with Mel Brooks in 1983.

Woman of the Year
BLOCKBUSTER CATEGORY: Classics
STARRING: Katharine Hepburn, Spencer Tracy
DIRECTED BY: George Stevens

Tracy and Hepburn debuted as one of Hollywood's most popular romantic teams in this witty, romantic comedy. It's a classic case of opposites attract when successful sportswriter Tracy meets, woos and weds world-famous, political columnist Hepburn, who knows nothing about sports - or domesticity! Memorable moments include Tracy trying to teach Hepburn about the game of baseball and Hepburn's famous kitchen scene. Hepburn also received an Oscar nomination for Best Actress.
OSCAR WIN: *Best Original Screenplay (Michael Kanin and Ring Lardner, Jr.)*

Yankee Doodle Dandy
BLOCKBUSTER CATEGORY: Musicals
STARRING: James Cagney, Joan Leslie, Walter Huston
DIRECTED BY: Michael Curtiz

Cagney exhibited some fancy footwork in his bang-up role as hoofer/singer/songwriter/actor/playwright George M. Cohan. Born on the Fourth of July, Cohan was immensely patriotic and the movie is a showcase for his melodious, flag-waving tunes, as well as a showcase for Cagney, who won an Oscar for his performance. The classic World War II-era film received seven Oscar nominations, including Best Picture, Director (Curtiz), Supporting Actor (Huston) and Original Story (Robert Buckner). Cagney reprised the role in THE SEVEN LITTLE FOYS (1955).
OSCAR WINS: *Best Actor (Cagney), Sound Recording, Scoring of a Musical*

Cabin in the Sky
BLOCKBUSTER CATEGORY: Musicals
STARRING: Eddie "Rochester" Anderson, Ethel Waters,
Lena Horne, Louis Armstrong, Cab Calloway
DIRECTED BY: Vincente Minnelli

Exuberant, extravagant musical in which guest appearances by such greats as Duke Ellington and Butterfly McQueen supplement an already all-star, all-black cast. Anderson, a gambler of questionable moral fiber, is torn between his wife (Waters) and the seductive charms of Horne. As might be expected from the quality of the cast, the music is nothing short of spectacular. Oscar-nominated for Best Song ("Happiness is Just a Thing Called Joe").

For Whom the Bell Tolls
BLOCKBUSTER CATEGORY: Not available on video
STARRING: Gary Cooper, Ingrid Bergman, Katina Paxinou
DIRECTED BY: Sam Wood

Ask not... it tolls for thee. This dramatic screen enactment of Ernest Hemingway's powerful novel of the Spanish Civil War, nominated as Best Picture of the year, is adventure at its finest. Cooper and Bergman both received Oscar nominations (Actor, Actress) as an American mercenary and his lovely, spectre-like love interest. The suspense is almost palpable as Cooper aids a group of overmatched, undertrained peasants in their attempt to destroy a strategic bridge. Also nominated for Best Cinematography, Interior Decoration, Scoring and Film Editing.
OSCAR WIN: *Best Supporting Actress (Paxinou)*

Heaven Can Wait
BLOCKBUSTER CATEGORY: Classics
STARRING: Don Ameche, Gene Tierney, Marjorie Main,
Charles Coburn
DIRECTED BY: Ernst Lubitsch

This is a truly tender and heartwarming comedy of a semi-repentant playboy (Ameche) and his quest (yes, quest) for the eternal damnation he believes he so dearly deserves. Flashbacks reveal that under his cavalier facade resides a warm and sensitive nature in subtle contrast to his forceful self-incriminations, and a touching, ill-fated love for Tierney. Oscar-nominated for Best Picture, Director (Lubitsch) and Cinematography.

Madame Curie
BLOCKBUSTER CATEGORY: Not available on video
STARRING: Greer Garson, Walter Pidgeon
DIRECTED BY: Mervyn LeRoy

Fresh from the previous year's Oscar blockbuster MRS. MINIVER, Garson and Pidgeon play the obsessed scientists who discover radium. Although conceived more to inform than to entertain, the film is nevertheless a deeply absorbing biography filled with drama and fascinating historical details. Nominated for Best Picture, Actor (Pidgeon), Actress (Garson), Cinematography, Interior Decoration, Sound Recording, Scoring.

The Ox-Bow Incident

BLOCKBUSTER CATEGORY: Classics
STARRING: Henry Fonda, Dana Andrews, Anthony Quinn,
Harry Morgan
DIRECTED BY: William Wellman

An Oscar nominee for Best Picture, this western makes a powerful social statement without being preachy or high-handed. When a local rancher is shot by cattle rustlers, a posse forms, more intent on punishing someone for the crime than on justice. That their captive suspects are unlikely to have committed the deed means little to the vigilantes, so long as the crime is avenged. Fonda plays a cowboy with a conscience.

Phantom of the Opera

BLOCKBUSTER CATEGORY: Horror
STARRING: Claude Rains, Suzannah Foster, Nelson Eddy
DIRECTED BY: Arthur Lubin

Universal Studios, which created the classic movie monsters of the 1930's and 40's, created its first Technicolor horror movie with this big-budget remake of the classic silent shocker. Claude Rains, the co-star of CASABLANCA (and, much earlier, THE INVISIBLE MAN), plays the Phantom, and for the first time we are told how he became the disfigured monster who haunts the Paris Opera House. Although the film contains bits of humor and some well-handled musical interludes with Nelson Eddy and Suzannah Foster, Universal never lets us forget it's a horror film. The Phantom's dropping of the opera house chandelier on the unsuspecting audience is a terror highlight. Oscar-nominated for scoring of a musical.
OSCAR WINS: *Cinematography - color, Art Direction - color*

The Seventh Victim

BLOCKBUSTER CATEGORY: Horror
STARRING: Kim Hunter, Tom Conway, Jean Brooks
DIRECTED BY: Mark Robson

A teen-age girl journeys to New York to search for her older sister, who has joined a group of devil worshippers in Greenwich Village - and disappeared. This quietly frightening chiller is one of the best of a series of landmark horror movies produced during the 1940's by Val Lewton. Other titles in this classic package include THE BODY SNATCHER (with Karloff and Lugosi) and the original version of THE CAT PEOPLE.

Shadow of a Doubt

BLOCKBUSTER CATEGORY: Alfred Hitchcock
STARRING: Joseph Cotten, Teresa Wright
DIRECTED BY: Alfred Hitchcock

A landmark work of suspense and undoubtedly one of Hitchcock's finest. Gordon McDonell was nominated for an Academy Award for Best Original Story, for his tale of a psychopath who, suspecting his apprehension is imminent, drops out of sight by dropping in on relatives in a small California town. His niece is fascinated by his worldly sophistication - and then she begins to suspect the truth.

1943

The Song of Bernadette

BLOCKBUSTER CATEGORY: Classics
STARRING: Jennifer Jones, Charles Bickford, Anne Revere,
               Gladys Cooper
DIRECTED BY: Henry King

The vehicle that made Jones a star. An inspiring retelling of the story of Bernadette Soubirous, later St. Bernadette, the French peasant girl who sees a vision of the Virgin Mary at Lourdes. Despite widespread skepticism, Bernadette refuses to recant her story, and eventually pilgrims flock to the healing spring which suddenly and inexplicably appeared at the site of the miraculous vision. The film was nominated for Best Picture, Director (King), Supporting Actor (Bickford), Screenplay (George Seaton), Supporting Actress (Cooper and Revere), Sound Recording and Film Editing.

OSCAR WINS: *Best Actress (Jones), Cinematography - b&w, Interior Decoration - b&w, Scoring*

Watch on the Rhine

BLOCKBUSTER CATEGORY: Classics
STARRING: Bette Davis, Paul Lukas, Lucile Watson
DIRECTED BY: Herman Shumlin

The good guys and the bad guys are sharply defined in this best of all the anti-Nazi films that sprung up in the wake of World War II. Lukas, a dedicated member of the German underground, retains his high moral principles despite the most sinister efforts of the agents of the Reich to silence him. Based on the play by Lillian Hellman. Watson was nominated for Best Supporting Actress; the film was also nominated for Best Picture and Dashiell Hammett's and Hellman's Screenplay.

OSCAR WIN: *Best Actor (Lukas)*

The Adventures of Mark Twain

BLOCKBUSTER CATEGORY: Classics
STARRING: Fredric March, Alexis Smith, Alan Hale
DIRECTED BY: Irving Rapper

By the time this ambitious biography was made, Fredric March had established himself as one of Hollywood's premier character stars, playing everything from Jekyll and Hyde (for which he won an Oscar) to Garbo's lover in ANNA KARENINA. This satisfying period drama attempts to include nearly every major event in the life of author, inventor and philosopher Samuel L. Clemens. March is in nearly every scene, abetted by such wonderful supporting players as John Carradine and C. Aubrey Smith. Oscar-nominated for Special Effects, Music, Interior Decoration - b&w.

Double Indemnity

BLOCKBUSTER CATEGORY: Mystery/Suspense
STARRING: Fred MacMurray, Barbara Stanwyck,
Edward G. Robinson
DIRECTED BY: Billy Wilder

Hubby's life insurance includes a double-indemnity clause if he dies falling from a moving train. Lovely wife Stanwyck and insurance agent MacMurray plan to see that the extra premium does not go to waste. One of the great and most influential *film noirs* of all time and one of Robinson's best efforts as MacMurray's boss, who finally unravels the case. Oscar-nominated for Best Picture, Director (Wilder), Actress (Stanwyck), Screenplay (Raymond Chandler and Billy Wilder), Cinematography, Sound Recording and Scoring.

Gaslight

BLOCKBUSTER CATEGORY: Classics
STARRING: Charles Boyer, Ingrid Bergman, Joseph Cotten,
Angela Lansbury
DIRECTED BY: George Cukor

Boyer, a charming London ne'er-do-well, marries the wealthy Bergman and hatches a scheme to make her believe she's going mad. Success is imminent until Cotten, a savvy detective, gets on the case. Lavish, atmospheric cinematography, which earned an Oscar nomination, heightens the mood and suspense of the film. Angela Lansbury's screen debut - and her first Academy Award nomination (Best Supporting Actress). Also nominated for Best Picture, Actor (Boyer), Screenplay (John L. Balderston, Walter Reisch and John Van Druten) and Cinematography. OSCAR WINS: *Best Actress (Bergman), Interior Decoration - b&w*

Going My Way

BLOCKBUSTER CATEGORY: Classics
STARRING: Bing Crosby, Barry Fitzgerald, Gene Lockhart,
William Frawley
DIRECTED BY: Leo McCarey

The classic Bing vehicle. Crosby is a young priest in a poor New York parish. Fitzgerald is the elderly pastor whose heart of gold is buried under many layers of time and disillusionment. Don't miss Bing's incomparable "Swinging on a Star" and "Too-ra-loo-ra-loo-ra." Oscar-nominated for Best Cinematography, Song ("Swinging

on a Star") and Film Editing.
OSCAR SWEEP: *Best Picture, Director (McCarey), Actor (Crosby), Supporting Actor (Fitzgerald), Original Story (McCarey), Screenplay (Frank Butter and Frank Cavett)*

Hail the Conquering Hero

BLOCKBUSTER CATEGORY: Comedy
STARRING: Eddie Bracken, Ella Raines, Raymond Walburn
DIRECTED BY: Preston Sturges
Eddie Bracken goes off to enlist in the Army during World War II. He's turned down, but when the small-town lad returns home, he's mistaken for a war hero. Before he knows what's happening, everything has snowballed too far for Eddie to tell the truth - and now he's scared he'll eventually be found out. Another in director Preston Sturges' winning series of 1940's comedies about average folks overwhelmed by extraordinary events. Oscar-nominated for Original Screenplay (Sturges).

Henry V

BLOCKBUSTER CATEGORY: Classics
STARRING: Laurence Olivier, Robert Newton, Leslie Banks
DIRECTED BY: Laurence Olivier
For the first screen adaptation of Shakespeare's immortal play, Olivier is brilliant - not only as Henry, but also as producer and director of this lavish spectacle. The film opens as a production at the famous Globe Theater, then evolves into a spectacular location film replete with sweeping, technicolor battle scenes. Oscar- nominated for Best Picture, Actor (Olivier), Scoring and Interior Decoration.
OSCAR WIN: A special Oscar to Olivier for "Outstanding Achievement as Actor, Producer and Director," given in 1946, when the movie was Oscar-eligible.

Jane Eyre

BLOCKBUSTER CATEGORY: Classics
STARRING: Orson Welles, Joan Fontaine, Margaret O'Brien
DIRECTED BY: Robert Stevenson
Charlotte Bronte's gothic romance novel stars Orson Welles as the brooding, stern Rochester. He also has a hand (uncredited) in the script and direction. Welles', scenes with Joan Fontaine (in the lead role) are so powerful it's impossible to think of any two other actors in the roles -which is what makes this a classic. The sweeping, romantic score is by future Hitchcock composer Bernard Herrmann.

Laura

BLOCKBUSTER CATEGORY: Classics
STARRING: Dana Andrews, Gene Tierney, Clifton Webb
DIRECTED BY: Otto Preminger
This must-see, moody, murder mystery - classic *film noir* - earned an Oscar nomination for Preminger and is considered his finest picture. A police detective (Andrews) investigates the murder of a beautiful young woman. In the course of his interviews and investigation, he finds himself falling in love with his pieced-together image of the young victim. Oscar-nominated for Director (Preminger), Supporting Actor (Webb), Screenplay (Jay Dratler, Samuel Hoffenstein and Betty Reinhardt) and Interior Decoration.
OSCAR WIN: *Best Cinematography - b&w*

Lifeboat

BLOCKBUSTER CATEGORY: Alfred Hitchcock
STARRING: Tallulah Bankhead, William Bendix, Walter Slezak
DIRECTED BY: Alfred Hitchcock

Hardly your typical Hitchcock, LIFEBOAT is particularly noteworthy because it was created and co-scripted by novelist John Steinbeck. Survivors of a German submarine attack on a passenger liner (including the submarine captain himself), vastly different in background and philosophy, are confined in a single lifeboat. They finally manage to tear down the walls and work together to survive. Oscar-nominated for Best Director (Hitchcock), Original Story (Steinbeck) and Cinematography.

Meet Me in St. Louis

BLOCKBUSTER CATEGORY: Musicals
STARRING: Judy Garland, Mary Astor, Margaret O'Brien,
Leon Ames
DIRECTED BY: Vincente Minnelli

One of the decade's brightest musicals. Just before the St. Louis World's Fair, Papa (Ames) would like to move the family to New York, but Mama (Astor) and the girls (Garland and O'Brien) are quite happy right here, thank you. The sparkling musical score, including "The Boy Next Door," is as nostalgic as it is wonderful. Oscar-nominated for Best Screenplay (Irving Brecher and Fred F. Finkelhoffe), Cinematography, Song ("The Trolley Song") and Scoring.
OSCAR WIN: *Special award - Margaret O'Brien, Outstanding Child Actress of 1944*

The Miracle of Morgan's Creek

BLOCKBUSTER CATEGORY: Classics
STARRING: Betty Hutton, Eddie Bracken, William Demarest,
Brian Donlevy
DIRECTED BY: Preston Sturges

Far more controversial when released than it would be today, this outrageous comedy was held back by censors for a year before it was allowed into the theaters. It seems small-town girl Trudy (Hutton) finds herself in the family way following a rollicking all-night party with some soldiers from the local army base. She seems to recall that she *may* have married a soldier sometime during the festivities. What she can't remember is, *which* soldier? Oscar-nominated for Best Original Screenplay (Sturges).

Murder, My Sweet

BLOCKBUSTER CATEGORY: Mystery/Suspense
STARRING: Dick Powell, Claire Trevor, Anne Shirley
DIRECTED BY: Edward Dmytryk

Former Busby Berkeley crooner Dick Powell shed his boy-next-door image forever in this raw, violent adaptation of Raymond Chandler's FAREWELL, MY LOVELY. As detective Phillip Marlowe, Powell runs afoul of gangsters, gun molls and drug-dealing psychopaths in his search for the elusive girlfriend of a local thug. Story first filmed as THE FALCON TAKES OVER (1942), then again under actual title in 1975 with Robert Mitchum.

National Velvet

BLOCKBUSTER CATEGORY: Classics
STARRING: Elizabeth Taylor, Mickey Rooney, Angela Lansbury,
   Anne Revere
DIRECTED BY: Clarence Brown

Wonderful family fare. A butcher's daughter (Taylor) and a homeless ex-jockey (Rooney) who, against all odds, train a horse to win the English Grand National Steeplechase. This is the showcase that launched Taylor's career. Oscar-nominated for Best Director (Brown) and Cinematography.
OSCAR WIN: *Best Supporting Actress (Revere)*

None But the Lonely Heart

BLOCKBUSTER CATEGORY: Classics
STARRING: Cary Grant, Ethel Barrymore, Barry Fitzgerald,
   Jane Wyatt
DIRECTED BY: Clifford Odets

Grant, remarkably convincing in this departure from light comedy, plays a London cockney, long on wits, but lamentably short on conscience - until he learns his poverty-stricken mother is dying of cancer. Grant earned an Oscar nomination for his most dramatic role.
OSCAR WIN: *Best Supporting Actress (Barrymore)*

Since You Went Away

BLOCKBUSTER CATEGORY: Classics
STARRING: Claudette Colbert, Joseph Cotten, Jennifer Jones,
   Lionel Barrymore, Shirley Temple, Hattie McDaniel,
   Agnes Moorehead, Monty Woolley
DIRECTED BY: John Cromwell

With World War II at its height in Europe, those left behind must cope as best they can - even when a beloved father is reported missing in action. This classic melodrama with its all-star cast offers an intimate, sentimental look back at an American small town in simpler times. Nominated for nine Academy Awards, including Best Picture, Actress (Colbert), Supporting Actress (Jones), Supporting Actor (Wooley), Cinematography, Interior Decoration, Film Editing and Special Effects.
OSCAR WIN: *Best Musical Score (Max Steiner)*

Thirty Seconds Over Tokyo

BLOCKBUSTER CATEGORY: Action/Adventure
STARRING: Van Johnson, Robert Walker, Spencer Tracy
DIRECTED BY: Mervyn LeRoy

This World War II adventure about the first Allied bombing raids over Japan remains one of the most thrilling war movies ever made. It's also one of the most intelligent, thanks to a thoughtful screenplay by Dalton Trumbo and impassioned direction by the great Mervyn LeRoy (LITTLE CAESAR). Spencer Tracy makes a cameo appearance as Gen. Jimmy Doolittle, and sharp-eyed movie buffs will spot Robert Mitchum in a small but key role. Oscar-nominated for Cinematography - b&w.
OSCAR WIN: *Special Effects*

1944

To Have And Have Not
BLOCKBUSTER CATEGORY: Classics
STARRING: Humphrey Bogart, Lauren Bacall, Walter Brennan
DIRECTED BY: Howard Hawks

In her film debut - at age 20 - Lauren Bacall provides the romantic attraction for hardbitten boat captain Humphrey Bogart, who finds himself seduced into aiding the French Resistance. Supposedly based on an Ernest Hemingway novel, it's really an excuse for director Howard Hawks (who would also direct Bogie and Bacall in THE BIG SLEEP) to remake CASABLANCA in a different setting. Novelist William Faulkner contributed to the spicy screenplay.

Wilson
BLOCKBUSTER CATEGORY: Not available on video
STARRING: Alexander Knox, Geraldine Fitzgerald,
Charles Coburn, Vincent Price
DIRECTED BY: Henry King

This accurate and well-balanced film biography of World War I President Woodrow Wilson (Knox) is absorbing as well as informative. Criticized during his presidency for some controversial judgements, Wilson was still a president of lofty ideals and noble vision. Excellent performances all around by this stellar cast. Oscar-nominated for Best Picture, Actor (Knox), Director (King), Scoring and Special Effects.
OSCAR WINS: *Best Original Screenplay (Lamar Trotti), Cinematography - color, Interior Decoration - color, Sound Recording, Film Editing.*

Anchors Aweigh

BLOCKBUSTER CATEGORY: Musicals
STARRING: Frank Sinatra, Gene Kelly, Kathryn Grayson,
　　　　　　Dean Stockwell
DIRECTED BY: George Sidney

Features one of the earliest, and still the most delightful, blending of real-life and cartoon characters when Kelly does a dance number with Jerry the mouse (half of the famous Tom and Jerry team). Sinatra and Kelly are sailors on leave in Hollywood where they befriend a little boy who wants to be a sailor, have the usual misadventures, and sing and dance their leave away. A lively, fun musical. Oscar-nominated for Best Picture, Actor (Kelly), Cinematography and Song ("I Fall In Love Too Easily").
OSCAR WIN: *Best Scoring of a Musical*

The Bells of St. Mary's

BLOCKBUSTER CATEGORY: Classics
STARRING: Bing Crosby, Ingrid Bergman
DIRECTED BY: Leo McCarey

This delightful follow-up to 1944's Oscar-sweeping GOING MY WAY, with eight Academy Award nominations of its own, is one of the few screen sequels that lives up to the original. Unconventional Father O'Malley (Crosby), the fortunes of his own parish secure, goes to an impoverished Catholic school to help Sister Superior (Bergman) raise much-needed construction money. A highlight is Bergman's attempt to teach a young student to box. Crosby charm is in top form in this warm, sentimental tale, nominated for Best Picture. Actor (Crosby), Actress (Bergman), Director (McCarey), Film Editing, Song ("Aren't You Glad You're You") and Scoring.
OSCAR WIN: *Best Sound Recording*

The Clock

BLOCKBUSTER CATEGORY: Drama
STARRING: Judy Garland, Robert Walker, James Gleason
DIRECTED BY: Vincente Minnelli

In New York City, a soldier on a two-day pass and a secretary meet and fall in love. That's the whole premise of this classic romance, astutely directed by Vincente Minnelli (the future husband of the film's star, Judy Garland). This is a charming and endearing love story.

Detour

BLOCKBUSTER CATEGORY: Classics
STARRING: Tom Neal, Ann Savage, Edmund McDonald,
　　　　　　Claudia Drake
DIRECTED BY: Edgar G. Ulmer

This classic *film noir* of intrigue and deception still enjoys a loyal following decades after its release, although it was filmed on a shoestring in just six days. An itinerant musician (Neal) is hitchhiking across the country when he is drawn into a diabolical scheme of murder and extortion. Savage is a scheming hustler who plans to use the hapless pianist in a plot to defraud a fortune from a widow. Remade in 1991.

1945

The Lost Weekend

BLOCKBUSTER CATEGORY: Classics
STARRING: Ray Milland, Jane Wyman, Howard Da Silva,
Phillip Terry
DIRECTED BY: Billy Wilder

A cinematic milestone when released, this powerful film handles the sensitive topic of alcoholism with skill and grace. Milland runs a harrowing gamut of emotions and personal struggle in his moving performance as a struggling writer fighting off his personal demons and the bottle. Da Silva is outstanding as a bartender; Wyman and Terry excel as the writer's girlfriend and brother. Oscar-nominated for Cinematography, Score and Editing.
OSCAR SWEEP: *Best Picture, Director (Wilder), Actor (Milland), Screenplay (Wilder and Charles Brackett)*

Mildred Pierce

BLOCKBUSTER CATEGORY: Classics
STARRING: Joan Crawford, Ann Blyth, Zachary Scott, Eve Arden,
Jack Carson
DIRECTED BY: Michael Curtiz

An unusual *film noir*. Crawford gives what is, perhaps, the finest performance of her career in this deeply moving exploration of the relationship between an impoverished divorcee, fighting her way up from waitress to restaurant owner, and her spoiled, demanding daughter (Blyth). Heartless lover Scott adds to her troubles. Best Supporting Actress nominations for both Arden and Blyth, as well as nominations for Best Picture, Screenplay and Cinematography.
OSCAR WIN: *Best Actress (Crawford)*

The Picture of Dorian Gray

BLOCKBUSTER CATEGORY: Classics
STARRING: George Sanders, Hurd Hatfield, Angela Lansbury,
Peter Lawford
DIRECTED BY: Albert Lewin

Gripping screen adaptation of Oscar Wilde's classic gothic tale about a self-absorbed and a voracious young man (Hatfield) who seems to stay forever youthful and vibrant, while his portrait, hidden away from prying eyes, grows old and misshapen, reflecting his true nature. Sparkling direction, excellent performances all around, and near-hypnotic narration by Cedric Hardwicke make this a must-see cinematic experience. Oscar-nominated for Best Supporting Actress (Lansbury) and Interior Decoration. The glimpses of Gray's deteriorating portrait are in Technicolor.
OSCAR WIN: *Best Cinematography (Harry Stradling)*

Scarlet Street

BLOCKBUSTER CATEGORY: Classics
STARRING: Edward G. Robinson, Dan Duryea, Joan Bennett,
Margaret Lindsay
DIRECTED BY: Fritz Lang

When this dark, textured drama was released, it was banned for a time in New York State because it violates the "crime doesn't pay" convention. Robinson is a timid husband and clerk whose sole pleasure in life is his painting. Almost accidentally, he rescues a beautiful, mysterious woman (Bennett) from a mugging, but his only reward is treachery and deception as the beauty and her boyfriend (Duryea) scheme to use him for their own wicked ends. A delicious double twist and an ironic ending.

Spellbound

BLOCKBUSTER CATEGORY: Alfred Hitchcock
STARRING: Gregory Peck, Ingrid Bergman, Michael Chekhov, Leo G. Carroll
DIRECTED BY: Alfred Hitchcock

Hitchcock at his finest. Salvador Dali collaborated on the eerie dream sequences in this dark, intriguing murder mystery about a psychiatrist (Bergman) who shields a patient (Peck) from the police while she searches for clues to the crime within his psyche. Plot twists and surprises to satisfy even the most demanding Hitchcock fan. Oscar-nominated for Best Picture, Director (Hitchcock), Supporting Actor (Chekhov), Cinematography and Special Effects.
OSCAR WIN: *Best Score (Miklos Rozsa)*

The Story of GI Joe

BLOCKBUSTER CATEGORY: Drama
STARRING: Burgess Meredith, Robert Mitchum, Freddie Steele
DIRECTED BY: William A. Wellman

Burgess Meredith is ideally cast as Ernie Pyle, the famed war correspondent, in this superior World War II drama. Robert Mitchum plays his first major screen role as one of the GI's whose stories Pyle recounts for his readers. This movie and BATTLEGROUND (1949) were both directed by the legendary action film director William A. Wellman, and they are among the most authentic World War II films ever made. Also known as G.I. JOE. Oscar-nominated for Supporting Actor (Mitchum), Screenplay (Leopold Atlas, Guy Endore, Philip Stevenson), Music, Song.

They Were Expendable

BLOCKBUSTER CATEGORY: Action/Adventure
STARRING: John Wayne, Donna Reed, Robert Montgomery, Ward Bond, Leon Ames
DIRECTED BY: John Ford

An inspiring, patriotic World War II story that nevertheless avoids the cliches and addresses the grim realities of war. Montgomery is a PT boat commander in the Pacific, modeled after real-life Congressional Medal of Honor recipient Captain John Bulkeley. Wayne is his eager second-in-command, frustrated by his squad's minor role in the action - until he finds himself outgunned and seriously overmatched by the powerful Japanese forces. Oscar-nominated for Special Effects, Sound.

A Tree Grows in Brooklyn

BLOCKBUSTER CATEGORY: Classics
STARRING: Dorothy McGuire, Joan Blondell, James Dunn, Peggy Ann Garner
DIRECTED BY: Elia Kazan

Kazan's first directional effort produced this uplifting drama about the coming of age in a turn-of-the-century Brooklyn tenement district of a young lady (Garner) with dreams of a better life. She idolizes the alcoholic father (Dunn), and resents the struggling mother (McGuire), whom the girl sees as a constant reminder of the harsh realities of a self-perpetuating trap of poverty. Frank Davis and Tess Slesinger were nominated for Best Screenplay.

OSCAR WINS: *Best Supporting Actor (Dunn), Outstanding Child Actress of the Year (Garner)*

Anna and the King of Siam

BLOCKBUSTER CATEGORY: Classics
STARRING: Irene Dunne, Rex Harrison, Linda Darnell
DIRECTED BY: John Cromwell

An exotic 19th-century romance best known today as the source for the 1956 musical, THE KING AND I. Happily the original version more than holds its own. British schoolteacher and governess Anna L. Owens (Irene Dunne) journeys to Siam in 1862 to tutor the king's 67 (!) children. Harrison, in his first Hollywood movie, is properly dashing and regal; it's impossible to think of anyone else in the role of the king. Oscar-nominated for Supporting Actress (Gale Sondergaard), Screenplay (Sally Benson, Talbot Jennings), Score (Bernard Hermann).
OSCAR WINS: *Cinematography - b&w, Art Direction*

The Best Years of Our Lives

BLOCKBUSTER CATEGORY: Classics
STARRING: Fredric March, Myrna Loy, Dana Andrews,
　　　　　　　Teresa Wright, Harold Russell
DIRECTED BY: William Wyler

One of Hollywood's finest moments. This powerful narrative follows three soldiers, an Air Corps captain (Andrews), a sergeant (March), and a sailor crippled in action (Russell, a real-life veteran and amputee), returning from World War II and trying to adjust to their post-war emotions and an unfamiliar civilian life. Although the era has changed, this drama is still fresh and relevant. Excellent direction, perfect pacing and superior acting dominate this Library of Congress National Film Registry selection. Oscar-nominated for Best Sound Recording.
OSCAR SWEEP: *Best Picture, Director (Wyler), Actor (March), Supporting Actor (Russell), Screenplay (Robert E. Sherwood), Editing, Musical Score and a Special Oscar to Russell for inspiring other World War II vets*

The Big Sleep

BLOCKBUSTER CATEGORY: Classics
STARRING: Humphrey Bogart, Lauren Bacall, Dorothy Malone,
　　　　　　　Regis Toomey
DIRECTED BY: Howard Hawks

In this suspenseful adaptation of Raymond Chandler's famous detective story, scripted by William Faulkner, Bogart is Philip Marlowe, private eye, hired to keep an eye on the shady daughter (Bacall) of a rich man. What wasn't in the bargain was the collection of assorted murders he encounters along the way. The remarkable chemistry between the stars helps make this atmospheric murder mystery an all-time classic and one of Bogart's best.

Brief Encounter

BLOCKBUSTER CATEGORY: Classics
STARRING: Trevor Howard, Celia Johnson, Joyce Carey
DIRECTED BY: David Lean

A tender love story that manages to be deeply romantic without being maudlin. A chance train-station encounter between a middle-class, middle-aged housewife (Johnson) and a married doctor (Howard) leads to a storybook love affair – touching, sweet in its near-innocence, but doomed from the start. This sensitive and well-crafted adaptation of the Noel Coward play earned Oscar nominations for Best Director (Lean), Actress (Johnson) and Screenplay (Anthony Havelock-Allan, Ronald Neame and Lean).

Duel in the Sun
BLOCKBUSTER CATEGORY: Westerns
STARRING: Jennifer Jones, Gregory Peck, Joseph Cotten
DIRECTED BY: King Vidor

The basic plot is simple enough: Two brothers, one good and one bad, vie for the affections of a half-breed Indian woman in the old west. But producer David O. Selznick used it as the backdrop for one of the most elaborately produced westerns ever made, a movie he hoped would top even his earlier masterpiece, GONE WITH THE WIND. A stellar supporting cast, including Lionel Barrymore and Lillian Gish, is in top form. The Technicolor photography has never been matched. Oscar-nominated for Best Actress (Jones), Supporting Actress (Gish).

Gilda
BLOCKBUSTER CATEGORY: Classics
STARRING: Rita Hayworth, Glenn Ford, George Macready
DIRECTED BY: Charles Vidor

Only Hayworth at her most seductive could have created the degree of sexual tension - without removing a single glove - that made this film so controversial. A casino owner (Macready) helps out a drifter (Ford), then hires him to protect his wife (Hayworth), unaware that the pair were once lovers and the drifter still carries a torch. The tightly interwoven relationships that develop among the three become ever more twisted and intricate right to the explosive climax.

Great Expectations
BLOCKBUSTER CATEGORY: Classics
STARRING: John Mills, Valerie Hobson, Alec Guinness,
Bernard Miles
DIRECTED BY: David Lean

Brilliant and faithful adaptation of the beloved Charles Dickens tale of Pip (Mills), the poor orphan who gets an unexpected boost in society from a mysterious escaped convict. The dreary Victorian atmosphere, superb period settings and excellent acting make this lavishly filmed spectacle the best Dickens movie adaptation ever. Oscar-nominated for Best Picture, Director (Lean) and Screenplay.
OSCAR WINS: *Best Cinematography - b&w, Art Direction - b&w*

It's a Wonderful Life
BLOCKBUSTER CATEGORY: Classics
STARRING: James Stewart, Donna Reed, Henry Travers,
Lionel Barrymore
DIRECTED BY: Frank Capra

A perennial Christmas favorite, but well worth watching any time of the year. George Bailey (Stewart) is a self-sacrificing, altruistic businessman in a small town who seems to be losing at every turn to rich, greedy Barrymore. Driven to despair by his self-perceived failures, Bailey is contemplating suicide until one Clarence Oddbody (Travers), a guardian angel of sorts, shows him what the town would have been like without him. Oscar-nominated for Best Picture, Director (Capra), and Actor (Stewart), Sound Recording and Film Editing.

The Jolson Story

BLOCKBUSTER CATEGORY: Classics
STARRING: Larry Parks, Evelyn Keyes, William Demarest
DIRECTED BY: Alfred E. Green

Larry Parks has the role of a lifetime in this top-drawer screen biography. He plays Al Jolson, who rose from being the son of a rabbi to a popular vaudeville singer to, in 1927, the star of the first talking picture, THE JAZZ SINGER. Jolson dubbed his own voice for the musical sequences of this big-budget show biz biography, but Parks delivers a *tour-de-force* performance nonetheless. The movie does a praiseworthy job of alternating between Jolson's exhilarating career climb and his troubled personal life. Songs include: "April Showers", "You Made Me Love You" and, of course, "My Mammy." Oscar-nominated for Best Actor (Parks), Supporting Actor (Demarest), Cinematography and Editing.
OSCAR WINS: *Best Musical Score, Best Sound Recording*

My Darling Clementine

BLOCKBUSTER CATEGORY: Westerns
STARRING: Henry Fonda, Victor Mature, Linda Darnell
DIRECTED BY: John Ford

In the turbulent Arizona of the late 1800's, a series of land wars, border feuds and murders finally leads to the famed gunfight at the OK Corral. The great western director John Ford (STAGECOACH) knew Wyatt Earp personally, and based some of this majestic western's screenplay upon the former Tombstone marshal's recollections. Henry Fonda and Victor Mature are ideally teamed as Earp and that magnet for trouble, gambler Doc Holliday. Also see: GUNFIGHT AT O.K. CORRAL.

Notorious

BLOCKBUSTER CATEGORY: Alfred Hitchcock
STARRING: Cary Grant, Ingrid Bergman, Claude Rains,
Louis Calhern
DIRECTED BY: Alfred Hitchcock

Dark, tingling suspense that could only come from Hitchcock. The scene is Rio de Janeiro, just after World War II - a haven for Nazis on the run. A U.S. double agent (Grant) finds Bergman, the daughter of a war criminal and, despite the steamy, tension-charged romance that ensues, blackmails her into marrying his quarry, a dangerous Nazi agent (Rains). Oscar-nominated for Best Supporting Actor (Rains) and Screenplay.

The Postman Always Rings Twice

BLOCKBUSTER CATEGORY: Drama
STARRING: John Garfield, Lana Turner, Cecil Kellaway
DIRECTED BY: Tay Garnett

A drifter (Garfield) falls under the spell of the sultry wife (Turner) of a diner owner, and together they bump off the unsuspecting husband. The censors of the day tried to keep this adaptation of pulp novelist James M. Cain's suspense classic off the screen, but Hollywood managed to make a sexy version of it anyway, by *not* showing the things that were explicit in the book. John Garfield, the Brando of his day, gives one of his strongest performances, and Turner is enticing as ever. Other versions: OSSESSIONE (Italy, 1942) and the 1981 American remake.

The Razor's Edge
BLOCKBUSTER CATEGORY: Classics
STARRING: Tyrone Power, Gene Tierney, Anne Baxter, Clifton Webb
DIRECTED BY: Edmund Goulding

Moving, ambitious screen adaptation of Somerset Maugham's masterpiece about a wealthy young man, disillusioned by the ravages of World War I, who sets out to discover some meaning in life - no matter how far and wide his search may take him. Remarkably faithful to the tone of the novel, the film manages to retain Maugham's dark, atmospheric mood and powerful characterizations. Oscar-nominated for Best Picture and Best Supporting Actor (Webb) and Interior Decoration.
OSCAR WIN: *Best Supporting Actress (Baxter)*

The Seventh Veil
BLOCKBUSTER CATEGORY: Classics
STARRING: James Mason, Herbert Lom, Ann Todd
DIRECTED BY: Compton Bennett

Stunning gothic romance stars Todd as an orphan raised by her bachelor cousin (Mason), who, although domineering and tyrannical, cultivates her considerable musical abilities. She leaves home, aspiring for a career as a concert pianist, but is torn between two suitors, her cousin, and a psychiatrist who helps her come to terms with her emotions. Masterful direction helps sustain the dark, gothic atmosphere throughout.
OSCAR WIN: *Best Original Screenplay (Muriel Box and Sidney Box)*

To Each His Own
BLOCKBUSTER CATEGORY: Not available on video
STARRING: Olivia de Havilland, John Lund, Roland Culver
DIRECTED BY: Mitchell Leisen

Evocative melodrama about an unwed mother (de Havilland) who reluctantly gives up her child, only to meet him by accident years later, when he's a soldier (Lund) during World War II - and a perfect likeness of his father. Posing as a long-lost aunt, she works her way back into his life. Oscar-nominated for Best Original Story.
OSCAR WIN: *Best Actress (de Havilland)*

The Yearling
BLOCKBUSTER CATEGORY: Family
STARRING: Gregory Peck, Claude Jarman, Jr., Jane Wyman
DIRECTED BY: Clarence Brown

A boy growing up on a Florida farm adopts a young deer and struggles to keep him amid pressure from his family. Generally considered one of the finest films of its kind, this drama was directed by one of the most powerful filmmakers on the MGM lot, Clarence Brown; he was able to persuade the studio to let him shoot it on actual Florida locations. Oscar-nominated for Best Picture, Director (Brown), Actor (Peck), Actress (Wyman), Film Editing.

OSCAR WINS: *Cinematography - color, Art Direction - color, Special Oscar to Claude Jarman, Jr., Outstanding Child Actor of 1946.*

The Bachelor and the Bobbysoxer
BLOCKBUSTER CATEGORY: Classics
STARRING: Cary Grant, Myrna Loy, Shirley Temple,
Harry Davenport, Rudy Vallee
DIRECTED BY: Irving Reis
A spinsterish lady judge orders a playboy to squire her teenage sister around town.
The teenaged girl is infatuated with the playboy and the judge thinks a close
association will cure her. The movie was the last to show these types in an innocent
light. Once the realistic 1950's and 60's hit, teenaged girls were no longer innocent
and playboys were much more worldly. Grant, Loy and Temple spoofed their own
former images in this wonderful comedy.
OSCAR WIN: *Best Original Screenplay (Sidney Sheldon)*

The Bishop's Wife
BLOCKBUSTER CATEGORY: Classics
STARRING: Cary Grant, Loretta Young, David Niven,
Gladys Cooper
DIRECTED BY: Henry Koster
The good news is that an angel (Grant) arrives straight from heaven to help out the
poor, overworked bishop (Niven). The bad news is that the bishop believes the
angel has designs on his wife - and why not? She's Loretta Young at her loveliest.
This timeless Christmas comedy classic will charm audiences of all ages with its
whimsical storyline and its convincing performances all around. Oscar-nominated
for Best Picture, Director (Koster), Score, Film Editing.
OSCAR WIN: *Best Sound Recording*

Black Narcissus
BLOCKBUSTER CATEGORY: Classics
STARRING: Deborah Kerr, Jean Simmons, Sabu, David Farrar,
Flora Robson
DIRECTED BY: Michael Powell and Emeric Pressburger
British nuns establish a mission in India and undergo obstacles inside and outside
the mission's walls. Rich Technicolor photography gives the film vivid life, and the
performers tackle soap opera elements in a very melodramatic setting. It
realistically shows that madness, jealousy, greed, passion and even murder can exist
in areas considered out of bounds - like a nunnery in India.
OSCAR WINS: *Best Cinematography - color, Art Direction/Set Decoration - color*

Body & Soul
BLOCKBUSTER CATEGORY: Drama
STARRING: John Garfield, Lilli Palmer, Hazel Brooks
DIRECTED BY: Robert Rossen
The first great expose of boxing corruption, this gritty melodrama stars Oscar-
nominated John Garfield as a kid who works his way up from the streets to become
a champion prizefighter. Lilli Palmer tries to help him escape the fight racket's
pitfalls. The ring sequences foreshadow the vivid brutality of RAGING BULL.
Oscar-nominated tor Best Actor (Garfield), Best Original Screenplay.
OSCAR WIN: *Best Editing*

1947

Dark Passage

BLOCKBUSTER CATEGORY: Classics
STARRING: Humphrey Bogart, Lauren Bacall, Agnes Moorehead, Bruce Bennett
DIRECTED BY: Delmer Daves

A man is unjustly accused of murdering his wife and undergoes plastic surgery in order to assume a new identity. He hides at his wife's girlfriend's apartment until he can locate the real killer. The film is still hailed for its intense cinematography that makes moodiness one of the characters. The complicated screenplay successfully competes with the Sam Spade and Phillip Marlow stories. Great chemistry between Bogart and Bacall. The story also inspired the long-running TV series, "The Fugitive."

A Double Life

BLOCKBUSTER CATEGORY: Classics
STARRING: Ronald Colman, Shelley Winters, Signe Hasso, Edmond O'Brien
DIRECTED BY: George Cukor

A prominent Broadway actor gets so involved in his acting roles that he begins to live them off-stage. When he suspects a woman of being unfaithful, he strangles her in a fit of madness while performing that very scene from *Othello*. A significant film for bringing an element of Shakespeare to mass entertainment. It is also essentially the story of *Dr. Jekyll and Mr. Hyde* reworked to suit the personalities and talents of an excellent cast. Oscar-nominated for Best Director, (Cukor)and Screenplay.
OSCAR WINS: *Best Actor (Colman), Musical Score*

The Farmer's Daughter

BLOCKBUSTER CATEGORY: Classics
STARRING: Loretta Young, Joseph Cotten, Ethel Barrymore, Charles Bickford
DIRECTED BY: H.C. Potter

A Swedish girl from Minnesota gets a job as a maid in a Congressman's home and decides to go into politics herself. A political spoof that hit a nerve in a pre-election year and is considered a classic because it typifies the political mood of the times so well. Oscar-nominated for Best Supporting Actor (Bickford).
OSCAR WIN: *Best Actress (Young)*

Gentleman's Agreement

BLOCKBUSTER CATEGORY: Not available in video
STARRING: Gregory Peck, Dorothy McGuire, Celeste Holm, John Garfield, Anne Revere
DIRECTED BY: Elia Kazan

A magazine writer pretends to be Jewish in order to uncover anti-Semitism in his business and social circles. A history-making film that exposed both overt and covert cases of anti-Semitism in all walks of life. Oscar-nominated for Best Actor (Peck), Actress (McGuire), Supporting Actress (Revere), Screenplay, Film Editing.
OSCAR SWEEP: *Best Picture, Director (Kazan), Supporting Actress (Holm)*

The Ghost and Mrs. Muir
BLOCKBUSTER CATEGORY: Classics
STARRING: Gene Tierney, Rex Harrison, George Sanders
DIRECTED BY: Joseph L. Mankiewicz
Rex Harrison is marvelous in a unique love story that was one of the first Hollywood movies to showcase the British star as a romantic leading man. Gene Tierney (LAURA) portrays a lonely widow, sheltered away in a cottage at the edge of a seacoast village, who is romanced by the ghost of a sea captain (Harrison). A charming, one-of-a-kind fantasy, a delicate and altogether satisfying blend of love story and ghost story. Quite different from the 60's TV sitcom loosely based on it. Classic score by Bernard Hermann. Oscar-nominated for Cinematography.

Kiss of Death
BLOCKBUSTER CATEGORY: Drama
STARRING: Victor Mature, Brian Donlevy, Colleen Gray
DIRECTED BY: Henry Hathaway
In this landmark gangster movie, Victor Mature plays an ex-con robber who must choose between a life of crime and the brutal consequences of turning his former cronies in to the cops. One of several late 40's melodramas by 20th Century-Fox that were shot on atmospheric, New York locations, it's also distinguished by Richard Widmark's frightening portrayal of one of the screen's first all-out psychopaths, a cackling maniac who shoves a wheelchair-bound woman down a flight of stairs. Oscar-nominated for Best Supporting Actor (Widmark), Original Screenplay.

Life With Father
BLOCKBUSTER CATEGORY: Classics
STARRING: William Powell, Irene Dunne, Edmund Gwenn
DIRECTED BY: Michael Curtiz
In turn-of-the-century New York, the bombastic - but lovable - patriarch of a large family creates a domestic furor through his stubborn ways. Howard Lindsay and Russel Crouse's Broadway stage hit is transformed into a nostalgic - and very funny - vehicle for a large stable of reliable stars, including Elizabeth Taylor in a small (but key) role. Oscar-nominated for Best Actor (Powell), Cinematography - color, Art Direction - color and Score (Max Steiner).

Miracle on 34th Street
BLOCKBUSTER CATEGORY: Classics
STARRING: Maureen O'Hara, John Payne, Edmund Gwenn,
Natalie Wood
DIRECTED BY: George Seaton
Kris Kringle lands a job as a department store Santa and guides customers to a competing department store when they can't find what they want. He also insists he is really Santa Claus, leading to a court trial to see if Santa really exists or not. A whimsical tale that keeps the Christmas spirit without playing down to its audience. The performers play their roles so straight they make Santa Claus believers out of the audience, and that is the secret to its perennial success. Oscar-nominated for Best Picture.
OSCAR SWEEP: *Best Supporting Actor (Gwenn), Original Story (Valentine Davies), Screenplay (Seaton)*

Monsieur Verdoux
BLOCKBUSTER CATEGORY: Classics
STARRING: Charlie Chaplin, Martha Raye, William Frawley
DIRECTED BY: Charlie Chaplin
Who but Chaplin could have made a comedy about Landru, the Parisian mass murderer who killed his many wives in order to collect on their insurance policies? Chaplin's black comedy sailed over the heads of most audiences when it was first released. Today, it's one of his most popular films. Oscar-nominated for Best Original Screenplay (Chaplin).

Odd Man Out
BLOCKBUSTER CATEGORY: Classics
STARRING: James Mason, Robert Newton, Dan O'Herlihy,
Kathleen Ryan
DIRECTED BY: Carol Reed
An Irish rebel leader commits a robbery and runs from the police. An exciting picture that socks home the ambiguity of law and order during war and revolution. It is also another major *film noir* that communicates suspense with intricate lighting, unusual camera angles and extreme close-ups of agonized faces. Another reason for its continued success is that it brought James Mason to Hollywood. Oscar-nominated for Best Film Editing.

Out of the Past
BLOCKBUSTER CATEGORY: Classics
STARRING: Kirk Douglas, Robert Mitchum, Jane Greer,
Rhonda Fleming
DIRECTED BY: Jacques Tourneur
A mob leader entices a former crook to go back into a life of crime by sending him on a wild goose chase. He wants the man to find his straying wife and hopes to catch them both in a clinch so he can kill them. This *film noir* masterpiece gave Jane Greer a villainess of the year award from several groups. It set a pattern for other gangland melodramas with its intricate plot of manipulation and intense character study of good guys and bad guys. Remade as Against All Odds (1984), also with Greer.

The Secret Life of Walter Mitty
BLOCKBUSTER CATEGORY: Comedy
STARRING: Danny Kaye, Virginia Mayo, Boris Karloff
DIRECTED BY: Norman Z. McLeod
Walter Mitty (Danny Kaye) is a bored office worker who daydreams his way into flights of derring-do, all of which are shown to us in the breathtaking Technicolor of the 40's. More than just a knockabout vehicle for Kaye's slapstick talents, this James Thurber adaptation influenced scores of later movies and TV shows, including BILLY LIAR, MONTY PYTHON and even "The Simpsons".

1947

¶¶

Unconquered

BLOCKBUSTER CATEGORY: Westerns
STARRING: Gary Cooper, Paulette Goddard, Howard da Silva
DIRECTED BY: Cecil B. DeMille

Cecil B. DeMille took a break from his Biblical epics to make this large-scale frontier saga about settlers battling Indians in the 1760's. Wrongly convicted of robbery, Goddard is banished from England and sent to America. There, she falls in love with Virginian Gary Cooper and is nearly killed after being captured by Indians. Only DeMille would think of casting Boris Karloff as an Indian chief, and manage to pull off the stunt. As always with DeMille, there are plenty of action scenes, all of them staged superbly. Oscar-nominated for Special Effects.

¶¶

Adventures of Don Juan

BLOCKBUSTER CATEGORY: Classics
STARRING: Errol Flynn, Viveca Lindfors, Robert Douglas
DIRECTED BY: Vincent Sherman

Errol Flynn's offscreen exploits as a ladies' man were making headlines in the 40's, so it's no surprise to find him portraying history's most celebrated skirt-chaser. What is surprising is that a film arriving so late in Flynn's days as a swashbuckler should be as terrific as thjs one. Acting, script and direction have a leisurely, tongue-in-cheek manner to them - yet there are plenty of swordfights and brawls for die-hard action fans. Look for Raymond Burr and perennial Flynn crony Alan Hale in the supporting cast. Oscar-nominated for Art Direction.
OSCAR WIN: *Costume Design - color*

Call Northside 777

BLOCKBUSTER CATEGORY: Drama
STARRING: James Stewart, Richard Conte, Lee J. Cobb
DIRECTED BY: Henry Hathaway

A reporter (Stewart), covering what appears to be a routine, open-and-shut case of murder, begins to believe the suspect is innocent and spends months trying to prove it. One of several dramas produced in the 40's by Louis de Rochemont, whose trademark was location filming - then rare among Hollywood studios - and an almost documentary sense of realism. The ball-of-twine mystery unravels with cool precision, and Stewart, cast against type, contributes one of his best performances.

Easter Parade

BLOCKBUSTER CATEGORY: Musicals
STARRING: Judy Garland, Fred Astaire, Peter Lawford,
Ann Miller
DIRECTED BY: Charles Walters

A lighthearted, tune-filled musical in the stellar MGM tradition. Astaire plays a dancing star who rejuvenates his tired career with a new partner, Judy Garland. Alas, he can't get ex-partner Ann Miller out of his system. Peter Lawford, then being groomed as a major MGM star, has a key supporting role. Irving Berlin provided one of his best scores. The cast performs several classic numbers, including "Stepping Out With My Baby," "Shaking the Blues Away," and on a glorious MGM re-creation of New York's Fifth Avenue, the famous title tune.
OSCAR WIN: *Scoring of a Musical Picture*

Forever Amber

BLOCKBUSTER CATEGORY: Classics
STARRING: Linda Darnell, Cornel Wilde, Richard Greene
DIRECTED BY: Otto Preminger

An early effort by director Otto Preminger (LAURA, ANATOMY OF A MURDER), which adapts a steamy costume romance novel that Hollywood was reluctant to tackle because of its racy content. Darnell dyed her hair blonde to play the scheming Amber, who rises to a position of influence in the reign of Charles II by seducing a number of men. A perfect example of role-reversal romance.

Hamlet

BLOCKBUSTER CATEGORY: Classics
STARRING: Laurence Olivier, Jean Simmons, Eileen Herlie,
Peter Cushing
DIRECTED BY: Laurence Olivier

A Danish prince avenges his father's murder in this lengthy Shakespearean tragedy.
Olivier cut out about half of the play, consolidated some characters and omitted
others and made the first truly successful film adaptation of Shakespeare. It
succeeds because Olivier made it move, focusing on action and not just soliloquies.
He literally adapted it to the medium of film, and it was Oscar-nominated for Best
Supporting Actress (Simmons), Director (Olivier) and Score.
OSCAR SWEEP: *Best Picture, Actor (Olivier), Art Direction/Set Decoration - b&w,
Costume Design - b&w*

I Remember Mama

BLOCKBUSTER CATEGORY: Classics
STARRING: Irene Dunne, Barbara Bel Geddes, Oscar Homolka
DIRECTED BY: George Stevens

In San Francisco in the early 1900's, several generations of a Norwegian immigrant
family are held together by the wisdom, wit and guidance of the family matriarch
(Dunne). First-rate, warm and altogether rewarding adaptation of Kathryn Forbes'
memoirs, with a big, ensemble cast and direction by the man responsible for
SHANE and A PLACE IN THE SUN. Oscar-nominated for Best Actress (Dunne),
Supporting Actress (Bel Geddes, Ellen Corby), Supporting Actor (Homolka),
Cinematography -b&w.

Johnny Belinda

BLOCKBUSTER CATEGORY: Classics
STARRING: Jane Wyman, Lew Ayres, Agnes Moorehead,
Charles Bickford
DIRECTED BY: Jean Negulesco

A deaf-mute farm girl is raped by the town bully and has a child. A country doctor
champions her cause and helps her keep the baby, causing the townspeople to think
he was the one who raped her. A significant movie because it deals openly with the
formerly taboo subject of rape and treats the handicapped heroine with more
compassion than usual. Oscar-nominated for Best Picture, Actor (Ayres),
Supporting Actor (Bickford), Supporting Actress (Moorehead), Director
(Negulesco), Screenplay, Cinematography, Art Direction/Set Decoration, Sound,
Score and Editing.
OSCAR WIN: *Best Actress (Wyman)*

Key Largo

BLOCKBUSTER CATEGORY: Drama
STARRING: Humphrey Bogart, Lauren Bacall, Edward G.
Robinson, Claire Trevor, Lionel Barrymore
DIRECTED BY: John Huston

One of the last great Bogart gangster classics, this suspense melodrama puts him
on the right side of the law, as a cynical World War II veteran. While a threatening
hurricane draws closer, a notorious mobster holds the inhabitants of a hotel captive

in the Florida Keys. Robinson, playing the final gangster role of his colorful career, pulls out all the stops as the sadistic villain. His climactic showdown with Bogart, a hero who refuses to be bullied, is raw and exciting. Bacall plays the daughter of hotel owner Barrymore, and Trevor is outstanding as Robinson's alcoholic gun moll. Adapted from Maxwell Anderson's play.

OSCAR WIN: *Best Supporting Actress (Trevor)*

Letter from an Unknown Woman

BLOCKBUSTER CATEGORY: Classics
STARRING: Joan Fontaine, Louis Jourdan, Mady Christians,
Marcel Journet
DIRECTED BY: Max Ophuls

A young girl falls madly in love with a concert pianist who is also a womanizer. She bears his child in secret and returns to him years later in the hope that he matured. But he doesn't even recognize her and thinks of her as another new conquest. The film is notable for the way it emphasizes romance through moody lighting effects, unusual camera angles and movement to showcase facial reactions, and the clever way it uses close-ups to make the audience feel part of the picture. Director Ophuls employs *film noir* techniques to enhance the romance and he was one of the first to do so.

Oliver Twist

BLOCKBUSTER CATEGORY: Classics
STARRING: Alec Guinness, Robert Newton, John Howard Davies,
Kay Walsh
DIRECTED BY: David Lean

A young boy in Victorian England escapes an orphanage because of cruel treatment and takes up with a gang of thieves. He witnesses the cruelty people use against one another when they're poor, destitute and desperate and sees the rich treat the poor with contempt. A masterpiece of filmmaking, just as the Dickens original is a masterpiece of writing. Both show the deplorable conditions of the times in a personal perspective. The story could have been set in today's tenements and be just as timely with these performances. Also see OLIVER!

The Pirate

BLOCKBUSTER CATEGORY: Musicals
STARRING: Judy Garland, Gene Kelly, Walter Slezak,
Gladys Cooper
DIRECTED BY: Vincente Minnelli

A street clown pretends to be a pirate in order to live up to a young girl's romantic wish. She, in turn, wants a reason to leave the stodgy, old man to whom she is engaged. When she finds out the pirate is a fake, she throws a tantrum, but he wins her in the end. A lavish musical that capitalizes on the singing and dancing talents of its stars to spoof swashbuckler movies. One of the first major parodies to use name stars, a name composer (Cole Porter) and a Broadway play (by S.N. Behrman) without compromising any of its ingredients. Oscar-nominated for Best Scoring of a Musical.

Red River

BLOCKBUSTER CATEGORY: Westerns
STARRING: John Wayne, Montgomery Clift, Joanne Dru,
Walter Brennan
DIRECTED BY: Howard Hawks

A tough Texas rancher blazes the Chisholm Trail to herd his cattle to Kansas. He brutalizes his men in an effort to get there with the herd of cattle intact and one of his underlings openly defies him by fighting with him in a climactic showdown. This movie deservedly earned acclaim for showing the bitter times of the Old West without resorting to maudlin sentiment. The story is similar to MUTINY ON THE BOUNTY (1935) with the same accent on masculine aggressiveness. Oscar-nominated for Best Original Story, Film Editing.

The Red Shoes

BLOCKBUSTER CATEGORY: Classics
STARRING: Moira Shearer, Anton Walbrook, Marius Goring,
Robert Helpmann
DIRECTED BY: Michael Powell and Emeric Pressburger

A young ballerina is torn between her love for a possessive young composer and a domineering dance impressario. Famous for being the first adult love story fashioned out of a child's fairy tale and the first successful commercial feature dealing with the ballet world, not to mention great color photography. Oscar-nominated for Best Picture, Story and Editing.
OSCAR WINS: *Best Art Direction/Set Decoration - color, Score*

The Search

BLOCKBUSTER CATEGORY: Not available on video
STARRING: Montgomery Clift, Ivan Jandl, Aline MacMahon,
Jarmila Novotna
DIRECTED BY: Fred Zinnemann

An American soldier cares for a youth who survived concentration camp torture in postwar Germany. The young boy's mother desperately searches for him and her search is juxtaposed with the soldier's compassionate caring. The first film to show the horrors of war through the beleaguered eyes of a child. It is also noteworthy for drawing a realistic picture of the kind of life the occupation forces were subjected to. Oscar-nominated for Best Actor (Clift) and Director (Zinnemann).
OSCAR WINS: *Best Story (Richard Schweizer and David Wechsler) and an Honorary Oscar for Best Juvenile Performance (Jandl).*

The Snake Pit

BLOCKBUSTER CATEGORY: Not available on video
STARRING: Olivia de Havilland, Celeste Holm, Mark Stevens,
Leo Genn
DIRECTED BY: Anatole Litvak

A young woman suffers a nervous breakdown and is committed to a mental institution where she undergoes treatment. The first movie to deal realistically with mental problems by showing the effect of treatment on the patient. It influenced mental health and "women-behind-bars" movies for years to come. Oscar-nominated for Best Picture, Actress, (de Havilland), Director (Litvak), Screenplay and Music Score.

1948

Sorry, Wrong Number
BLOCKBUSTER CATEGORY: Mystery
STARRING: Barbara Stanwyck, Burt Lancaster, Ann Richards
DIRECTED BY: Anatole Litvak
A bedridden woman accidentally overhears a phone conversation in which her husband reveals that he is planning to kill her. Lucille Fletcher's virtual one-woman show had been dramatized many times on radio during the 40's; Fletcher herself expanded it for this 89-minute movie version, which netted Barbara Stanwyck an Oscar nomination for her portrayal of the potential victim.

The Treasure of the Sierra Madre
BLOCKBUSTER CATEGORY: Classics
STARRING: Humphrey Bogart, Walter Huston, Tim Holt,
Bruce Bennett
DIRECTED BY: John Huston
Three men hunt for gold in Mexico, embittered by a boss who stole their wages and bandits who try to steal their new-found riches. One of the most powerful indictments of greed with a storyline that compares individual greed for gold with the avarice of Big Business and the first to put those traits in a personal perspective. Oscar-nominated for Best Picture. John Huston directed his father to an Oscar.
OSCAR WINS: *Best Director (John Huston), Supporting Actor (Walter Huston), Screenplay (John Huston)*

Unfaithfully Yours
BLOCKBUSTER CATEGORY: Classics
STARRING: Rex Harrison, Linda Darnell, Kurt Krueger
DIRECTED BY: Preston Sturges
Probably the last great movie written and directed by Preston Sturges - whose series of 40's comedies were without equal - this wonderful film is also a great early vehicle for Rex Harrison. The future star of MY FAIR LADY plays a popular orchestra conductor who thinks his sexy wife, Linda Darnell, is having an affair. Naturally, she isn't. The film's highlight is a scene in which Harrison feverishly conducts the orchestra, while we see what he's really thinking about: an assortment of creative ways to bump off Darnell and her "lover."Remade in 1984.

1949

All the King's Men
BLOCKBUSTER CATEGORY: Classics
STARRING: Broderick Crawford, Mercedes McCambridge,
John Ireland, Joanne Dru, John Derek,
Shepperd Strudwick, Anne Seymour
DIRECTED BY: Robert Rossen
A detailed account of a corrupt politician based on the life and career of Huey Long.
The movie is based on a Pulitzer Prize-winning novel that fictionalized the
characters, but was true to the era. One of the first movies to indict a modern day
politician by showing his personal weaknesses in vivid detail. Each performance
rings true as a reminder that corruption is present, accounted for and punishable.
Oscar-nominated for Best Supporting Actor (Ireland), Director (Rossen),
Screenplay and Film Editing.
OSCAR SWEEP: Best Picture, Actor (Crawford), Supporting Actress (McCambridge)

Battleground
BLOCKBUSTER CATEGORY: Classics
STARRING: Van Johnson, Ricardo Montalban, John Hodiak,
Denise Darcel, James Whitmore, George Murphy,
Marshall Thompson, Richard Jaeckel
DIRECTED BY: William Wellman
A reenactment of the Battle of the Bulge, with sidelights that develop the
personalities of each soldier and how the war affects him. A significant movie
because it was produced long after World War II and had some of the same morale-
building ingredients of wartime pictures. Unlike the wartime films, it didn't exploit
the personalities in the name of sentiment. Instead, it painted a truer picture of men
in wartime. Oscar-nominated for Best Picture and Supporting Actor (Whitmore).
OSCAR WINS: Best Story & Screenplay (Robert Pirosh), Cinematography - b&w

The Bicycle Thief
BLOCKBUSTER CATEGORY: Foreign
STARRING: Lamberto Magiorani, Lianella Carell, Enzo Staiola,
Elena Altieri
DIRECTED BY: Vittorio Di Sica
In post-World War II Italy, a billboard painter searches for his stolen bicycle. He
takes his young son with him and they see the effects the war had on the people
during their search. A major film that established "movie realism" with stark
photography which exposed the bitterness in people's faces after they've suffered
deprivation. Gritty scenes of actual street people enforced the realistic work. Oscar-
nominated for Best Screenplay.
*OSCAR WIN: Special Oscar to the Italian Film Industry for the Best Foreign
Language movie released in the U.S. in 1949*

Champion
BLOCKBUSTER CATEGORY: Classics
STARRING: Kirk Douglas, Lola Albright, Arthur Kennedy,
Marilyn Maxwell, Ruth Roman, Paul Stewart
DIRECTED BY: Mark Robson
An unscrupulous boxer fights his way to the top regardless of who stands in his

way. The movie established Kirk Douglas as a major dramatic actor. It is noteworthy for the way it shows the parallels between corruption in the sports world and corruption in business and politics, and the way first place winners control and manipulate those around them. Oscar-nominated for Best Actor (Douglas), Supporting Actor (Kennedy), Screenplay, Cinematography and Score.
OSCAR WIN: *Best Film Editing*

The Heiress

BLOCKBUSTER CATEGORY: Classics
STARRING: Olivia de Havilland, Montgomery Clift, Ralph Richardson, Miriam Hopkins, Mona Freeman, Vanessa Brown, Ray Collins
DIRECTED BY: William Wyler
A fortune hunter courts an unattractive heiress. Her father suspects his motives and threatens to disinherit her, so the fortune hunter leaves. He returns when the father dies to court the heiress, but she gets retribution. A commercial success in spite of downbeat ingredients, proving that the public will accept a film on its dramatic, thought-provoking merits when done well. Oscar-nominated for Best Picture, Supporting Actor (Richardson), Director (Wyler) and Cinematography.
OSCAR WINS: *Best Actress (de Havilland), Art Direction/Set Decoration - b&w, Score (Aaron Copland), Costume Design - b&w*

I Was A Male War Bride

BLOCKBUSTER CATEGORY: Not available on video
STARRING: Cary Grant, Ann Sheridan, Marion Marshall
DIRECTED BY: Howard Hawks
Cary Grant in Army drag - wig and all! He's a French soldier, married to female GI Ann Sheridan, who must disguise himself as a WAC in order to sneak into the U.S. Rapid-fire dialogue carries the plot, and Grant makes the most of the absurd comic premise.

Intruder In The Dust

BLOCKBUSTER CATEGORY: Not available on video
STARRING: David Brian, Claude Jarman, Jr., Juan Hernandez
DIRECTED BY: Clarence Brown
Superior book adaptation, handsomely shot on location, of a boy's attempts to stop the lynching of a black man wrongly accused of murder in a Southern village. Based on a William Faulkner novel, this top-rank movie, the IN THE HEAT OF THE NIGHT of its day, tackles a controversial subject without a hint of stereotype.

Jolson Sings Again

BLOCKBUSTER CATEGORY: Musicals
STARRING: Larry Parks, Barbara Hale, William Demarest
DIRECTED BY: Henry Levin
THE JOLSON STORY (1946) left Al Jolson with his career in high gear but his personal life a shambles. This satisfying sequel ties up the loose ends, and is an entertaining musical drama on its own terms. Larry Parks sings "Baby Face," "Back In Your Own Back Yard" and again makes a first-rate Jolson. Oscar-nominated for Best Story and Screenplay (Sidney Buchman), Cinematography - color, Scoring of a Musical.

A Letter to Three Wives

BLOCKBUSTER CATEGORY: Not available on video
STARRING: Ann Southern, Linda Darnell, Jeanne Crain, Kirk Douglas, Jeffrey Lynn, Paul Douglas, Thelma Ritter, Connie Gilchrist, Barbara Lawrence
DIRECTED BY: Joseph L. Mankiewicz

Three women receive a letter from a mutual friend who tells them she will run away with one of their husbands. Flashbacks dramatize each woman's marriage as they reflect on what went wrong. A comedy in spite of its subject matter and one of the first to also be a constructive morality lesson to wives who take their husbands for granted. An unusual movie because it criticizes wives and shows respect for them at the same time. Oscar-nominated for Best Picture.
OSCAR WINS: *Best Director (Mankiewicz), Screenplay (Mankiewicz)*

Samson & Delilah

BLOCKBUSTER CATEGORY: Classics
STARRING: Victor Mature, Hedy Lamarr, George Sanders
DIRECTED BY: Cecil B. DeMille

Just when audiences thought they had Cecil B. DeMille figured out, he surprised them with this movie. Instead of the Biblical extravaganza everyone expected, this is a surprising low-key historical spectacle - well acted by Victor Mature and Hedy Lamarr in the title roles, and particularly by George Sanders. The movie has aged well, and contains plenty of big-budget scenes that are distinctively DeMille's - Samson's fight with a lion, and the explosive climax. Oscar-nominated for Cinematography, Music, Special Effects.
OSCAR WINS: *Art Direction - color and Costume Design - color*

Sands of Iwo Jima

BLOCKBUSTER CATEGORY: Action/Adventure
STARRING: John Wayne, Forrest Tucker, John Agar
DIRECTED BY: Allan Dwan

A hard-bitten Marine sergeant leads his squad on a near-suicide mission to an occupied island in the closing days of World War II. John Wayne was nominated for his first Oscar in this flag-waving, grippingly realistic war saga, which contains some of the most powerful battle footage ever put on film. Additional Oscar-nominations: Editing, Sound, Motion Picture Story (Harry Brown).

She Wore a Yellow Ribbon

BLOCKBUSTER CATEGORY: Westerns
STARRING: John Wayne, Joanne Dru, John Agar, Victor McLaglen, George O'Brien, Ben Johnson, Harry Carey, Jr., Mildred Natwick
DIRECTED BY: John Ford

A cavalry officer is about to retire, but won't do it as long as Indians are a threat to the Army. One of the last major movies to showcase the romantic, free-enterprising feeling of the Old West and one of the best movies about old-fashioned heroics. Photographed like a colorful painting.
OSCAR WIN: *Best Cinematography - color*

The Stratton Story

BLOCKBUSTER CATEGORY: Not available on video
STARRING: James Stewart, June Allyson, Frank Morgan,
Agnes Moorehead, Bill Williams
DIRECTED BY: Sam Wood

The true story of Monty Stratton, a Texas farm boy and baseball star who had his leg amputated below the knee at the height of his fame. He continued to play baseball and retrained himself to overcome his handicap. Noteworthy because it took the spotlight away from disabled war heros and put it on those in everyday life.
OSCAR WIN: *Best Motion Picture Story (Douglas Morrow)*

Twelve O'Clock High

BLOCKBUSTER CATEGORY: Classics
STARRING: Gregory Peck, Dean Jagger, Hugh Marlowe,
Gary Merrill, Millard Mitchell, Paul Stewart,
Robert Arthur, John Kellogg, John Zilly
DIRECTED BY: Henry King

A World War II veteran visits an airfield where he was stationed and reflects about the war and the problems of leadership. Noted in movie history as the first effective film to show the importance of leadership and the stresses it has on men. The focus in not on battle, but there is enough action to highlight the need for intelligent military training in wartime. Oscar-nominated for Best Picture and Actor (Peck).
OSCAR WINS: *Best Supporting Actor (Jagger), Sound*

White Heat

BLOCKBUSTER CATEGORY: Classics
STARRING: James Cagney, Virginia Mayo, Edmond O'Brien,
Margaret Wycherly, Steve Cochran, John Archer,
Fred Clark, Paul Guilfoyle
DIRECTED BY: Raoul Walsh

A psychotic gangster is overly attached to his mother. In prison he learns that his enemies killed her and it pushes him over the edge. He escapes to get revenge and meets more violence than he bargained for. Significant because it revived the once-popular gangster movie genre. Considered the epitome of gangster pictures and Cagney's best. Oscar-nominated for Best Motion Picture Story.

All About Eve
BLOCKBUSTER CATEGORY: Classics
STARRING: Bette Davis, Celeste Holm, Anne Baxter, Gary Merrill, George Sanders, Hugh Marlowe, Gregory Ratoff, Marilyn Monroe, Thelma Ritter
DIRECTED BY: Joseph L. Mankiewicz

Here's a gripping story of trust...and betrayal. An aging actress of the stage (Davis) mentors a young woman (Baxter) who, cunningly, plans to replace her. Davis and Baxter turn in dynamic portrayals of women on opposite ends of the integrity spectrum. Look for Monroe in an early performance. Oscar-nominated for Best Actress (Davis and Baxter), Cinematography, Art Direction/Set Decoration, Score and Editing.
OSCAR SWEEP: *Best Picture, Supporting Actor (Sanders), Director (Mankiewicz), Screenplay (Mankiewicz), Sound, Costume Design - b&w*

The Asphalt Jungle
BLOCKBUSTER CATEGORY: Classics
STARRING: Sterling Hayden, Jean Hagen, Marilyn Monroe, Louis Calhern, Sam Jaffe, James Whitmore, Marc Lawrence
DIRECTED BY: John Huston

A detailed account of the plotting of a crime, the reason why it will ultimately fail and the agony of the chase when police apprehend the thieves. The first film to put the perspective of sympathy on the thieves by showing their frustrated efforts and subtly comparing them to the efforts of the working man to succeed in his job. Noted also for catapulting Marilyn Monroe to fame as a sex symbol. Oscar-nominated for Best Supporting Actor (Jaffe), Director (Huston), Screenplay and Cinematography.

Born Yesterday
BLOCKBUSTER CATEGORY: Classics
STARRING: Judy Holliday, William Holden, Broderick Crawford, Howard St. John
DIRECTED BY: George Cukor

An uncultured mobster wants his naive mistress to acquire some sophistication - so he hires a tutor. The tutor and the girl fall in love after he enlightens her about the illegal activities of her gangland boyfriend. A pioneering feminist film that redefined the ditzy blonde and showed she had brains. It also poked fun at male chauvinism and glorified romance. Oscar-nominated for Best Picture, Director (Cukor) and Screenplay.
OSCAR WIN: *Best Actress (Holliday)*

Cheaper By The Dozen
BLOCKBUSTER CATEGORY: Not available on video
STARRING: Clifton Webb, Myrna Loy, Jeanne Crain
DIRECTED BY: Walter Lang

Delightful turn-of-the-century comedy, comparing favorably to the classic LIFE WITH FATHER, with stuffy Clifton Webb as head of a family of 12 children, Myrna Loy as his long-suffering wife.

Cinderella

BLOCKBUSTER CATEGORY: Kids
STARRING: The voices of Ilene Woods, Verna Felton,
William Phipps, Eleanor Audley, Rhoda Williams,
Lucille Bliss
DIRECTED BY: Wilfred Jackson, Hamilton Luske, Clyde Geronimi

The fairy tale of a scullery maid who gets her wish to go to a fancy ball and wins her
Prince Charming. Embellished with delightful music and comic animal figures who
have human characteristics. The most successful version of the often-filmed tale
because Disney sparked it with personality just like he did with SNOW WHITE
AND THE SEVEN DWARFS (1937). A landmark animated film because it has an
adult following as well as a children's following. Oscar-nominated for Best Sound,
Song ("Bibbidi Bobbidi Boo") and Musical Scoring.

Cyrano de Bergerac

BLOCKBUSTER CATEGORY: Classics
STARRING: Jose Ferrer, Mala Powers, William Prince,
Morris Carnovsky, Elena Verdugo
DIRECTED BY: Michael Gordon

A 17th-century swordsman with an oversized nose is hopelessly in love with a
beautiful woman but feels she would never have him. He releases his romantic
ardor by helping a younger, more handsome man win her by using poetry to woo
her on the younger man's behalf. A distinguished film which proved that classic
stage fare does not have to be wordy, stodgy or stagey. Remade as ROXANNE
(1987) and again in the original French in 1990.
OSCAR WIN: *Best Actor (Jose Ferrer)*

Father of the Bride

BLOCKBUSTER CATEGORY: Classics
STARRING: Spencer Tracy, Elizabeth Taylor, Joan Bennett,
Billie Burke, Don Taylor, Russ Tamblyn,
Leo G. Carroll
DIRECTED BY: Vincente Minnelli

A bride's father recounts all the problems, expenses and calamities that occurred
between the time his daughter announced she found a fiance until she said "I do." A
significant film of the 1950's because it redefined the role of the father of the family
in satiric terms. It used the same methods TV used to show him as a bumbler, but
made him sympathetic and warmly identifiable instead. Oscar-nominated for Best
Screenplay.

Harvey

BLOCKBUSTER CATEGORY: Not available on video
STARRING: James Stewart, Josephine Hull, Cecil Kellaway,
Peggy Dow
DIRECTED BY: Henry Koster

A friendly alcoholic insists that an invisible six-foot-high pookah (rabbit) is his best
friend. His widowed sister thinks he should be committed to an asylum; then the
alcoholic convinces the head administrator that the pookah, Harvey, is his friend,

too. A thinking person's comedy that posed the question of who is insane and who is sane without talking down to the audience. Happiness is a state of mind and the film points it out emphatically. Oscar-nominated for Best Actor (Stewart).
OSCAR WIN: *Best Supporting Actress (Hull)*

In a Lonely Place
BLOCKBUSTER CATEGORY: Drama
STARRING: Humphrey Bogart, Gloria Grahame, Frank Lovejoy
DIRECTED BY: Nicholas Ray
Cast squarely against type, Bogart plays a bad-tempered screenwriter who may or may not be the murderer of a Beverly Hills hatcheck girl. Grahame (offscreen wife of the movie's director, Nicholas Ray) is the neighbor who falls for Bogie and wants to believe he's innocent. A still-powerful mystery that is the first of several movies about outcasts and outsiders directed by Ray, who is best known for REBEL WITHOUT A CAUSE.

King Solomon's Mines
BLOCKBUSTER CATEGORY: Classics
STARRING: Deborah Kerr, Stewart Granger, Richard Carlson, Hugo Haas
DIRECTED BY: Compton Bennett and Andrew Marton
A woman hires a hunter to find her husband in the African jungles. He disappeared while searching for the fabled King Solomon mine of gold and jewels. A rousing adventure that combines a travelog on sights of mysterious Africa and an exciting fight for survival while trying to find riches. The movie set standards for adventure tales unmatched until RAIDERS OF THE LOST ARK (1981).
OSCAR WINS: *Best Cinematography - color, Film Editing*

Panic in the Streets
BLOCKBUSTER CATEGORY: Classics
STARRING: Richard Widmark, Paul Douglas, Barbara Bel Geddes, Jack Palance, Zero Mostel
DIRECTED BY: Elia Kazan
A doctor joins forces with the police to find mobsters on the loose. One of the crooks is infected with a highly contagious disease and doesn't know it. The suspense builds as they try to catch him before he starts an epidemic and before the public responds with hysteria. This important movie combines the elements of documentary-style filmmaking with cinematic techniques to give the impression of realism. It set the pattern for cops and robbers movies.
OSCAR WIN: *Best Motion Picture Story (Edna and Edward Anhalt)*

Sunset Boulevard
BLOCKBUSTER CATEGORY: Classics
STARRING: Gloria Swanson, William Holden, Erich von Stroheim, Nancy Olson, Jack Webb, Fred Clark, Franklyn Barnum, Cecil B. DeMille, Buster Keaton, Anna Q. Nilsson, Hedda Hopper
DIRECTED BY: Billy Wilder

1950

An out-of-work screenwriter is hired by an old-time movie queen to write a script for her comeback. She insists that he move in with her, and her decadent style of living becomes his downfall. This black comedy - which also works as a melodrama - signified the break between old-time Hollywood glamour and the new-found realism of the 50's. Oscar-nominated for Best Picture, Actor (Holden), Actress (Swanson), Supporting Actor (von Stroheim), Supporting Actress (Olson), Director (Kazan), Cinematography and Editing. Registered as a national treasure with the Library of Congress.
OSCAR WINS: *Best Story & Screenplay (Billy Wilder, Charles Brackett & D.M. Marshman, Jr.), Art Direction/Set Decoration, Score*

1951

The African Queen

BLOCKBUSTER CATEGORY: Classics
STARRING: Humphrey Bogart, Katharine Hepburn,
Robert Morley
DIRECTED BY: John Huston

A spinsterish missionary is stranded at her African mission when the Germans attack during World War I. She escapes with a hobo-like sea captain on an old tugboat. Their unlikely pairing changes him from a boozer to a romantic and her from an uptight spinster into a romantic. Notable for pairing such extreme personalities and allowing them to spoof their movie images. Oscar-nominated for Best Actress (Hepburn), Director (Huston) and Screenplay.
OSCAR WIN: *Best Actor (Bogart)*

Alice in Wonderland

BLOCKBUSTER CATEGORY: Kids
STARRING: Voices of Kathryn Beaumont, Ed Wynn,
Richard Haydn
DIRECTED BY: Clyde Geronimi, Hamilton Luske, Wilfred Jackson

One of the great Walt Disney cartoon triumphs, combining new, "streamlined" animation style of the 50's with a breezy condensing of Lewis Carroll's fantasy yarn. A visual treat in vivid color, the movie makes the most of Carroll's mindspinning excursion into the world of the Mad Hatter and Cheshire Cat.

An American in Paris

BLOCKBUSTER CATEGORY: Musicals
STARRING: Gene Kelly, Leslie Caron, Georges Guetary,
Oscar Levant, Nina Foch
DIRECTED BY: Vincente Minnelli

A former soldier (Kelly) lives in Paris to paint. He meets a French waif (Caron) and falls in love with her. Later, a wealthy American matron tries to woo him away from the waif. A movie milestone because it is the first successful film to have an 18-minute artistic ballet. Oscar-nominated for Director (Minnelli) and Film Editing.
OSCAR SWEEP: *Best Picture, Story & Screenplay (Alan Jay Lerner), Cinematography - color, Score, Costume Design and an Honorary Oscar to Gene Kelly for his acting, dancing and choreography*

A Christmas Carol

BLOCKBUSTER CATEGORY: Classics
STARRING: Alastair Sim, Patrick Macnee, Peter Bull,
Mervyn Johns
DIRECTED BY: Brian Desmond-Hurst

A faithful rendition of the Dickens classic in which a miser is visited by the ghosts of his past, present and future to shame him into becoming a more benevolent creature. Notable for Sims' performance of Scrooge as a more realistic, more human and more identifiable character for the audience. The screenplay is by Noel Langley, who co-penned THE WIZARD OF OZ (1939) and the style is evident.

The Day the Earth Stood Still

BLOCKBUSTER CATEGORY: Science Fiction
STARRING: Michael Rennie, Patricia Neal, Hugh Marlowe,
    Sam Jaffe, Billy Gray
DIRECTED BY: Robert Wise

An alien lands in Washington, D.C. and warns the people to stop experimenting with nuclear weapons before the world is destroyed. An historically important film because it is the first big budget production to logically dramatize the idea that aliens might help, not destroy, the earth. It is also the first successful mystery-melodrama developed from a science fiction story without dependence on special effects.

The Lavender Hill Mob

BLOCKBUSTER CATEGORY: Classics
STARRING: Alec Guinness, Stanley Holloway, Sidney James,
    Audrey Hepburn (cameo)
DIRECTED BY: Charles Crichton

A meek bank clerk forms a band of thieves to steal a million pounds of gold bullion, shape it into miniature Eiffel Towers and smuggle it out of England. This first "caper" movie is an unusual blend of comedy, satire and action-adventure. It set a precedent for Hollywood writers who have been copying its theme and premise ever since. Oscar-nominated for Best Actor (Guinness).
OSCAR WIN: *Best Story & Screenplay (T.E.B. Clarke)*

A Place in the Sun

BLOCKBUSTER CATEGORY: Classics
STARRING: Elizabeth Taylor, Montgomery Clift, Shelley Winters,
    Anne Revere
DIRECTED BY: George Stevens

A naive country boy (Clift) visits his wealthy city cousins hoping to get a job to improve his social status. He has an affair with a co-worker, but tries to drop her for a glamorous society woman (Taylor). An important movie milestone because it introduced the first rebel without a cause of the 1950's. Don't miss Taylor in one of her first adult dramas and first pairing with Clift. Oscar-nominated for Best Picture, Actor (Clift) and Actress (Winters).
OSCAR SWEEP: *Best Director (Stevens), Screenplay (Michael Wilson, Harry Brown), Cinematography - b&w, Score, Editing, Costume Design - b&w*

Quo Vadis

BLOCKBUSTER CATEGORY: Classics
STARRING: Robert Taylor, Deborah Kerr, Peter Ustinov
DIRECTED BY: Mervyn LeRoy

First, and most influential, of the 50's Biblical spectacles. Robert Taylor stars as a Roman soldier, during the reign of Nero, who must come to terms with his love for Christian slave Deborah Kerr. Produced on location in Rome, with a cast of thousands (a concept that would be achieved in later movies), this exciting movie contains several sequences that have yet to be topped. A particular standout is the climactic burning of Rome, which took over two weeks to shoot. Oscar-nominated for Best Picture, Supporting Actor (Ustinov), Cinematography - color, Film Editing, Music, Art Direction, Costume Design - color (Gennand Ustinov).

Rashomon

BLOCKBUSTER CATEGORY: Foreign
STARRING: Toshiro Mifune, Machiko Kyo, Masayuki Mori,
Takashi Shimura
DIRECTED BY: Akira Kurosawa

Four people in a medieval Japanese town are questioned about a rape they witnessed. Each gives a different version of what happened, forcefully dramatizing the delicacy of truth in human nature. One of the first Oriental features to win Western acclaim.

OSCAR WIN: *Honorary award to the Japanese Film Industry for the most outstanding Foreign Language movie released in the United States in 1951.*

Strangers on a Train

BLOCKBUSTER CATEGORY: Alfred Hitchcock
STARRING: Robert Walker, Farley Granger, Ruth Roman,
Leo G. Carroll
DIRECTED BY: Alfred Hitchcock

A psychopath wants to get rid of a parent and proposes to "exchange murders" with a tennis pro who wants a divorce from his wife. The psycho kills the wife, then demands that the pro return the favor in one of Hitchcock's most suspenseful films. Notable for the way Hitchcock puts the audience in the character's shoes, providing an understanding of motives regardless of immorality. Oscar-nominated for Best Cinematography.

A Streetcar Named Desire

BLOCKBUSTER CATEGORY: Classics
STARRING: Marlon Brando, Vivien Leigh, Karl Malden,
Kim Hunter
DIRECTED BY: Elia Kazan

A faded Southern belle visits her sister in New Orleans and taunts her brother-in-law about his slovenly ways. This movie proved that the Broadway stage did not have a monopoly on tragedy as entertainment. Filled with action generated by forceful personalities, biting dialogue and expert filmmaking. Oscar-nominated for Best Picture, Director (Kazan), Screenplay, Cinematography, Sound, Score, Costume Design.

OSCAR SWEEP: *Best Actress (Leigh), Supporting Actor (Malden), Supporting Actress (Hunter), Art Direction/Set Decoration - b&w*

The Thing (From Another World)

BLOCKBUSTER CATEGORY: Science Fiction
STARRING: Kenneth Tobey, James Arness, Margaret Sheridan
DIRECTED BY: Christian Nyby

Scientists discover an alien in the Arctic Circle and thaw him out. The alien tries to kill them one-by-one in a tense, melodramatic, intellectual staging of an old-fashioned horror tale. Significant because it capitalized on the nation's fear of atomic/extraterrestrial horrors after World War II, without resorting to fantasy-like special effects. The plot, direction and acting appeal more to the intellect than later films of its type. Produced by Howard Hawks. Remade in 1982.

The Bad and the Beautiful

BLOCKBUSTER CATEGORY: Classics
STARRING: Kirk Douglas, Lana Turner, Dick Powell,
Gloria Grahame
DIRECTED BY: Vincente Minnelli

An ambitious moviemaker uses and abuses his friendships in order to get to the top. Flashbacks show what his writers, directors and stars thought about him and why in moody vignettes. It initiated a pattern of expose films about different industries and is notable because Hollywood began exposing corruption by scrutinizing itself. Oscar-nominated for Best Actor (Douglas).
OSCAR WINS: *Best Supporting Actress (Grahame), Screenplay (Charles Schnee), Cinematography - b&w, Art Direction/Set Decoration - b&w, Costume Design - b&w*

Come Back, Little Sheba

BLOCKBUSTER CATEGORY: Classic
STARRING: Burt Lancaster, Shirley Booth, Terry Moore,
Richard Jaeckel
DIRECTED BY: Daniel Mann

An aging alcoholic makes life miserable for his dowdy wife after their shotgun marriage prevents him from pursuing a medical career. One of the very few heavy stage dramas translated intact to the movie screen with the star (Booth) who made it work onstage. Noted for being one of the most successful movies aimed at a middle-aged audience, but which also pleased younger audiences. Oscar-nominated for Supporting Actress (Moore) and Editing.
OSCAR WIN: *Best Actress (Booth)*

The Crimson Pirate

BLOCKBUSTER CATEGORY: Classics
STARRING: Burt Lancaster, Nick Cravat, Eva Bartok,
Christopher Lee
DIRECTED BY: Robert Siodmak

A swashbuckling spoof. A buccaneer captures a ship headed for the Caribbean and learns that the islanders plan to rebel against their French rulers. The buccaneer intends to profit from the situation by pitting both sides against the other. Noteworthy as the first pirate picture to succeed since World War II features a scientist who develops a super-weapon that looks suspiciously like an atom bomb, also making this the first movie to spoof the atomic issue.

The Greatest Show on Earth

BLOCKBUSTER CATEGORY: Classics
STARRING: Charlton Heston, Betty Hutton, James Stewart,
Cornel Wilde, Dorothy Lamour, Gloria Grahame,
Emmett Kelly
DIRECTED BY: Cecil B. DeMille

A circus manager has difficulty moderating the competition between performers, their love affairs and their ways of coping with their mistakes. A giant train wreck puts everything in perspective in the only circus movie to succeed on a big scale. Important in movie history as the first all-star disaster film, starting a string of multi-star, bigger-than-life films for the rest of the decade and beyond. Oscar-nominated

for Director (DeMille), Editing and Costume Design.
OSCAR WINS: *Best Picture (De Mille's only!), Motion Picture Story (Fredric Frank, Theodore St. John and Frank Cavett)*

High Noon

BLOCKBUSTER CATEGORY: Westerns
STARRING: Gary Cooper, Grace Kelly, Katy Jurado,
Lloyd Bridges, Lon Chaney, Jr., Lee Van Cleef,
Henry Morgan
DIRECTED BY: Fred Zinnemann

A frontier marshal's wedding day is interrupted and the townspeople desert him when he hears that a convict he imprisoned is coming after him. A memorable western that is a somber character study, not a colorful shoot-'em-up. It set a new standard for macho movies and also provided a new perspective on the way people felt about the law and themselves. Oscar-nominated for Best Picture, Director (Zinnemann) and Screenplay. Registered as a national treasure with the Library of Congress.
OSCAR WINS: *Best Actor (Cooper), Song ("Do Not Forsake Me, Oh My Darlin"), Score and Editing*

Ivanhoe

BLOCKBUSTER CATEGORY: Classics
STARRING: Robert Taylor, Elizabeth Taylor, Joan Fontaine
DIRECTED BY: Richard Thorpe

Robert Taylor, one of the screen's most dashing male stars, plays the title role in this filmed-on-location adaptation of Sir Walter Scott's novel of medieval England. Along with the expected scenes of knights on horseback, duels and daring rescues, we get a script that succeeds in giving us a feel for the historical climate of the period. The color photography is magnificent. Oscar-nominated for Best Picture, Cinematography, Music Score.

Limelight

BLOCKBUSTER CATEGORY: Classics
STARRING: Charlie Chaplin, Claire Bloom, Buster Keaton
DIRECTED BY: Charles Chaplin

Another Chaplin masterpiece, this is the PYGMALION-like fable of a broken-down music hall performer (Chaplin) who builds the confidence of a lovely newcomer (Claire Bloom) and is himself restored in the process. Many classic scenes, including the treat of seeing Chaplin and silent film colleague Buster Keaton finally performing together.
OSCAR WIN: *Best Musical Score (Chaplin, his only award won in competition, awarded 21 years later because the film wasn't eligible until 1972!)*

Monkey Business

BLOCKBUSTER CATEGORY: Classics
STARRING: Cary Grant, Ginger Rogers, Marilyn Monroe,
Charles Coburn
DIRECTED BY: Howard Hawks

A scientist discovers a youth serum that is mistakenly taken by his wife and boss. When the scientist takes it, he reverts to his own youth and starts chasing his secretary. The fast pace keeps the audience from taking it too seriously, and the personalities give it magnetism. The movie is still imitated in the various body-switch movies of the 1980's.

Moulin Rouge

BLOCKBUSTER CATEGORY: Classics
STARRING: Jose Ferrer, Colette Marchand, Zsa Zsa Gabor,
Suzanne Flon, Christopher Lee, Peter Cushing
DIRECTED BY: John Huston
A biography of Toulouse-Latrec, the 19th century French painter whose views of life were reflected in his work. This memorable movie recreated the moral decay of Toulouse-Latrec's era in vibrant color. Oscar-nominated for Best Picture, Actor (Ferrer), Supporting Actress (Marchand), Director (Huston) and Editing.
OSCAR WINS: *Art Direction/Set Decoration - color, Costume Design - color*

The Quiet Man

BLOCKBUSTER CATEGORY: Classics
STARRING: John Wayne, Maureen O'Hara, Victor McLaglen,
Barry Fitzgerald
DIRECTED BY: John Ford
An American boxer (Wayne) is disillusioned with himself and life in general when he accidently kills an opponent in the ring. He moves to Ireland and falls in love with O'Hara and has to fight her brother who objects to him. One of the most beautifully photographed movies of all time and a landmark in Wayne's career. He proved he could believably play a romantic and retain his machismo at the same time. Oscar-nominated for Supporting Actor (McLaglen), Screenplay, Art Direction/Set Decoration and Sound.
OSCAR WINS: *Best Director (Ford), Cinematography - color*

Singin' in the Rain

BLOCKBUSTER CATEGORY: Musicals
STARRING: Gene Kelly, Debbie Reynolds, Donald O'Connor,
Jean Hagen, Cyd Charisse, Rita Moreno
DIRECTED BY: Gene Kelly and Stanley Donen
A movie queen's career is about to be destroyed by the talkies. She forces the studio to hire a girl to re-dub her voice, realizing that the girl is the one her boyfriend picked when he ditched the movie queen. The best satire Hollywood did on itself, punctuated with happy, optimistic, toe-tapping tunes and successfully combining ballet, ballads and comic musical numbers with pratfalls and big-scale production numbers. Oscar-nominated for Supporting Actress (Hagen) and Scoring of a Musical. Registered as a national treasure with the Library of Congress.

Son of Paleface

BLOCKBUSTER CATEGORY: Comedy
STARRING: Bob Hope, Jane Russell, Roy Rogers
DIRECTED BY: Frank Tashlin

One of those rare sequels that's as good as the original. Four years earlier, Bob Hope starred in PALEFACE as a cowardly cowboy who somehow becomes a hero. This follow-up again co-stars Jane Russell, and again pits our spineless hero against some ruthless outlaws - but an emphasis on outright parody makes this spoof a delightful surprise. Roy Rogers is wonderfully deadpan in a role that lets Rogers spoof himself. The direction by former cartoon animator Frank Tashlin allows for plenty of sight gags - such as Bob waking up in bed with Trigger! Oscar-nominated for Best Song.

Viva Zapata!

BLOCKBUSTER CATEGORY: Westerns
STARRING: Marlon Brando, Anthony Quinn, Jean Peters,
   Joseph Wiseman
DIRECTED BY: Elia Kazan

An exciting drama about a Mexican's rise from poverty to presidency. A hard-hitting character study that combines good acting with action. Unlike other films about revolution, this one goes into detail about the strengths and weaknesses of both the established government and the revolutionaries. Oscar-nominated for Best Actor (Brando), Story & Screenplay (John Steinbeck), Art Direction/Set Decoration and Score.

OSCAR WIN: *Best Supporting Actor (Quinn)*

1953

The Band Wagon
BLOCKBUSTER CATEGORY: Musicals
STARRING: Fred Astaire, Cyd Charisse, Nanette Fabray, Jack Buchanan
DIRECTED BY: Vincente Minnelli
This was one of the last of the all-star musical spectacles from the studio that specialized in them (MGM). It is also a tribute to the standard behind-the-scenes musical and the "let's-put-on-a-show" youth musicals with its story of a has-been movie star (Astaire) who goes to Broadway to regenerate his career. He clashes with his leading lady (Charisse) just like the backstage musical stars did, and, like them, falls in love. Oscar-nominated for Best Story & Screenplay (Betty Comden, Adolphe Green), Costume Design, Scoring of a Musical.

The Big Heat
BLOCKBUSTER CATEGORY: Classics
STARRING: Glenn Ford, Lee Marvin, Gloria Grahame, Carolyn Jones
DIRECTED BY: Fritz Lang
A cop investigates the suicide of one of his cohorts even though his superiors try to stop him. The first major film to deal with police corruption. The movie was inspired by the timely crime activities exposed by the Kefauver Committee and has never lost its timeliness.

From Here to Eternity
BLOCKBUSTER CATEGORY: Classics
STARRING: Burt Lancaster, Deborah Kerr, Montgomery Clift, Frank Sinatra, Donna Reed, Ernest Borgnine
DIRECTED BY: Fred Zinnemann
Here's the story of peacetime soldiers whose aimless lives take new form when war breaks out. It delves into the personality clashes, tempestuous love affairs and hunger for power of men and women in the military. This is the first World War II film of the 1950's that regenerated a feeling of patriotism. Kerr and Lancaster's famous beach scene is a sizzler. Oscar-nominated for Best Actor (Lancaster and Clift), Actress (Kerr) and Score.
OSCAR SWEEP: *Best Picture, Director (Zinnemann), Supporting Actor (Sinatra), Supporting Actress (Reed), Screenplay, Cinematography, Editing, Sound Recording*

Gentlemen Prefer Blondes
BLOCKBUSTER CATEGORY: Musicals
STARRING: Jane Russell, Marilyn Monroe, Charles Coburn
DIRECTED BY: Howard Hawks
On a transatlantic cruise yacht, two showgirls (Marilyn Monroe, Jane Russell) set out to snare a pair of rich husbands. Their episodic misadventures slow down briefly enough for a bevy of delightful tunes, including "Diamonds Are a Girl's Best Friend." Not content merely to settle for a breezy musical, director Howard Hawks - adapting a memoir by Anita Loos - transformed this popular film into a very funny satire of manners and morals.

House of Wax

BLOCKBUSTER CATEGORY: Horror
STARRING: Vincent Price, Frank Lovejoy, Phyllis Kirk,
Carolyn Jones, Charles Bronson
DIRECTED BY: Andre de Toth

A mad professor goes on a killing spree to get models for his waxworks. A police detective goes after him with a vengeance when his girlfriend figures out the professor's scheme. Price devours the scenery in the role that began his reign as the King of Horror. Although originally distinguished by its color 3-D innovations, it's just as much fun without them. Don't miss this enjoyable remake of MYSTERY OF THE WAX MUSEUM (1933).

Julius Caesar

BLOCKBUSTER CATEGORY: Classics
STARRING: Marlon Brando, Louis Calhern, James Mason,
John Gielgud, Greer Garson, Deborah Kerr
DIRECTED BY: Joseph L. Mankiewicz

Julius Caesar copes with the envy of his contemporaries and the corruption of his government. A successful version of Shakespeare that captured moviegoers' fancy with its cast of modern players who put life into Shakespeare's poetry. The film relies on the dramatic text, but underscores it with distinctive camera angles and a fast pace to give it the appeal of a modern adventure. Oscar-nominated for Best Picture, Actor (Brando), Cinematography and Score.
OSCAR WIN: *Best Art Direction/Set Decoration - b&w*

Lili

BLOCKBUSTER CATEGORY: Family
STARRING: Leslie Caron, Mel Ferrer, Zsa Zsa Gabor
DIRECTED BY: Charles Walters

Charming, one-of-a-kind love story that introduced Leslie Caron to American audiences. In the title role, she plays a 16-year-old girl who joins a travelling carnival, where she endures an unhappy romance with a magician (Jean-Pierre Aumont) while a shy puppeteer (Mel Ferrer) dreams of winning her heart. The movie has an unforced sentimentality to it and, though it isn't really a musical, closes with a ballet that is one of the screen highlights of the 50's. Oscar-nominated for Best Actress (Caron), Director (Walters), Screenplay Adaptation (Helen Deutsch), Cinematography - color, Art Direction/Set Decoration.
OSCAR WIN: *Best Musical Score*

Mogambo

BLOCKBUSTER CATEGORY: Classics
STARRING: Clark Gable, Grace Kelly, Ava Gardner
DIRECTED BY: John Ford

An action-packed remake of the early 30's classic RED DUST, with Clark Gable repeating his role and the added bonus of color photography and location shooting in Africa. The original movie was set in Saigon. Relocating the remake to Africa and rewriting it to give the film a safari setting opened the way for some memorable action scenes. Oscar-nominated for Best Actress (Gardner), Supporting Actress (Kelly).

Peter Pan

BLOCKBUSTER CATEGORY: Kids
STARRING: Voices of Bobby Driscoll, Kathryn Beaumont,
Hans Conreid
DIRECTED BY: Hamilton Luske, Clyde Geronimi,
Wilfred Jackson

Walt Disney's cartoon feature based on James M. Barrie's story is a perfect companion piece to the Mary Martin TV version, also on video. Peter sweeps three children from the rigid boredom of Victorian London to mythical Neverland, where they battle pirates and still get home before their parents know they're gone. The visual treat of a bird's-eye-view, in cartoon Technicolor, of London as Peter sings "You Can Fly" is one of the classic highlights of Disney cartoons.

The Robe

BLOCKBUSTER CATEGORY: Classics
STARRING: Richard Burton, Jean Simmons, Victor Mature
DIRECTED BY: Henry Koster

Richard Burton, in his first major Hollywood movie, stars as a Roman centurion whose pagan ways are shaken by Christ's crucifixion. Not a dated Biblical opus, this is a thoughtful, exciting adaptation of Lloyd C. Douglas' novel. The duel between Burton and Jeff Morrow is an action highlight. Burton's performance netted him an Oscar-nomination, and the Art Direction was also nominated, as was the film for Best Picture.
OSCAR WIN: *Costume Design - color*

Roman Holiday

BLOCKBUSTER CATEGORY: Classics
STARRING: Gregory Peck, Audrey Hepburn, Eddie Albert,
Margaret Rawlings
DIRECTED BY: William Wyler

A bored princess escapes from her room while visiting Italy. A newspaper writer sees her and tries to get an interview without telling her who he is. This sophisticated and witty reworking of the Cinderella story with modern characters is one a modern audience can identify with. Also a throwback to old-fashioned romance, an ingredient missing from movies after the war ended - a welcome treat for movie fans that was kept fresh by its lively cast. Oscar-nominated for Best Picture, Director (Wyler), Supporting Actor (Albert), Screenplay, Cinematography, Art Direction/Set Decoration and Editing.
OSCAR SWEEP: *Best Actress (Hepburn), Motion Picture Story (Ian McLellan Hunter), Costume Design - b&w*

Shane

BLOCKBUSTER CATEGORY: Westerns
STARRING: Alan Ladd, Jean Arthur, Van Heflin, Jack Palance,
Brandon de Wilde, Ben Johnson, Nancy Kulp,
Edgar Buchanan, Elisha Cook, Jr.
DIRECTED BY: George Stevens

A lone frontiersman stumbles on a poor homesteading family in the Old West. He stays to help them fight the cattle barons trying to take over their land and becomes

a father figure to the farmer's son and a love object to the farmer's wife. A picturesque old-fashioned western told in a way that was not done before: through the eyes of a child. Oscar-nominated for Best Picture, Director (Stevens), Supporting Actor (Palance and de Wilde) and Screenplay.
OSCAR WIN: *Best Cinematography - color*

Stalag 17

BLOCKBUSTER CATEGORY: Classics
STARRING: William Holden, Otto Preminger, Don Taylor, Peter Graves, Robert Strauss, Harvey Lembeck, Richard Erdman, Sig Ruman
DIRECTED BY: Billy Wilder

A serio-comic treatment of life inside a Nazi P.O.W. camp when the inmates try to find out who the Nazi stooge is in their midst. This movie signaled a change in philosophy about World War II because it was the first major war movie treated with humor, yet socking home a strong dramatic message about the importance of teamwork. Oscar-nominated for Best Director and Supporting Actor (Strauss).
OSCAR WIN: *Best Actor (Holden)*

Titanic

BLOCKBUSTER CATEGORY: Not available on video
STARRING: Barbara Stanwyck, Clifton Webb, Robert Wagner, Audrey Dalton
DIRECTED BY: Jean Negulesco

The story of the doomed ship from the perspective of the passengers. Their plights are foremost and the sinking of the ship merely a backdrop. Notable for using a real-life tragedy to make a fictional story about everyday people effective. Oscar-nominated for Art Direction/Set Decoration.
OSCAR WIN: *Best Story & Screenplay (Charles Brackett, Walter Reisch, Richard Breen)*

War of the Worlds

BLOCKBUSTER CATEGORY: Science Fiction
STARRING: Gene Barry, Les Tremayne, Ann Robinson, Robert Cornthwaite
DIRECTED BY: Byron Haskin

A reworking of H.G. Wells' old-time science fiction thriller about an alien invasion. A shocker because it links new-found nuclear weaponry to an old-time and well-known story. This movie is well-known for its dazzling special effects, which made it a forerunner of many futuristic stories even though it is set in the present. Nominated for Best Sound and Editing.
OSCAR WIN: *Best Special Effects*

The Barefoot Contessa

BLOCKBUSTER CATEGORY: Classics
STARRING: Humphrey Bogart, Edmond O'Brien, Ava Gardner,
Rossano Brazzi
DIRECTED BY: Joseph L. Mankiewicz

A tempermental Spanish dancer becomes a Hollywood star and gets involved in a
world of deceptive glamour that turns out to be self-destructive. An atmospheric
movie that is filled with cynical dialogue and treats Hollywood with more disdain
than usual. Many moviegoers felt Gardner was playing a character patterned after
herself. Oscar-nominated for Best Story & Screenplay.
OSCAR WIN: *Best Supporting Actor (O'Brien)*

Broken Lance

BLOCKBUSTER CATEGORY: Westerns
STARRING: Spencer Tracy, Robert Wagner, Jean Peters,
Richard Widmark, Katy Jurado
DIRECTED BY: Edward Dmytryk

A cattle baron tries to keep his family together, but each of his sons go in a different
direction when they challenge his authority. The film applies the basic theme of
Shakespeare's King Lear to the Old West and shows that people don't change much
from generation to generation. Oscar-nominated for Best Supporting Actress
(Jurado). Remake of HOUSE OF STRANGERS, an Edward G. Robinson crime
movie.
OSCAR WIN: *Best Motion Picture Story (Philip Yordan)*

The Caine Mutiny

BLOCKBUSTER CATEGORY: Classics
STARRING: Humphrey Bogart, Fred MacMurray, Van Johnson,
Jose Ferrer, Lee Marvin, E.G. Marshall, Tom Tully,
Claude Akins
DIRECTED BY: Edward Dmytryk

A modern-day sea story with old-fashioned elements. The crew mutinies against
their eccentric ship captain and has him tried for insane activities. One of the first
movies to even hint there may be unstable people in the Navy, which initially
banned it for that reason. The film works because it relies on the quirks of human
nature for its drama. Oscar-nominated for Best Picture, Actor (Bogart), Supporting
Actor (Tully), Screenplay, Sound, Score and Editing.

The Country Girl

BLOCKBUSTER CATEGORY: Classics
STARRING: Bing Crosby, Grace Kelly, William Holden,
Anthony Ross
DIRECTED BY: George Seaton

The embittered wife of a former stage star is of little moral support to her alcoholic
husband when he tries a comeback. This movie catapulted Grace Kelly into the
"actress" category. This version of Clifford Odets' play about self-sacrifice, the
human will and the power of self-esteem made the public take her more seriously.
Oscar-nominated for Best Picture, Actor (Crosby), Director (Seaton),
Cinematography and Art Direction/Set Decoration.
OSCAR WIN: *Best Actress (Kelly)*

1954

The Glenn Miller Story
BLOCKBUSTER CATEGORY: Musicals
STARRING: James Stewart, June Allyson, Harry Morgan
DIRECTED BY: Anthony Mann

During the 50's, James Stewart and director Anthony Mann teamed for eight superb films, most of them westerns (WINCHESTER 73', THE MAN FROM LARAMIE, etc.). One of the exceptions was this first-rate biography of bandleader Miller, who created the most distinctive sound of the big band era before dying in a plane crash during World War II. This movie is the most imaginative and entertaining of several show biz biographies made during the 50's, and Stewart's performance is one of his best. Oscar-nominated for Story & Screenplay (Valentine Davies and Oscar Brodney), Scoring of a Musical Picture.
OSCAR WIN: *Best Sound*

On the Waterfront
BLOCKBUSTER CATEGORY: Classics
STARRING: Marlon Brando, Eva Marie Saint, Lee J. Cobb,
Rod Steiger, Karl Malden, Pat Henning,
Leif Erickson, John Hamilton, Tony Galento
DIRECTED BY: Elia Kazan

An ex-boxer works for racketeers on the waterfront and unwittingly gets involved in murder. He falls in love with the victim's sister and tries to stand up to the mob even though his own brother is involved with them. A movie milestone that teaches a lesson in morality and uncovers weaknesses in the union system without indicting the whole system. Oscar-nominated for Supporting Actor (Cobb, Steiger and Malden) and Score. Registered as a national treasure with the Library of Congress.
OSCAR SWEEP: *Best Picture, Actor (Brando), Supporting Actress (Saint), Director (Kazan), Story & Screenplay (Budd Schulberg), Cinematography - b&w, Art Direction/Set Decoration - b&w, Editing*

Rear Window
BLOCKBUSTER CATEGORY: Alfred Hitchcock
STARRING: James Stewart, Grace Kelly, Raymond Burr,
Thelma Ritter
DIRECTED BY: Alfred Hitchcock

A man with a broken leg and confined to his apartment spies on his neighbors through a telescope. He has reason to believe one of them is a murderer. When the killer realizes he is being watched, he goes after him. Top-notch Hitchcock suspense that taps the Peeping Tom instinct in the movie audience and enables it to identify with a man unable to run or walk while seeing all the dangers from his viewpoint. Oscar-nominated for Best Director (Hitchcock), Screenplay (John Michael Hayes), Cinematography and Sound.

Sabrina
BLOCKBUSTER CATEGORY: Classics
STARRING: Humphrey Bogart, Audrey Hepburn, William Holden,
John Williams
DIRECTED BY: Billy Wilder

A chauffeur's teenage daughter leaves America for France. She comes back a grown woman and the playboy son of her employer's family makes a play for her. His straight-laced businessman brother tries to stop them from having an affair. A breezy comedy that clicked more because of casting than plot. The movie gets laughs with performers who defy their previous types. Oscar-nominated for Best Actress (Hepburn), Director (Wilder), Screenplay, Cinematography and Art Direction/Set Decoration.
OSCAR WIN: *Costume Design - b&w*

Seven Brides for Seven Brothers
BLOCKBUSTER CATEGORY: Musicals
STARRING: Howard Keel, Jane Powell, Russ Tamblyn, Julie Newmar
DIRECTED BY: Stanley Donen
Six backwoods brothers kidnap six pretty girls from the nearby town. They envy their oldest brother's marriage and want wives of their own. A snow-storm barricades their farm from vengeful fathers and boyfriends through the winter. By spring, the girls decide to stay and become brides. An energetic musical in which the inspired dancing is integrated into the story better that any musical before or since. Oscar-nominated for Best Picture, Screenplay, Cinematography and Editing.
OSCAR WIN: *Scoring of a Musical Picture*

The Seven Samurai
BLOCKBUSTER CATEGORY: Foreign
STARRING: Toshiro Mifune, Takashi Shimura, Yoshio Inaba
DIRECTED BY: Akira Kurosawa
In 16th-century Japan, a village hires seven mercenaries to protect its inhabitants against the marauding bandits who loot it every year. Packed with some of the most alarming action scenes ever filmed, this Japanese melodrama proved so popular all over the world that it was remade in the U.S. as the classic western, THE MAGNIFICENT SEVEN, and as BATTLE BEYOND THE STARS (Science-Fiction). Oscar-nominated for Art Direction/Set Decoration , Costume Design.

A Star is Born
BLOCKBUSTER CATEGORY: Classics
STARRING: Judy Garland, James Mason, Jack Carson, Charles Bickford
DIRECTED BY: George Cukor
A movie star discovers a talented young girl and helps her start a movie career. They marry and, as her star rises, his falls. Another movie that succeeds by analyzing the movie business. This one differs from most because it stars Judy Garland in her last big musical role and audiences had the feeling she was playing out her own life story. Oscar-nominated for Best Actor (Mason), Actress (Garland), Art Direction/Set Decoration, Song ("The Man That Got Away"), Score and Costume Design.

1954

Them!

BLOCKBUSTER CATEGORY: Science Fiction
STARRING: Edmund Gwenn, James Whitmore, Joan Weldon, James Arness
DIRECTED BY: Gordon Douglas

Experimental atom bomb blasts cause a colony of ants to grow to a 15-foot height. They menace the southwestern area of the United States and a scientist joins forces with the police in Los Angeles to stop them. A real shocker! Significant because it used a detective-story format in the sci-fi genre. Oscar-nominated for Special Effects.

20,000 Leagues Under the Sea

BLOCKBUSTER CATEGORY: Science Fiction
STARRING: Kirk Douglas, Peter Lorre, James Mason
DIRECTED BY: Richard Fleischer

Walt Disney assembled an all-star cast for this spectacular, multi-million dollar rendition of Jules Verne's classic adventure novel. At the turn of the century, the fanatical Capt. Nemo (Mason), whose wife and children were killed in a military disaster, uses his deadly submarine, "The Nautilus," to destroy warships. The only survivors of one such attack are a scientist (Lukas), his aide (Lorre), and a roughneck sailor (Douglas). The unlikely trio are taken captive by Nemo and his crew, which exposes them - and us - to a fantastic world of terror and excitement, both above and below the sea. These include attacks by island cannibals, an eerie burial on the ocean floor, and the movie's climactic highlight: a frightening attack upon "The Nautilus" by a giant, monster squid, during a typhoon. 20,000 Leagues Under the Sea begins with a fiery attack by "The Nautilus" on an unsuspecting Navy schooner, and the thrills never let up from that point on. This was the first major assignment for director Richard Fleischer, whose lengthy career also included FANTASTIC VOYAGE.
OSCAR WINS: *Art Direction/Set Decoration - color, Special Effects*

White Christmas

BLOCKBUSTER CATEGORY: Musicals
STARRING: Bing Crosby, Danny Kaye, Rosemary Clooney
DIRECTED BY: Michael Curtiz

One of the most popular of all holiday-theme musicals is HOLIDAY INN (1942), with Bing Crosby and Fred Astaire. In 1954, Hollywood decided to remake it - and pulled out all the stops to do so, shooting the new version in Technicolor, and adding a batch of new tunes by the original movie's composer, the great Irving Berlin. Crosby is teamed this time with Danny Kaye; they portray Army buddies who transform a struggling hotel into a holiday resort. Rosemary Clooney (at the peak of her career) and Vera-Ellen provide the romantic interest, and there is welcome comic support from such familiar character actors as Grady Sutton (a familiar face from his W.C. Fields comedies), Sig Ruman (the blustery sergeant from Billy Wilder's STALAG 17) and Dean Jagger as the hotel owner... who also happens to be Crosby and Kaye's ex-commander! A perennial holiday favorite!

1954

The Wild One

BLOCKBUSTER CATEGORY: Classics
STARRING: Marlon Brando, Mary Murphy, Lee Marvin
DIRECTED BY: Laslo Benedek

This first melodrama about motorcycle gangs terrorizing a small town was based on a series of news magazine articles, and intended as a serious social tract. Today, that aspect of the movie is forgotten and it's enjoyed as the first Hell's Angels movie and a terrific vehicle for Marlon Brando. Asked by leading lady Mary Murphy what he's rebelling against, Brando sneers,"Whadda ya got?" His fight with rival gang leader Lee Marvin is the movie's centerpiece.

Bad Day at Black Rock

BLOCKBUSTER CATEGORY: Classics
STARRING: Spencer Tracy, Ernest Borgnine, Anne Francis,
Robert Ryan, Dean Jagger, Walter Brennan,
Lee Marvin, John Ericson, Russell Collins
DIRECTED BY: John Sturges

A one-armed man stops at a desolate California town and makes the residents
nervous when he starts asking questions about a Japanese farmer who had long-
since disappeared. A monumental movie that used the detective story format to
analyze the guilt Americans felt for dropping the atom bomb on Hiroshima and
Nagasaki. It is also an important indictment of the McCarthy era in which everyone
feared the country would become a police state. Oscar-nominated for Best Actor
(Tracy), Director (Sturges) and Screenplay.

Battle Cry

BLOCKBUSTER CATEGORY: Action/Adventure
STARRING: Van Heflin, Tab Hunter, Dorothy Malone
DIRECTED BY: Raoul Walsh

Leon Uris' mammoth bestseller becomes a sprawling, effective World War II saga
about young men who enlist in the Marines and the effect the war has on them. The
entire ritual is here - boot camp, the first pass home, and finally, going to war. And
it's all in the capable hands of director Raoul Walsh, an action specialist whose films
include some of Cagney and Bogart's classics. Oscar-nominated for Best Score.

East of Eden

BLOCKBUSTER CATEGORY: Classics
STARRING: James Dean, Raymond Massey, Jo Van Fleet,
Richard Davalos, Julie Harris, Burl Ives,
Albert Dekker
DIRECTED BY: Elia Kazan

Two brothers compete for their father's attention and one of them succeeds in
destroying the other's faith in family relationships. This movie defines the
Generation Gap by using a World War I setting to parallel feelings of the 1950's
when the young generation tried to assert itself by condemning old-fashioned
values. Also popular because it introduced James Dean. Oscar-nominated for Best
Actor (Dean), Director (Kazan) and Screenplay (Paul Osborn).
OSCAR WIN: *Best Supporting Actress (Van Fleet)*

Lady and the Tramp

BLOCKBUSTER CATEGORY: Kids
STARRING: The voices of Peggy Lee, Barbara Luddy,
Bill Thompson, Stan Freberg, Bill Baucon,
Verna Felton, Alan Reed, George Givot, Lee Miller
DIRECTED BY: Hamilton Luske, Clyde Geronimi, Wilfred Jackson

A mongrel dog sees a lady dog in distress and helps her. A romance develops and
the film works just as well as a love story as it does a family animated feature for the
kids. Good music, appropriate voices and colorful settings enable the audience to
identify with the animals as much as they would with human beings. The film was
the first Cinemascope feature-length cartoon and the first Disney film that switched
the focus from human beings to animal characters while keeping both in the show.

Lola Montes

BLOCKBUSTER CATEGORY: Foreign
STARRING: Martine Carol, Anton Walbrook, Peter Ustinov,
Oskar Werner
DIRECTED BY: Max Ophuls

A circus performer reflects on her life as the mistress of influential men. Filmed in a florid style with many of the unusual camera techniques director Ophlus was known for. Long dissolves from one scene to another, moody lighting effects and extreme close-ups make it highly stylized and unusual for a romantic film.

Marty

BLOCKBUSTER CATEGORY: Classics
STARRING: Ernest Borgnine, Betsy Blair, Esther Minciotti,
Joe Mantell
DIRECTED BY: Delbert Mann

A lonely, homely butcher unexpectedly finds romance with a very plain-looking woman. This is notable for being the first Oscar winner derived from an original TV movie. A classic of its type that gives everyone in the audience someone with whom they can readily identify. Oscar-nominated for Best Supporting Actor (Mantell), Cinematography and Art Direction/Set Decoration.
OSCAR SWEEP: *Best Picture, Actor (Borgnine), Director (Mann), Screenplay (Paddy Chayefsky)*

Mister Roberts

BLOCKBUSTER CATEGORY: Classics
STARRING: Henry Fonda, James Cagney, William Powell,
Jack Lemmon, Betsy Palmer, Ward Bond,
Martin Milner, Nick Adams, Philip Carey
DIRECTED BY: John Ford and Mervyn LeRoy

A restless officer copes with petty personality problems and mischief aboard his ship while yearning to be in combat instead. A successful blend of comedy and drama that revived a feeling of patriotism and honor for the military long after World War II when these feelings were no longer in vogue. Oscar-nominated for Best Picture and Sound.
OSCAR WIN: *Best Supporting Actor (Lemmon)*

The Night of the Hunter

BLOCKBUSTER CATEGORY: Classics
STARRING: Robert Mitchum, Shelley Winters, Lillian Gish,
Billy Chapin
DIRECTED BY: Charles Laughton

An ex-convict posing as a preacher marries his former cellmate's widow and menaces her children in an effort to find money the cellmate had hidden. An allegory about good and evil that uses the Depression as a symbol of punishment. A classic mystery-suspense story with highly stylized camera angles and lighting to show fear through a child's eyes.

Oklahoma!
BLOCKBUSTER CATEGORY: Musicals
STARRING: Gordon MacRae, Shirley Jones, Rod Steiger
DIRECTED BY: Fred Zinneman
Rodgers and Hammerstein's musical love story, set in the American heartland, has
much to recommend it: Gordon MacRae and Shirley Jones in top voice, Agnes
DeMille's sweeping choreography, and some winning backup performances by the
actors - chiefly Rod Steiger and Gloria Grahame - that you wouldn't expect to find in
a musical. Songs include: "Oh, What a Beautiful Mornin'," "The Surrey with the
Fringe On Top" and "I Cain't Say No." Oscar-nominated for Best Cinematography .
OSCAR WINS: *Best Score, Sound*

Picnic
BLOCKBUSTER CATEGORY: Classics
STARRING: William Holden, Kim Novak, Susan Strasberg,
Rosalind Russell, Betty Field, Arthur O'Connell,
Nick Adams, Verna Felton, Cliff Robertson
DIRECTED BY: Joshua Logan
A wanderer drifts into a small town and looks up an old school friend. He stirs up
the emotions of the women in town and causes a school teacher to vent her
frustrations and his friend's sweetheart to vent her subdued passions. Effective by
being sexy without being graphic. This is the movie that changed the sentimental
perspective of small-town living by showing the sophisticated passions that exist in
rural America. Oscar-nominated for Best Picture, Supporting Actor (O'Connell),
Director (Logan) and Score.
OSCAR WIN: *Best Editing*

Rebel Without A Cause
BLOCKBUSTER CATEGORY: Classics
STARRING: James Dean, Natalie Wood, Sal Mineo, Jim Backus,
Dennis Hopper
DIRECTED BY: Nicholas Ray
An alienated teenager tries to fit into the high school crowd in a new town by
meeting the challenges of his clannish age group. This is the movie which defined
the youth of the 1950's and showed the breakdown between the generations that
developed after World War II and is the prototype for all teenage exploitation
movies made since. Oscar-nominated for Best Supporting Actor (Mineo),
Supporting Actress (Wood) and Motion Picture Story (Ray).

The Rose Tattoo
BLOCKBUSTER CATEGORY: Not available on video
STARRING: Anna Magnani, Burt Lancaster, Marisa Pavan,
Ben Cooper, Jo Van Fleet, Virginia Grey
DIRECTED BY: Daniel Mann
A simple-minded, but fun-loving truckdriver courts a lonely widow and brings her
out of deep mourning. A successful movie that applied Italian neo-realism to a
Hollywood-style movie. It was also the first movie, based on a Tennessee Williams
play, to compare the earthy European sexiness to Hollywood-style sophistication
and glamour, encouraging other European types to carve a Hollywood career.

Oscar-nominated for Best Picture, Supporting Actress (Pavan), Score, Costume Design and Editing.
OSCAR WINS: *Best Actress (Magnani), Art Direction/Set Decoration - b&w, Cinematography - b&w*

The Seven-Year Itch
BLOCKBUSTER CATEGORY: Comedy
STARRING: Tom Ewell, Marilyn Monroe, Evelyn Keyes
DIRECTED BY: Billy Wilder
Stuffy, married businessman Tom Ewell settles in for several weeks of boredom while the family is off on summer vacation, only to discover that Marilyn Monroe inhabits the apartment upstairs. The first of Monroe's top-drawer comedies for director Billy Wilder (they later teamed for SOME LIKE IT HOT), this features one of the most striking images from a Monroe movie: her white dress billowing above her legs as she walks over a Manhattan subway grating.

To Catch a Thief
BLOCKBUSTER CATEGORY: Alfred Hitchcock
STARRING: Cary Grant, Grace Kelly, John Williams
DIRECTED BY: Alfred Hitchcock
A mysterious cat burglar stalks the Riviera at the height of tourist season, and the most likely suspect is the notorious thief, "The Cat" (Grant), who swears he has retired. Grant balances searching for the real thief with his romantic pursuit of vacationing Grace Kelly in one of Alfred Hitchcock's most delightful essays in sexy suspense. And you'll never guess the identity of the culprit! Oscar-nominated for Art Direction and Costume Design.
OSCAR WIN: *Cinematography - color*

Anastasia

BLOCKBUSTER CATEGORY: Not available on video
STARRING: Ingrid Bergman, Yul Brynner, Helen Hayes,
Akim Tamiroff
DIRECTED BY: Anatole Litvak

A con man rescues a derelict from suicide and convinces her that she is the survivor of the massacre of the Russian Romanovs. He coaches her in the ways of the Princess Anastasia to convince distant relatives that she is heir to the Czar's fortunes. This movie reinstated Ingrid Bergman as a major Hollywood actress after a brief period of blacklisting. Oscar-nominated for Best Score.
OSCAR WIN: *Best Actress (Bergman)*

Around the World in 80 Days

BLOCKBUSTER CATEGORY: Classics
STARRING: David Niven, Cantinflas, Shirley MacLaine,
Robert Newton, with cameo bits by major stars from
both Hollywood and Europe
DIRECTED BY: Michael Anderson

Straight-laced Phineas Fogg accepts a bet that he can't go around the world in 80 days. He experiences outrageous adventures that represent different movie genres and the film succeeds as a live-action cartoon poking fun at different adventure types. This is the closest thing to a three-ring circus that the movie industry has produced. Oscar-nominated for Best Director (Anderson), Art Direction/Set Decoration and Costume Design.
OSCAR SWEEP: *Best Picture, Screenplay (James Poe, John Farrow, S.J. Perelman), Cinematography - color, Editing and Score*

Forbidden Planet

BLOCKBUSTER CATEGORY: Science Fiction
STARRING: Walter Pidgeon, Anne Francis, Leslie Nielsen
DIRECTED BY: Fred M. Wilcox

An exploratory spaceship from Earth is drawn to a mysterious planet where the only inhabitants are a scientist and his daughter. One of the most imaginative and ambitious sci-fi movies of the 50's, with gorgeous color, eye-popping special effects, a groundbreaking electronic music score - and a plot derived from Shakespeare's *The Tempest*! Oscar-nominated for Best Special Effects.

Friendly Persuasion

BLOCKBUSTER CATEGORY: Classics
STARRING: Gary Cooper, Dorothy McGuire, Anthony Perkins,
Marjorie Main
DIRECTED BY: William Wyler

A Quaker family tries to maintain its identity and hold onto its traditions at the outbreak of the Civil War. A subtle anti-war film that drew parallels between the agonies of the Civil War with wars of the 20th century that took sons away from their homes and parents. Oscar-nominated for Best Picture, Director (Wyler), Supporting Actor (Perkins), Screenplay, Sound Recording and Song ("Thee I Love").

Giant

BLOCKBUSTER CATEGORY: Classics
STARRING: Elizabeth Taylor, Rock Hudson, James Dean, Sal Mineo, Earl Holliman, Carroll Baker, Dennis Hopper, Chill Wills, Mercedes McCambridge, Jane Withers, Paul Fix, Alexander Scourby
DIRECTED BY: George Stevens

An epic film, based on Edna Ferber's sprawling novel, that shows the growth of the oil and cattle industries in Texas through the passionate affairs, marriages and political philosophies of two generations. One of the first movies focusing on prejudice against Hispanics in the Southwest and using the film medium to describe and condemn social practices. Dean turns in a compelling performance (modeled after Howard Hughes) in his final film. Oscar-nominated for Best Picture, Actor (Hudson and Dean), Supporting Actress (McCambridge), Screenplay, Art Direction/Set Decoration, Score, Editing and Costume Design.
OSCAR WIN: *Best Director (Stevens)*

High Society

BLOCKBUSTER CATEGORY: Musicals
STARRING: Bing Crosby, Grace Kelly, Frank Sinatra
DIRECTED BY: Charles Walters

A musical remake of THE PHILADELPHIA STORY (1940), with the added bonus of some Cole Porter tunes - most memorably "True Love." Society snob Grace Kelly is about to marry stuffed shirt John Lund, until ex-husband Bing Crosby turns up to bring her back down to Earth. Frank Sinatra inherits the James Stewart role from the original, a snoopy reporter determined to get a story. Oscar-nominated for Motion Picture Story (withdrawn because it was confused with a Bowery Boys comedy of the same name!), Scoring of a Musical, Song ("True Love").

Invasion of the Body Snatchers

BLOCKBUSTER CATEGORY: Science Fiction
STARRING: Dana Wynter, Kevin McCarthy, Carolyn Jones, King Donovan
DIRECTED BY: Don Siegel

A doctor is dumbfounded when the residents of his town turn into emotionless people overnight. He finds that aliens are creating malevolent clones and tries to stop them before they overtake him and the world. An indictment against the McCarthy era and its methods, masquerading as a horror film. Remade in 1978.

The King and I

BLOCKBUSTER CATEGORY: Musicals
STARRING: Yul Brynner, Deborah Kerr, Rita Moreno
DIRECTED BY: Walter Lang

A widowed Englishwoman goes to Siam to teach the royal family's children and teaches the king some lessons, too. A rich musical transferred intact from its Broadway success and one of the first to be praised for using cinematic techniques to enhance a stage musical. Oscar-nominated for Best Picture, Actress (Kerr), Director (Lang) and Cinematography.

1956

OSCAR WINS: *Best Actor (Brynner), Art Direction/Set Decoration - color, Sound Recording, Scoring of a Musical, Costume Design - color*

Lust for Life
BLOCKBUSTER CATEGORY: Classics
STARRING: Kirk Douglas, Anthony Quinn, Everett Sloane, Niall McGinnis
DIRECTED BY: Vincente Minnelli

A detailed account of the life of Vincent Van Gogh, spotlighting the events that made him a desperate, frustrated man. The movie brings the life and times of a famous painter to life through his paintings. Filmed mostly where Van Gogh lived and worked with scenic backgrounds that were actually used by him. Oscar-nominated for Best Actor (Douglas), Screenplay (Norman Corwin) and Art Direction/Set Decoration.
OSCAR WIN: *Best Supporting Actor (Quinn)*

The Man Who Knew Too Much
BLOCKBUSTER CATEGORY: Alfred Hitchcock
STARRING: James Stewart, Doris Day, Brenda DeBanzie, Daniel Gelin
DIRECTED BY: Alfred Hitchcock

A youngster is kidnapped while vacationing in Morocco with his parents. The rescue attempt involves an international spy ring and a plot to assassinate a government official. Notable as a suspense picture that didn't compromise family entertainment values. Doris Day's version of "Que Sera, Sera" is a classic. The only Hitchcock movie he remade himself to utilize technical effects he couldn't use for his 1934 version.
OSCAR WIN: *Best Song ("Que Sera, Sera")*

Moby Dick
BLOCKBUSTER CATEGORY: Action/Adventure
STARRING: Gregory Peck, Richard Basehart, Leo Genn
DIRECTED BY: John Huston

Ray Bradbury wrote the script for this adaptation of Herman Melville's novel, and John Huston (THE AFRICAN QUEEN) directed it, so expect something striking and unusual. Gregory Peck is cast against type as Capt. Ahab, complete with beard and jagged scar down one side of his face. The scenes of the giant, white whale bearing down on the crew in their tiny boats are as frightening as ever. Screenplay by Huston and Ray Bradbury.

The Searchers
BLOCKBUSTER CATEGORY: Westerns
STARRING: John Wayne, Vera Miles, Jeffrey Hunter, Ward Bond, Natalie Wood
DIRECTED BY: John Ford

A man searches for his niece who had been kidnapped by Indians as a child. After many years he finds her completely assimilated into the Indian way of life. One of Wayne's first character roles and distinctive for the way Ford blended majestic scenery with the plot. The vast panorama dwarfed the human story to symbolize the significance of one man's problems in the scheme of nature. Registered as a national treasure with the Library of Congress.

The Ten Commandments
BLOCKBUSTER CATEGORY: Classics
STARRING: Charlton Heston, Yul Brynner, Anne Baxter,
Edward G. Robinson, Yvonne DeCarlo,
Cedric Hardwicke, Debra Paget, John Derek
DIRECTED BY: Cecil B. DeMille

An epic treatment of the Book of Exodus, detailing the life of Moses from his infant days when discovered in the bullrushes by the Pharoah's daughter to his leadership as an older man. DeMille remade his silent version using more people, more effects and more flamboyance. Known for the way DeMille created identifiable characters out of Biblical legends and eye-popping technical effects to show the parting of the Red Sea and the burning bush. Oscar-nominated for Best Picture, Cinematography, Art Direction/Set Decoration, Sound Recording, Editing and Costume Design.
OSCAR WIN: *Best Special Effects*

The Bridge on the River Kwai

BLOCKBUSTER CATEGORY: Action/Adventure
STARRING: Alec Guinness, Jack Hawkins, William Holden,
Sessue Hayakawa
DIRECTED BY: David Lean

This film, based on the novel by Pierre Boulle, demonstrates superb acting and compelling direction in its depiction of World War II drama. Guinness is a determined British officer captured by the Japanese. The movie develops into a gripping story of morality through a series of ironic twists and relentless suspense. Guiness agonizes over engineering the construction of a bridge in Burma only to see the creation destroyed by his allies. Oscar-nominated for Best Supporting Actor (Hayakawa).

OSCAR SWEEP: *Best Picture, Director (Lean), Actor (Guinness), Screenplay-adapted (Pierre Boulle, uncredited - Dalton Trumbo), Cinematography - color, Editing, Score*

Designing Woman

BLOCKBUSTER CATEGORY: Not available on video
STARRING: Gregory Peck, Lauren Bacall, Delores Gray
DIRECTED BY: Vincente Minnelli

Gregory Peck is perfectly cast as a sports reporter who marries a dress designer in this hilarious farce. Bacall is sophisticated in the role of the designer. She and Peck soon discover that they have little in common. Minnelli shows his flair for comedy in his clever direction.

OSCAR WIN: *Best Screenplay (George Wells)*

A Face in the Crowd

BLOCKBUSTER CATEGORY: Classics
STARRING: Andy Griffith, Patricia Neal, Walter Matthau
DIRECTED BY: Elia Kazan

Glumly searching for a story in the backwoods South, a radio producer (Neal) finds a charismatic drunk recovering from a hangover in a small-town jail. She transforms him into an overnight sensation: radio and TV superstar "Lonesome Rhodes." The NETWORK of its day, this superb drama, magnificently acted by Andy Griffith, is the screen's best expose of the corrupting power of the media.

The Incredible Shrinking Man

BLOCKBUSTER CATEGORY: Science Fiction
STARRING: Grant Williams, Randy Stuart, April Kent
DIRECTED BY: Jack Arnold

Williams is exposed to a radioactive gas that causes him to shrink in size. The combination of an interesting sci-fi script with inventive photography showcases a view of the world from a different perspective. This film is a fascinating thriller even though it was produced with a modest budget.

Jailhouse Rock

BLOCKBUSTER CATEGORY: Elvis Presley
STARRING: Elvis Presley, Judy Tyler, Dean Jones,
Mickey Shaughnessy
DIRECTED BY: Richard Thorpe

Of all the Presley films, this is perhaps the most stylish. Presley struts through this movie with his typical bravado and cockiness as Vince Everett, a con with a talent, convicted of manslaughter. As he plays his guitar for his fellow inmates, it becomes clear that this movie was an early appeal to the newly forming rock and roll audience.

Peyton Place

BLOCKBUSTER CATEGORY: Not available on video
STARRING: Lana Turner, Arthur Kennedy, Hope Lange, Diane Varsi, Russ Tamblyn
DIRECTED BY: Mark Robson

This story of scandal and sex in a small New England community is handled with flair and fine performances. The Peyton Place residents exhibit the dark side of every man as they wind their ways through a series of impressive stories with unusual twists. Oscar-nominated for Best Picture, Director (Robson), Actress (Turner), Supporting Actor (Kennedy, Tamblyn), Supporting Actress (Lange, Varsi), Screenplay (John Hayes) and Cinematography.

Raintree County

BLOCKBUSTER CATEGORY: Classics
STARRING: Elizabeth Taylor, Montgomery Clift, Lee Marvin, Rod Taylor, Eva Marie Saint, Agnes Moorehead
DIRECTED BY: Edward Dmytryk

Taylor garnered an Academy Award nomination for Best Actress for her extraordinary portrayal of a Civil War-era Southern belle accustomed to getting what she wants. What she wants is Clift and, despite his relationship with a school sweetheart, she gets him. Happiness, however, is short-lived. Midway through the shooting of this beautifully crafted tale, Clift was involved in a disfiguring car crash; observant viewers will spot the effects in the later-filmed scenes. Oscar-nominated for Best Score and Art Direction.

Sayonara

BLOCKBUSTER CATEGORY: Classics
STARRING: Marlon Brando, Miyoshi Umeki, Red Buttons, Miiko Taka
DIRECTED BY: Joshua Logan

Brando portrays an Air Force pilot who falls in love with a Japanese entertainer after the Korean War. Umeki and Buttons provide solid support in this story of life and love in the Far East. Oscar-nominated for Best Actor (Brando), Director (Logan), Screenplay (Paul Osborn), Cinematography and Film Editing.
OSCAR WINS: *Best Supporting Actor (Buttons), Supporting Actress (Umeki), Art Direction - color, Sound*

The Spirit of St. Louis

BLOCKBUSTER CATEGORY: Classics
STARRING: James Stewart, Patricia Smith, Murray Hamilton
DIRECTED BY: Billy Wilder

James Stewart portrays Charles Lindbergh in this spirited production of Lindy's solo 33 1/2-hour airplane flight from New York to Paris in 1927. Stewart carries the film with his *tour-de-force* performance of a man on a mission as he is featured in many solo scenes flying across the Atlantic Ocean. Oscar-nominated for Best Special Effects.

The Three Faces of Eve

BLOCKBUSTER CATEGORY: Not available on video
STARRING: Joanne Woodward, Lee J. Cobb, David Wayne,
Nancy Kulp
DIRECTED BY: Nunnally Johnson
Woodward stars in this compelling, true drama about a woman with three different personalities. Cobb is brilliant as the psychiatrist who struggles to cure her. This film is poignant in its incisive depiction of schizophrenia.
OSCAR WIN: *Best Actress (Woodward)*

12 Angry Men

BLOCKBUSTER CATEGORY: Drama
STARRING: Henry Fonda, Lee J. Cobb, E.G. Marshall,
Jack Warden, Martin Balsam, Jack Klugman
DIRECTED BY: Sidney Lumet
This superb drama features Fonda as the moral conscience of a jury instructed to decide the fate of a teenager accused of murdering his father. Through his persistence, Fonda turns this standard courtroom drama into superb theater as he pleads with his fellow jurors to maintain sober judgement in their rush to decide the defendant's fate. Oscar-nominated for Best Picture, Director (Lumet) and Screenplay (Reginald Rose).

Witness for the Prosecution

BLOCKBUSTER CATEGORY: Mystery/Suspense
STARRING: Charles Laughton, Tyrone Power, Marlene Dietrich,
Elsa Lanchester
DIRECTED BY: Billy Wilder
This film, based on a play by Agatha Christie, includes a series of intriguing twists and turns in the story of an alleged killer (Power) defended by Laughton. The clever dialogue helps to enhance this suspenseful courtroom drama. Oscar-nominated for Best Picture, Director (Wilder), Actor (Laughton), Supporting Actress (Lanchester) and Film Editing.

1958

Auntie Mame
BLOCKBUSTER CATEGORY: Classics
STARRING: Rosalind Russell, Forrest Tucker, Peggy Cass
DIRECTED BY: Morton DaCosta

Russell is unstoppable in the *tour-de-force* performance as an eccentric aunt who is both colorful and sensitive as she grooms a young boy with her love-of-life philosophy and happy-go-lucky flair. The supporting cast turns in fine characterizations in this delightful film. Oscar-nominated for Best Picture, Actress (Russell), Supporting Actress (Cass), Cinematography, Art Direction and Film Editing. Remade as MAME.

The Big Country
BLOCKBUSTER CATEGORY: Westerns
STARRING: Gregory Peck, Jean Simmons, Charlton Heston,
Carroll Baker, Burl Ives
DIRECTED BY: William Wyler

This film is an entertaining spectacle of western life. Peck portrays a sailor who is caught up in a feud over water rights when he returns to settle on his land. Heston and Ives are brilliant in supporting roles that highlight top performances by a talented and engaging cast. Oscar-nominated for Best Score.
OSCAR WIN: *Best Supporting Actor (Ives)*

Cat on a Hot Tin Roof
BLOCKBUSTER CATEGORY: Classics
STARRING: Elizabeth Taylor, Paul Newman, Burl Ives
DIRECTED BY: Richard Brooks

This exceptional portrayal of Tennessee Williams' compelling play is noted for powerful performances by the entire cast. Taylor is brilliant as the wife of the troubled Newman and Ives' "Big Daddy" is considered one of the finest domineering patriarch roles in film history. Oscar-nominated for Best Picture, Director (Brooks), Actor (Newman), Actress (Taylor), Screenplay (Brooks and James Poe) and Cinematography.

The Defiant Ones
BLOCKBUSTER CATEGORY: Drama
STARRING: Tony Curtis, Sidney Poitier, Theodore Bikel,
Cara Williams
DIRECTED BY: Stanley Kramer

Curtis and Poitier portray escaped convicts chained together as they attempt to outmaneuver the police in this gripping drama of racial conflict and suspense. The performances are powerful and the subject matter is on the cutting edge in this brilliant film. Oscar-nominated for Best Picture, Director (Kramer), Actor (Curtis, Poitier), Supporting Actor (Bikel) and Supporting Actress (Williams).
OSCAR WIN: *Best Screenplay (Nathan Douglas and Harold Smith)*

1958

Gigi

BLOCKBUSTER CATEGORY: Musicals
STARRING: Leslie Caron, Louis Jourdan, Maurice Chevalier,
Hermione Gingold
DIRECTED BY: Vincente Minnelli

This high-spirited Lerner and Loewe musical features many memorable songs and
fine, upbeat performances. Caron is unforgettable as the young French girl who
becomes a fascinating woman capable of intriguing the handsome Jourdan.
Chevalier sings the memorable "Thank Heaven For Little Girls" in this wonderful
turn-of-the-century film.
OSCAR SWEEP: *Best Picture, Director (Minnelli), Screenplay (Alan Lerner),
Cinematography - color, Art Direction, Scoring of a Musical, Song ("Gigi"), Film
Editing, Costume Design, Honorary Oscar (Chevalier)*

I Want to Live!

BLOCKBUSTER CATEGORY: Classics
STARRING: Susan Hayward, Simon Oakland
DIRECTED BY: Robert Wise

Susan Hayward is brilliant in her Academy Award-winning performance as a
prostitute executed in the gas chamber for her role in a murder. The film is based
on the true story of Barbara Graham and provides an explicit and gripping insight
into the system of crime and punishment. Oscar-nominated for Best Director
(Wise), Screenplay (Nelson Gidding and Don Mankiewicz), Cinematography,
Sound and Film Editing.
OSCAR WIN: *Best Actress (Hayward)*

Indiscreet

BLOCKBUSTER CATEGORY: Classics
STARRING: Cary Grant, Ingrid Bergman, Cecil Parker
DIRECTED BY: Stanley Donen

In London, an American diplomat romances - then drops - a European actress, but
finds he can't get her out of his system. Cary Grant and Ingrid Bergman, the lovers
of Hitchcock's NOTORIOUS, are reunited, this time for a romantic comedy by the
director of SINGIN' IN THE RAIN.

The Last Hurrah

BLOCKBUSTER CATEGORY: Classics
STARRING: Spencer Tracy, Jeffrey Hunter, Dianne Foster
DIRECTED BY: John Ford

In this superb adaptation of Edwin O'Connor's novel of Boston politics, Spencer
Tracy gives one of his best performances as a beloved politician running for
reelection against a corrupt political machine. John Ford (STAGECOACH, THE
MAN WHO SHOT LIBERTY VALANCE) took a break from westerns to direct this
movie, and he cast it with some of his favorite actors from years past. Basil
Rathbone, Pat O'Brien and John Carradine are among the old pros given plumb
roles in this classic about the changing of the guard in the era of modern politics.

1958

A Night to Remember
BLOCKBUSTER CATEGORY: Classics
STARRING: Kenneth Moore, Honor Blackman, David McCallum
DIRECTED BY: Roy Baker
This film depicts the sinking of the Titanic. It approaches the subject in a semi-documentary fashion and is based on the book by Walter Lord. During the course of the movie, many scenes of personal heroism and valor are captured in the agonizing attempt to rescue passengers from the ill-fated vessel which struck an iceberg in 1912 on its maiden voyage.

No Time For Sergeants
BLOCKBUSTER CATEGORY: Classics
STARRING: Andy Griffith, Myron McCormick, Nick Adams
DIRECTED BY: Mervyn LeRoy
Draftees Andy Griffith and Nick Adams make life miserable for their long-suffering sergeant, Myron McCormick, in what is basically a dry run for every Army sitcom that turned up on TV for the next 20 years. Griffith also met his future TV co-star, Don Knotts, on this film.

Separate Tables
BLOCKBUSTER CATEGORY: Classics
STARRING: Burt Lancaster, Rita Hayworth, David Niven,
Deborah Kerr, Wendy Hiller
DIRECTED BY: Delbert Mann
This sensitive portrayal about guests at a British seaside resort, based on the play by Terence Rattigan, is presented in an emotionally gripping and subtle manner. The direction and acting are compelling as the story weaves a tale of conflict and lost hope. The entire cast is in top form throughout this splendid feature. Oscar-nominated for Best Picture, Actress (Kerr), Screenplay (Rattigan and John Gay), Cinematography and Scoring.
OSCAR WINS: *Best Actor (Niven), Best Supporting Actress (Hiller)*

South Pacific
BLOCKBUSTER CATEGORY: Musicals
STARRING: Rossano Brazzi, Mitzi Gaynor, John Kerr
DIRECTED BY: Joshua Logan
Author James Michener wrote a Pulitzer Prize-winning book of short stories, *Tales of the South Pacific*. Rodgers and Hammerstein turned it into a hugely successful Broadway musical. This is the screen version, shot on location and retaining all of the songs from the stage success, including "Bali H'ai," "Some Enchanted Evening" and "Happy Talk." Oscar-nominated for Cinematography - color, Scoring of a Musical.
OSCAR WIN: *Best Sound*

Touch of Evil
BLOCKBUSTER CATEGORY: Classics
STARRING: Charlton Heston, Marlene Dietrich, Orson Welles,
Joseph Cotten, Zsa Zsa Gabor, Janet Leigh
DIRECTED BY: Orson Welles

1958

Heston plays a Mexican policeman south of the border in this dark thriller of drugs and police corruption in a tiny border town. This was Welles' first American production in over a decade and exemplifies his love of shadows, framing and camera movement. The opening tracking shot is a movie landmark. Co-star Welles offers a compelling performance as a bad cop and Dietrich is wonderful in her cameo as a mysterious madam. This deftly directed, crafty tale makes for fascinating drama.

Vertigo
BLOCKBUSTER CATEGORY: Alfred Hitchcock
STARRING: James Stewart, Kim Novak
DIRECTED BY: Alfred Hitchcock

James Stewart portrays a detective caught in a web of fear and self-destruction in this analysis of terror. Stewart's fear of heights is compounded by a complex series of plot twists and sensual heat provided by Novak. As usual, Hitchcock provides a dark study into the paranoia and insecurity of the common man. The closing sequences are some of the most remarkable in the thriller genre. Registered as a national treasure with the Library of Congress. Oscar-nominated for Best Art Direction and Sound.

Anatomy of a Murder

BLOCKBUSTER CATEGORY: Mystery/Suspense
STARRING: James Stewart, Ben Gazzara, Lee Remick, Eve Arden,
Arthur O'Connell, George C. Scott
DIRECTED BY: Otto Preminger

This astounding courtroom drama, adapted from Robert Traver's novel, is a study in small-town law and justice. Stewart plays the clever attorney who defends an Army officer accused of murdering a bartender. George C. Scott portrays the prosecuting attorney. Oscar-nominated for Best Picture, Actor (Stewart), Supporting Actor (O'Connell, Scott), Screenplay (Wendell Mayes), Cinematography and Film Editing.

Ben-Hur

BLOCKBUSTER CATEGORY: Action/Adventure
STARRING: Charlton Heston, Haya Harareet, Jack Hawkins,
Stephen Boyd, Hugh Griffith, Martha Scott
DIRECTED BY: William Wyler

This epic spectacular about the life of an aristocratic Jew persecuted by the Romans is portrayed brilliantly by Heston in the title role. The action sequences and dramatic cinematography highlight this superb film. The climactic chariot race scene is one of the most memorable and exciting in movie history. Oscar-nominated for Best Screenplay (Karl Tunberg).
OSCAR SWEEP: *Best Picture, Director (Wyler), Actor (Heston), Supporting Actor (Griffith), Cinematography - color, Art Direction - color, Sound, Scoring, Film Editing, Special Effects, Costume Design - color*

Black Orpheus

BLOCKBUSTER CATEGORY: Foreign
STARRING: Breno Mello, Marpessa Dawn
DIRECTED BY: Marcel Camus

A black tram driver accidentally kills his girlfriend in this Academy Award-winning foreign film from France. The tram driver seeks to be with his love and does so by killing himself to be with her. Set during the Rio Carnival, this was the most popular foreign film ever, until the late 70's. Its climactic color photography is a movie landmark.
OSCAR WIN: *Best Foreign Film*

The Diary of Anne Frank

BLOCKBUSTER CATEGORY: Classics
STARRING: Millie Perkins, Joseph Schildkraut, Shelley Winters,
Ed Wynn
DIRECTED BY: George Stevens

This gripping sensitive film depicts the account of Anne Frank and her family, Dutch Jews who hid from the Nazis for two years in a factory loft. Based on the touching diary of Anne Frank, who died in a Nazi concentration camp, the film dramatizes the emotional and physical scars incurred from the horror of that wartime period. Oscar-nominated for Best Picture, Director (Stevens), Supporting Actor (Wynn), Scoring and Costume Design.

1959

Imitation of Life
BLOCKBUSTER CATEGORY: Drama
STARRING: Lana Turner, John Gavin, Sandra Dee
DIRECTED BY: Douglas Sirk
Fannie Hurst's famous story, previously filmed with Claudette Colbert, is updated and given big-budget treatment. Lana Turner is a workaholic actress, Sandra Dee her troubled daughter, and Juanita Moore is Turner's close friend. A key subplot involves Susan Kohner as Moore's daughter, a black girl trying to pass for white. Oscar-nominated for Supporting Actress (Kohner, Moore).

North by Northwest
BLOCKBUSTER CATEGORY: Alfred Hitchcock
STARRING: Cary Grant, Eva Marie Saint, James Mason, Leo G. Carroll, Martin Landau
DIRECTED BY: Alfred Hitchcock
This Hitchcock thriller is a non-stop action adventure of romance, comedy and terror. Grant portrays a dashing businessman pursued by foreign agents. The scene in which Grant is attacked by a crop-dusting plane is unforgettable. This is Hitchcock at his devious best and paved the way for the box office success of the James Bond films. Oscar-nominated for Best Story & Screenplay (Ernest Lehman), Art Direction and Film Editing.

The Nun's Story
BLOCKBUSTER CATEGORY: Religion
STARRING: Audrey Hepburn, Peter Finch, Edith Evans, Peggy Ashcroft
DIRECTED BY: Fred Zinnemann
Hepburn portrays a young nun in the Belgian Congo who eventually leaves the convent for a conventional life. Finch plays a physician with his usual dramatic flair as Hepburn struggles through the conditions of her existence. Oscar-nominated for Best Picture, Director (Zinnemann), Actress (Hepburn), Screenplay (Robert Anderson), Cinematography, Sound, Scoring and Film Editing.

Operation Petticoat
BLOCKBUSTER CATEGORY: Classics
STARRING: Cary Grant, Tony Curtis, Dina Merrill
DIRECTED BY: Blake Edwards
Enormously popular Navy comedy with Cary Grant as a submarine commander who's exasperated because his battle-weary sub has been drydocked. Enter Tony Curtis, a slick operator who scams his way to getting Grant everything he needs. The movie's title refers to Grant and Curtis' run-ins with the crew of nurses whom they pursue for most of the movie. A fast-paced comedy from the director who would soon launch the PINK PANTHER movies with Peter Sellers.

Pillow Talk
BLOCKBUSTER CATEGORY: Comedy
STARRING: Doris Day, Rock Hudson, Tony Randall,
Thelma Ritter
DIRECTED BY: Michael Gordon

Falling in love on the telephone is the premise of this lighthearted romantic comedy. Hudson and Day are adorable as the couple who cannot stand each other, yet cannot live without each other. Randall runs interference in this clever story that spun off a series of similarly themed pictures. Oscar-nominated for Best Actress (Day), Supporting Actress (Ritter), Art Direction and Scoring.
OSCAR WIN: *Best Story & Screenplay (Russell Rouse, Clarence Greene, Stanley Shapiro and Maurice Richlin)*

Rio Bravo
BLOCKBUSTER CATEGORY: Westerns
STARRING: John Wayne, Dean Martin, Ricky Nelson,
Angie Dickinson, Walter Brennan
DIRECTED BY: Howard Hawks

John Wayne is in fine form as he plays the sheriff struggling to prevent a killer's escape from jail. Hawks captured the Old West as no other director could and cast Martin and Nelson in interesting roles that played comfortably with Wayne's lawman. Dickinson is intriguing as the love interest in one of her first performances.

Room at the Top
BLOCKBUSTER CATEGORY: Classics
STARRING: Laurence Harvey, Simone Signoret,
Hermione Baddeley
DIRECTED BY: Jack Clayton

This film depicts British industrial life as Harvey portrays a factory clerk who shuns his love (Signoret) for the owner's daughter. The story, based on John Braine's novel, is vivid and poignant. Oscar-nominated for Best Picture, Actor (Harvey), Director (Clayton), Supporting Actress (Baddeley).
OSCAR WINS: *Best Actress (Signoret), Screenplay (Neil Patterson)*

Sleeping Beauty
BLOCKBUSTER CATEGORY: Kids
STARRING: Voices of Mary Costa, Bill Shirley, Eleanor Audley
DIRECTED BY: Clyde Geronimi

This subject is Disney's source of greatest success: fairy tales. Imprisoned in a castle surrounded by a forest of thorns and untold hidden horrors, a sleeping princess must be rescued by the prince who loves her. Climaxed by an exciting battle between the prince and a fire-breathing dragon. The lush music score, adapted from Tchaikovsky was Oscar-nominated.

Some Like It Hot

BLOCKBUSTER CATEGORY: Comedy
STARRING: Jack Lemmon, Tony Curtis, Marilyn Monroe,
George Raft, Joe E. Brown, Pat O'Brien
DIRECTED BY: Billy Wilder

This hilarious farce about two unemployed musicians is a non-stop comedy. Curtis and Lemmon are on the run from mobsters after witnessing a gangland slaying and, disguised as women, join an all-girl orchestra. Monroe is brilliant as the campy innocent. Registered as a national treasure with the Library of Congress. Oscar-nominated for Best Director (Wilder), Actor (Lemmon), Screenplay (Wilder and I.A.L. Diamond), Cinematography and Art Direction.
OSCAR WIN: *Best Costume Design - b&w*

The Alamo

BLOCKBUSTER CATEGORY: Westerns
STARRING: John Wayne, Laurence Harvey, Richard Widmark
DIRECTED BY: John Wayne

Big, boisterous and often incredibly exciting, this epic western traces the events leading up to the struggle for Texas independence and the bloody battle at the Alamo. The first movie directed by John Wayne (with an assist, uncredited, from his mentor, John Ford), this also gives the Duke one of his best roles: Davy Crockett. The home video version is issued in the "Letterbox" format to present the entire, widescreen picture - especially helpful for the climactic siege on the Alamo. Oscar-nominated for Best Picture, Supporting Actor (Chill Wills), Cinematography, Film Editing, Score.
OSCAR WIN: *Best Sound*

The Apartment

BLOCKBUSTER CATEGORY: Comedy
STARRING: Jack Lemmon, Shirley MacLaine, Fred MacMurray,
Jack Kruschen
DIRECTED BY: Billy Wilder

Jack Lemmon portrays a lonely, vulnerable office worker who allows his apartment to be used for the extramarital activities of his supervisors. Sadness and humor combine beautifully in this deftly directed comedy-drama that features memorable performances and skillful writing. Oscar-nominated for Best Actor (Lemmon), Actress (MacLaine), Supporting Actor (Kruschen) and Sound.
OSCAR SWEEP: *Best Picture, Director (Wilder), Screenplay (Wilder and I.A.L. Diamond), Film Editing*

Bells Are Ringing

BLOCKBUSTER CATEGORY: Musicals
STARRING: Judy Holliday, Dean Martin, Fred Clark
DIRECTED BY: Vincente Minnelli

Tune-filled throwback to the glory days of Hollywood musicals. It's also the last film starring the great Judy Holliday (BORN YESTERDAY, SOLID GOLD CADILLAC), whose death in 1965 ended a flourishing career. Holliday recreates her Broadway role as a telephone operator who falls in love with Dean Martin over the phone lines. The Betty Comden-Adolph Green score includes the title tune and "Just In Time," among many hummable favorites. Oscar-nominated for Scoring of a Musical.

Butterfield 8

BLOCKBUSTER CATEGORY: Classics
STARRING: Elizabeth Taylor, Laurence Harvey, Dina Merrill,
Mildred Dunnock
DIRECTED BY: Daniel Mann

Taylor plays a promiscuous woman in this film, based on John O'Hara's novel. The supporting cast is solid and delivers fine performances as Taylor strives to leave her past. Harvey portrays the wealthy, disillusioned married man Taylor falls in love with. Oscar-nominated for Best Cinematography. High quality, old-fashioned soap opera.
OSCAR WINS: *Best Actress (Taylor)*

1960

Elmer Gantry

BLOCKBUSTER CATEGORY: Classics
STARRING: Burt Lancaster, Jean Simmons, Arthur Kennedy,
Shirley Jones, Dean Jagger, Patti Page
DIRECTED BY: Richard Brooks

Based on the Sinclair Lewis novel, ELMER GANTRY is an intriguing story of evangelism, sin, despair and hypocrisy. Lancaster is brilliant in his Academy Award-winning title role and the supporting cast delivers fine performances all around. Jones is especially sharp as Gantry's former girlfriend turned prostitute. Oscar-nominated for Best Picture and Scoring.

OSCAR WINS: Best Actor (Lancaster), Supporting Actress (Jones), Screenplay (Brooks)

Exodus

BLOCKBUSTER CATEGORY: Drama
STARRING: Paul Newman, Eva Marie Saint, Ralph Richardson
DIRECTED BY: Otto Preminger

Mammoth, 3 1/2-hour opus combines human drama with battle action in adapting Leon Uris' bestselling novel about creation of modern Israel. Paul Newman is a resistance fighter, Eva Marie Saint a devoted nurse on the opposite side. The big-star cast includes Peter Lawford, Lee J. Cobb and Sal Mineo. Oscar-nominated for Supporting Actor (Mineo), Cinematography.

OSCAR WIN: Best Musical Score

Inherit the Wind

BLOCKBUSTER CATEGORY: Classics
STARRING: Spencer Tracy, Fredric March, Gene Kelly, Dick York
DIRECTED BY: Stanley Kramer

This film, an adaptation of the famous 1925 Scopes "monkey trial" in Tennessee, features brilliant performances and a tightly woven, fascinating script. Tracy, portraying Clarence Darrow, and March, as William Jennings Bryan, eloquently argue Darwin's theory of evolution in the small town courtroom. The supporting cast is excellent in this poignant piece. Oscar-nominated for Best Actor (Tracy), Screenplay (Nathan Douglas and Harold Jacob Smith), Cinematography (Ernest Laszlo) and Film Editing.

Peeping Tom

BLOCKBUSTER CATEGORY: Horror
STARRING: Carl Boehm, Moira Shearer, Anna Massey
DIRECTED BY: Michael Powell

The British PSYCHO. This movie depicts a film studio employee obsessed by the desire to murder beautiful women and capture the terror on their faces in a photograph. This compelling - and extremely controversial in its day - suspense thriller is distinguished by director Powell's flashes of brilliance throughout.

Psycho

BLOCKBUSTER CATEGORY: Alfred Hitchcock
STARRING: Anthony Perkins, Janet Leigh, Vera Miles,
John Gavin, Martin Balsam
DIRECTED BY: Alfred Hitchcock

The famous shower scene is just one of the cinematic thrills in this classic Hitchcock study in horror. Anthony Perkins portrays the eerie manager of the Bates Motel, obsessively loyal to his "mother." An absolute must for fans of terror, this film is the great-granddaddy of the 80's slasher films and still packs a punch. Oscar-nominated for Best Director (Hitchcock), Supporting Actress (Leigh), Cinematography and Art Direction.

Spartacus

BLOCKBUSTER CATEGORY: Action/Adventure
STARRING: Kirk Douglas, Laurence Olivier, Peter Ustinov,
Charles Laughton, Tony Curtis, Herbert Lom
DIRECTED BY: Stanley Kubrick

This epic, a historical study of slaves in revolt in Rome, is both grand and glorious as it celebrates the wonderful excess of large-scale movie making. Douglas is stunning in the title role and is supported by wonderful performances in the characterizations of his fellow cast members. Oscar-nominated for Film Editing, Score.
OSCAR WINS: *Best Supporting Actor (Ustinov), Cinematography, Art Direction, Costumes - color*

The Sundowners

BLOCKBUSTER CATEGORY: Drama
STARRING: Robert Mitchum, Deborah Kerr, Glynis Johns,
Peter Ustinov
DIRECTED BY: Fred Zinnemann

This film explores the life of a sheepherding family in Australia during the 1920's. The movie is characterized by sound, efficient performances and beautiful location photography. Oscar-nominated for Best Picture, Director (Zinnemann), Actress (Kerr), Supporting Actress (Johns), Screenplay (Isobel Lennart).

The Time Machine

BLOCKBUSTER CATEGORY: Science Fiction
STARRING: Rod Taylor, Yvette Mimieux, Alan Young,
Sebastian Cabot
DIRECTED BY: George Pal

This sci-fi thriller is set in the late 1800's and features a time-travelling scientist (Taylor) who ventures to the future world only to find cannibalism and destruction. The time machine itself is a marvel of gadgets and special effects which help to make this film one of the best of its kind. From H. G. Wells' novel.
OSCAR WIN: *Best Special Effects*

1960

Wild River

BLOCKBUSTER CATEGORY: Not available on video
STARRING: Montgomery Clift, Lee Remick, Jo Van Fleet
DIRECTED BY: Elia Kazan

This film, based on the novels, *Mud on the Stars* by William Bradford Huie and *Dunbar's Cove* by Borden Deal, was filmed on location in Tennessee and features powerful performances by Clift and Remick struggling to deal with the changes faced by a small town. Kazan's direction is bold in this relentless drama of a Tennessee Valley Authority inspector who encounters a local who will not leave her home although the valley is to be flooded.

1961

The Absent Minded Professor

BLOCKBUSTER CATEGORY: Family
STARRING: Fred MacMurray, Nancy Olson, Keenan Wynn
DIRECTED BY: Robert Stevenson

An unexpected smash hit, this proved to be one of the most popular comic fantasies of the 60's. MacMurray is a college prof who accidentally invents "flubber," an elastic mud that defies gravity. In the movie's big scene, the college basketball team uses the tricky substance to float above the heads of their arch rivals and win the big game. Oscar-nominated for Cinematography, Special Effects.

Breakfast at Tiffany's

BLOCKBUSTER CATEGORY: Comedy
STARRING: Audrey Hepburn, George Peppard, Mickey Rooney
DIRECTED BY: Blake Edwards

Truman Capote's story formed the basis of this romantic comedy. Eccentric Holly Golightly (Hepburn) is a small-town girl who journeys to Manhattan seeking her fortune - and the right man (Peppard). New York has never looked more appealing, there's a splendid Henry Mancini score, and Mickey Rooney is delightful as Holly's perennially irritated Oriental (!) neighbor. Oscar-nominated for Best Actress (Hepburn), Screenplay (George Axelrod), Art Direction/Set Decoration .
OSCAR WINS: *Best Music Score (Mancini), Best Song ("Moon River")*

The Guns of Navarone

BLOCKBUSTER CATEGORY: Action/Adventure
STARRING: Gregory Peck, David Niven, Anthony Quinn,
                 Stanley Baker
DIRECTED BY: J. Lee Thompson

A top cast propels this action-packed World War II adventure based on the novel by Alistair MacLean. The suspense builds and the drama explodes in this finely crafted story of Allied commandos on a death-defying mission to destroy the German guns located in a fortress above the Aegean Sea. Oscar-nominated for Best Picture, Director (Thompson), Screenplay, Sound, Scoring and Film Editing.
OSCAR WIN: *Best Special Effects*

The Hustler

BLOCKBUSTER CATEGORY: Drama
STARRING: Paul Newman, Jackie Gleason, George C. Scott,
                 Piper Laurie
DIRECTED BY: Robert Rossen

Newman is convincing as a hustling pool shark, Eddie, in this stark seedy, film of gambling and competition. Gleason is brilliant in a supporting role as Minnesota Fats. Newman reprised his role as Eddie in THE COLOR OF MONEY (1986). Oscar-nominated for Best Picture, Director (Rossen), Actor (Newman), Actress (Laurie), Supporting Actor (Gleason, Scott) and Screenplay.
OSCAR WINS: *Best Cinematography - b&w, Art Direction - b&w*

Judgment at Nuremberg

BLOCKBUSTER CATEGORY: Drama
STARRING: Spencer Tracy, Maximilian Schell, Marlene Dietrich,
Burt Lancaster, Richard Widmark, Judy Garland,
Montgomery Clift
DIRECTED BY: Stanley Kramer

This film captures, in semi-documentary fashion, the trials of Nazi crimes against humanity. Schell is outstanding as the defense attorney and his is one of several brilliant performances throughout the movie. The star-studded cast delivers a memorable and moving view of Nazi Germany and the rationalization of horror. Oscar-nominated for Best Picture, Director (Kramer), Actor (Tracy), Supporting Actor (Clift), Supporting Actress (Garland), Cinematography, Art Direction, Film Editing and Costume Design.
OSCAR WINS: *Best Actor (Schell), Screenplay (Abby Mann)*

La Dolce Vita

BLOCKBUSTER CATEGORY: Foreign
STARRING: Marcello Mastroianni, Anita Ekberg
DIRECTED BY: Federico Fellini

Mastroianni portrays a journalist who winds his way through the jaded cafe society of decadent Rome. This dark character study of scandal and culture illustrates Fellini's brilliance as a director of unique images and powerful dialogue. The blatant episodes of hedonistic lust depict shock over substance in this fascinating film. Oscar-nominated for Best Director (Fellini), Screenplay and Art Direction.
OSCAR WIN: *Best Costume Design - b&w*

The Misfits

BLOCKBUSTER CATEGORY: Drama
STARRING: Clark Gable, Marilyn Monroe, Montgomery Clift
DIRECTED BY: John Huston

This film, an intriguing character study by playwright Arthur Miller, is a compelling look into the lives of western adventurers rounding up wild horses in the desert. Monroe is a sullen divorcee who teams with Gable and Clift in this haunting study. Gable and Monroe both died shortly after this film was completed.

One, Two, Three

BLOCKBUSTER CATEGORY: Comedy
STARRING: James Cagney, Arlene Francis, Red Buttons
DIRECTED BY: Billy Wilder

This smart comedy, set in West Berlin during the Cold War, finds Cagney as a Coca-Cola executive promoting his product to the communists. The effective plot provides plenty of laughs and clever satire as Cagney masters the one-liner throughout. Wilder's upbeat direction reinforces his gift for comedy. Oscar-nominated for Best Cinematography.

A Raisin in the Sun

BLOCKBUSTER CATEGORY: Drama
STARRING: Sidney Poitier, Ruby Dee, Claudia McNeil,
Lou Gossett
DIRECTED BY: Daniel Petrie

This landmark film is one of the first to deal with the black experience in a sensitive manner. It is the story of a black family in Chicago and their struggles to live in an all-white neighborhood. The story is poignant and Poitier's performance is gripping. Sharp dialogue highlights this film adapted from the Broadway play by Lorraine Hansberry.

Splendor in the Grass

BLOCKBUSTER CATEGORY: Classics
STARRING: Natalie Wood, Warren Beatty, Pat Hingle,
Audrey Christie
DIRECTED BY: Elia Kazan

This William Inge story about two people falling in love is skillfully directed by Kazan. Wood and Beatty tenderly portray the young lovers who are separated by their unfeeling parents with disastrous results, in this 1920's characterization. This is Beatty's film debut and he delivers a careful, splendid performance. Oscar-nominated for Best Actress (Wood).
OSCAR WIN: Best Screenplay (William Inge)

Two Women

BLOCKBUSTER CATEGORY: Foreign
STARRING: Sophia Loren, Eleonora Brown, Jean-Paul Belmondo
DIRECTED BY: Vittorio De Sica

Loren's gripping and passionate performance became the first, and is still the only, delivered in a foreign language to be awarded an Academy Award. Her portrayal of an Italian widow, tormented by the harsh realities of wartime Rome, garnered her considerable notice as a serious actress. Eleonora Brown is sensitive as Loren's daughter in this moving study of relationships and trauma.
OSCAR WIN: Best Actress (Loren)

West Side Story

BLOCKBUSTER CATEGORY: Musicals
STARRING: Natalie Wood, Richard Beymer, Russ Tamblyn,
Rita Moreno, George Chakiris
DIRECTED BY: Robert Wise and Jerome Robbins

This classical musical adaptation of the Romeo and Juliet theme is stunning for its vibrant and lavish production numbers and Jerome Robbins' choreography. Set in a New York ghetto, this story of rival gangs and starcrossed love features many fine performances and powerful music by Leonard Bernstein and Stephen Sondheim. Oscar-nominated for Best Screenplay (Ernest Lehman).
OSCAR SWEEP: Best Picture, Supporting Actor (Chakiris), Supporting Actress (Moreno), Director (Wise and Robbins), Cinematography, Art Direction, Sound, Scoring, Film Editing, Costume Design

Birdman of Alcatraz

BLOCKBUSTER CATEGORY: Drama
STARRING: Burt Lancaster, Edmond O'Brien, Telly Savalas
DIRECTED BY: John Frankenheimer

A convict, sentenced to a life term at Alcatraz for murder, adopts a small bird that flies into his cell, and, over the years, uses his time and solitude to become a noted ornithologist. From this slim premise, Lancaster and director Frankenheimer (THE MANCHURIAN CANDIDATE) fashion a magnificent film about a man's evolution from bitter outcast to respected author. Based on the true story of Robert Stroud. Oscar-nominated for Best Actor (Lancaster), Supporting Actor (Savalas), Cinematography.

Days of Wine and Roses

BLOCKBUSTER CATEGORY: Drama
STARRING: Jack Lemmon, Lee Remick, Charles Bickford,
             Jack Klugman
DIRECTED BY: Blake Edwards

This compelling story illustrates the life of a slick public relations executive who becomes slowly absorbed into the stark world of alcoholism. Lemmon gives a brilliant performance as the disillusioned executive and Remick, as his wife, turns in a stunning acting job as she is caught up in the relentless fall. This is one of Hollywood's best efforts in treating this delicate subject. Oscar-nominated for Best Actor (Lemmon), Actress (Remick), Art Direction and Costume Design.
OSCAR WIN: *Best Song ("Days of Wine and Roses")*

Divorce - Italian Style

BLOCKBUSTER CATEGORY: Not available on video
STARRING: Marcello Mastroianni, Stefania Sandrelli
DIRECTED BY: Pietro Germi

This import from Italy had the prestige of being one of the most distinguished foreign films of the decade. The story focuses on a Sicilian nobleman's explanation of how he planned the seduction and murder of his wife by a jealous lover. It is an interesting black comedy that satirizes Italian culture and values. Oscar-nominated for Best Actor (Mastroianni) and Director (Germi).
OSCAR WIN: *Best Screenplay (Ennio de Concini, Alfredo Giannetti and Pietro Germi)*

Dr. No

BLOCKBUSTER CATEGORY: Action/Adventure
STARRING: Sean Connery, Ursula Andress, Joseph Wiseman,
             Jack Lord
DIRECTED BY: Terence Young

The first James Bond movie, introducing Sean Connery as 007, establishes the basics about the famed British agent - his license to kill, preference in guns and martinis, and his eye for the ladies. It's also a top-drawer adventure thriller on its own terms, apart from the series that followed. Bond is sent to Jamaica to investigate another secret agent's disappearance, and winds up matching wits with the title villain (a mad scientist played with icy precision by Wiseman), while finding time along the way to romance the lovely Andress. Jack Lord, pre-"Hawaii Five-O," plays Bond's CIA crony, Felix Leiter. It's the most polished, assured debut movie for any long-running series, and many 007 fans consider it the best Bond of all.

Lawrence of Arabia

BLOCKBUSTER CATEGORY: Action/Adventure
STARRING: Peter O'Toole, Omar Sharif, Arthur Kennedy, Claude Rains, Anthony Quinn, Alec Guinness
DIRECTED BY: David Lean

The grand, sweeping saga of T.E. Lawrence (O'Toole), the World War I British military officer dispatched to Arabia. He decides to remain and, living as a tribal desert warrior, successfully bridges centuries-old rivalries to unite Arab factions against the Turks. Despite wrenching self-doubts, Lawrence becomes a larger-than-life legend in his own lifetime. Magnificent desert landscapes and thrilling battle scenes make LAWRENCE a cinematic experience that's not to be missed. Oscar-nominated for Best Actor (O'Toole), Supporting Actor (Sharif) and Screenplay. Restored in 1989 to its full length, running time and wide-screen presentation. OSCAR SWEEP: *Best Picture, Director (Lean), Score, Cinematography - color, Art Direction, Editing, Sound*

Lolita

BLOCKBUSTER CATEGORY: Drama
STARRING: James Mason, Shelley Winters, Sue Lyon, Peter Sellers, Diana Decker
DIRECTED BY: Stanley Kubrick

Based on the cunning Vladimir Nabokov novel, this film is a sensational screen version about a professor (Mason) who is obsessed with the fourteen-year-old Lolita. He is so infatuated that he marries the girl's mother to be near the child, constantly being followed by the jealous Trilby (Sellers, with an impeccable American accent). The movie is both clever and dramatic in its handling of the subject matter and the performances are first class. The first truly controversial Stanley Kubrick film. Oscar-nominated for Best Screenplay.

Long Day's Journey into Night

BLOCKBUSTER CATEGORY: Drama
STARRING: Ralph Richardson, Katharine Hepburn, Jason Robards, Dean Stockwell
DIRECTED BY: Sidney Lumet

This powerful drama was brilliantly adapted to the screen from Eugene O'Neill's play. The story of a Connecticut family besieged by drug and alcohol problems focuses tightly on the strange relationships of the family and their efforts to maintain dignity in their crumbling world. Performances are moving and the direction is sharp throughout. Oscar-nominated for Best Actress (Hepburn).

The Longest Day

BLOCKBUSTER CATEGORY: Action/Adventure
STARRING: John Wayne, Robert Ryan, Rod Steiger, Peter Lawford
DIRECTED BY: Ken Annakin, Andrew Marton, Bernhard Wicki

An all-star cast recreates, with incredible excitement and astonishing accuracy, the Allied invasion of Normandy that helped turn the tide of World War II. For years,

this breathtaking film was a dream project of studio mogul Darryl F. Zanuck. Three directors and five writers adapted Cornelius Ryan's bestselling book, constructing the movie as a series of connecting episodes, which build suspense at a deliberate pace. Despite the movie's nearly three-hour length, you're never bored. Keep an eye out for Sean Connery, Richard Burton and Robert Wagner among the troops. Oscar-nominated for Best Picture, Art Direction/Set Decoration, Editing.
OSCAR WINS: *Cinematography - b&w, Special Effects*

The Man Who Shot Liberty Valance

BLOCKBUSTER CATEGORY: Westerns
STARRING: John Wayne, James Stewart, Vera Miles
DIRECTED BY: John Ford
A senator (Stewart) arrives by train at a small western town to attend the funeral of a near-forgotten gunfighter (Wayne), his friend from years earlier. As he is greeted by the puzzled townspeople, the senator thinks back to their first meeting - and their run-in with a mad-dog gunslinger, Liberty Valance (Lee Marvin). John Ford directed westerns better than anyone else, and in this masterpiece he reflects not only on the western movie, but the whole concept of the American frontier. A must.

The Manchurian Candidate

BLOCKBUSTER CATEGORY: Mystery/Suspense
STARRING: Frank Sinatra, Janet Leigh, Laurence Harvey,
   Angela Lansbury
DIRECTED BY: John Frankenheimer
A proud American public gives returning Korean War vet Harvey a hero's welcome, not suspecting the truth: he had been brainwashed by his captors and sent to assassinate a popular politician. Only his pal Sinatra, in perhaps his finest dramatic role, suspects that it is not what it seems - but Sinatra is tortured by demons of his own. A gripping edge-of-your-seat thriller with overtones of political satire and social commentary. Uncanny similarities to the Kennedy assassination, which it predates by a year. Oscar-nominated for Best Supporting Actress (Lansbury) and Film Editing.

The Miracle Worker

BLOCKBUSTER CATEGORY: Drama
STARRING: Anne Bancroft, Patty Duke
DIRECTED BY: Arthur Penn
This film is the intriguing account of Helen Keller (Duke) and her remarkable struggle to overcome the physical challenges of being deaf, mute and blind. Anne Bancroft is absorbing as Keller's teacher, a strong-willed and determined woman who works to communicate with the child. Oscar-nominated for Best Director, Screenplay (William Gibson) and Costume Design.
OSCAR WINS: *Best Actress (Bancroft), Supporting Actress (Duke)*

1962

The Music Man

BLOCKBUSTER CATEGORY: Musicals
STARRING: Robert Preston, Shirley Jones, Hermione Gingold,
Paul Ford
DIRECTED BY: Morton Da Costa

This thoroughly enjoyable musical extravaganza explodes with joy and laughter.
Preston is irresistible as a slick con man who organizes a high school band in Iowa
only to sell them musical instruments. Adapted from Meredith Wilson's Broadway
production, this film is filled with great performances and wonderful music. Every
song seems to be a show-stopper in this turn-of-the-century period piece. Oscar-
nominated for Best Picture, Art Direction, Sound, Film Editing and Costume
Design.
OSCAR WIN: *Best Score*

Sweet Bird of Youth

BLOCKBUSTER CATEGORY: Classics
STARRING: Paul Newman, Geraldine Page, Ed Begley, Rip Torn,
Shirley Knight
DIRECTED BY: Richard Brooks

This screen adaptation of Tennessee Williams' classic exploration of attitudes in a
small Southern town features fine performances and exquisite character
development from an all-star cast. Newman is a cynical Hollywood gigolo returning
home with an aging, washed-up glamour queen in tow. A malcontent, his
homecoming rekindles old conflicts with the populace in general and the powerful,
corrupt political boss in particular. Nominated for Best Actress (Page) and
Supporting Actress (Knight).
OSCAR WIN: *Best Supporting Actor (Begley)*

To Kill a Mockingbird

BLOCKBUSTER CATEGORY: Drama
STARRING: Gregory Peck, Mary Badham, Robert Duvall
DIRECTED BY: Robert Mulligan

Highly controversial at the time of its release. This is the story - as seen through the
eyes of his daughter - of a lawyer (Peck) in a small Southern town, unpopularly
defending a black man accused of rape. Much soul-searching and exploration of
personal values is experienced by this widowed father of two, who must contend
with threats against his family as well as his own conscience. Earned Oscar
nominations for Best Picture, Supporting Actress (Badham), Director (Mulligan),
Cinematography and Score. From the novel by Harper Lee.
OSCAR SWEEP: *Best Actor (Peck), Screenplay (Horton Foote), Art Direction - b&w*

What Ever Happened to Baby Jane?

BLOCKBUSTER CATEGORY: Mystery/Suspense
STARRING: Bette Davis, Joan Crawford, Victor Buono
DIRECTED BY: Robert Aldrich

A horrifying, suspense-filled mystery about an erstwhile child film star (Davis) who viciously and systematically tortures her wheelchair-bound sister (Crawford), jealous of her more successful movie career. Regarded as a dark classic today, the film revitalized Davis' acting career while setting the stage for a whole genre of chillers featuring Hollywood's *grand dames*. Oscar-nominated for Best Actress (Davis), Supporting Actor (Buono), Cinematography and Sound.
OSCAR WIN: *Best Costume Design - b&w*

1963

The Birds

BLOCKBUSTER CATEGORY: Alfred Hitchcock
STARRING: Rod Taylor, Tippi Hedren, Suzanne Pleshette,
Jessica Tandy, Veronica Cartwright
DIRECTED BY: Alfred Hitchcock

This thriller, about a small California coastal town under attack by thousands of birds, is filled with gripping suspense and relentless terror. Hitchcock is again brilliant in his direction and does not cease to provide remarkable special effects and a strong dose of shock tactics. The soundtrack contains no music, just the chilling sounds of the title characters heightening the terror. Oscar-nominated for Special Visual Effects.

Charade

BLOCKBUSTER CATEGORY: Drama
STARRING: Cary Grant, Audrey Hepburn, Walter Matthau
DIRECTED BY: Stanley Donen

Breezy, Hitchcock-style romantic suspense. The murdered husband of Audrey Hepburn has stashed a fortune in jewels somewhere in Paris - but where? Cary Grant helps her find the gems, and the two of them are just one step ahead of killers who want the jewels for themselves. Look for James Coburn and George Kennedy in supporting roles. You'll never guess the identity of the villain. Henry Mancini composed the catchy score. Oscar-nominated for Best Song ("Charade").

Cleopatra

BLOCKBUSTER CATEGORY: Drama
STARRING: Elizabeth Taylor, Richard Burton, Rex Harrison,
Pamela Brown, Roddy McDowell
DIRECTED BY: Joseph L. Mankiewicz

This movie heralds back to the glory era of Hollywood combining big budgets and big sets to create a giant spectacular of a film. Grand in scale and fun to look at. Taylor portrays a stunning Cleopatra and Harrison commands a strong presence as Julius Caesar. Although the expense and length were excessive, the result was epic. Oscar-nominated for Best Picture, Actor (Harrison), Sound, Score and Film Editing. OSCAR WINS: *Best Cinematography - color, Art Direction - color, Costume Design - color, Visual Effects*

From Russia with Love

BLOCKBUSTER CATEGORY: Action/Adventure
STARRING: Sean Connery, Robert Shaw, Daniela Bianchi,
Bernard Lee, Lois Maxwell
DIRECTED BY: Terence Young

Perhaps the best of the James Bond films. Connery reprises his role here as the suave British secret agent with a license to kill. 007 must tackle trained assassins and escape with a Russian decoding machine in the process. The gripping train scene, featuring Shaw as the murderous Russian agent, is as suspenseful as the spy genre can be.

1963

The Great Escape
BLOCKBUSTER CATEGORY: Action/Adventure
STARRING: Steve McQueen, James Garner,
Richard Attenborough, James Donald,
Charles Bronson, Donald Pleasence, James Coburn
DIRECTED BY: John Sturges
This is a non-stop action adventure that features powerful actors and thrilling
excitement. It is the true story of Allied prisoners attempting to escape from a
German POW camp during World War II. The action is daring and bold as the all-
star cast weaves a fascinating tale of wartime drama. Oscar-nominated for Best Film
Editing.

The Haunting
BLOCKBUSTER CATEGORY: Mystery/Suspense
STARRING: Julie Harris, Claire Bloom, Russ Tamblyn,
Lois Maxwell
DIRECTED BY: Robert Wise
Based on the Shirley Jackson novel, *The Haunting of Hill House*, this film is a
sinister depiction of a Victorian gothic New England home. The eerie atmosphere is
a movie landmark and the haunted house is as much a "character" as the human
stars. Wise directs this production with a keen elegance as the spooky Bloom and
frail Harris reveal their considerable talents throughout. Harris is especially
appealing in the role of a chaste heroine.

How the West Was Won
BLOCKBUSTER CATEGORY: Westerns
STARRING: Debbie Reynolds, Henry Fonda, Carroll Baker,
Lee J. Cobb, Karl Malden, Gregory Peck,
John Wayne, James Stewart, George Peppard,
Spencer Tracy (narration)
DIRECTED BY: Henry Hathaway, John Ford and George Marshall
This lavish production involves an extensive and engaging cast as they portray
generations of a farming family working their way west from New England. This
adventurous effort is big and bold as the story weaves its way through pioneering
the Old West. Oscar-nominated for Best Picture, Cinematography, Art Direction,
Score and Costume Design.
OSCAR WINS: *Best Screenplay (James R. Webb), Sound and Film Editing*

Hud
BLOCKBUSTER CATEGORY: Drama
STARRING: Paul Newman, Patricia Neal, Melvyn Douglas,
Brandon de Wilde
DIRECTED BY: Martin Ritt
Newman is outstanding as the irresponsible son of a Texas rancher and Neal is
excellent as the understanding housekeeper. The entire cast shines in this hard-
working character portrayal that is a study on family relationships and dynamics.
Oscar-nominated for Best Actor (Newman), Director (Ritt), Screenplay and Art
Direction.
OSCAR WINS: *Best Actress (Neal), Supporting Actor (Douglas) and
Cinematography - b&w*

It's a Mad, Mad, Mad, Mad World

BLOCKBUSTER CATEGORY: Comedy
STARRING: Spencer Tracy, Jimmy Durante, Milton Berle,
Sid Caesar, Ethel Merman, Buddy Hackett,
Mickey Rooney, Jack Benny, Jerry Lewis,
Phil Silvers, Jonathan Winters
DIRECTED BY: Stanley Kramer

This no-holds-barred comedy farce is an assault on the senses as practically every movie funnyman appears to deliver a line or a pratfall. The story concerns finding money hidden from a robbery and stars Tracy as a detective after the loot. Slapstick zaniness and wild chases abound. The stunts are marvelous. Oscar-nominated for Best Song ("It's a Mad, Mad, Mad, Mad World"), Sound, Score, Cinematography and Film Editing.
OSCAR WIN: *Best Sound Effects*

Lilies of the Field

BLOCKBUSTER CATEGORY: Drama
STARRING: Sidney Poitier, Lilia Skala, Lisa Mann, Stanley Adams
DIRECTED BY: Ralph Nelson

This well-paced, sentimental drama stars Poitier who helps a group of German nuns build a chapel in New Mexico. The performances are marvelous and the scale small in this pleasant and enjoyable film. Oscar-nominated for Best Picture, Supporting Actress (Skala), Screenplay and Cinematography.
OSCAR WIN: *Best Actor (Poitier)*

Tom Jones

BLOCKBUSTER CATEGORY: Classics
STARRING: Albert Finney, Susannah York, Edith Evans, Hugh
Griffith, Diane Cilento, Joyce Redman
DIRECTED BY: Tony Richardson

This film, based on Henry Fielding's novel, chronicles the free-spirited life of an 18th century runabout. Finney is splendid in the title role as his sexual exploits and culinary tastes are showcased in a passionate display of exuberance and joy. The supporting cast is marvelous as they join in the act. Oscar-nominated for Best Actor (Finney), Supporting Actor (Griffth), Supporting Actress (Cilento, Evans and Redman) and Art Direction.
OSCAR SWEEP: *Best Picture, Director (Richardson), Screenplay (John Osborne), Score*

Becket

BLOCKBUSTER CATEGORY: Drama
STARRING: Richard Burton, Peter O'Toole, John Gielgud,
Pamela Brown
DIRECTED BY: Peter Glenville

A fascinating look at Thomas A' Becket, Archbishop of Canterbury (Burton), and Henry II of England (O'Toole), whose remarkable but tumultuous friendship ultimately dissolved in conflicts over Church and Crown. Based on the play by Jean Anouilh, this lavish historical drama is full of energy and period splendor, enhanced by exceptional performances by the protagonists. Oscar-nominated for Best Picture, Actor (O'Toole), Supporting Actor (Gielgud), Director (Glenville), Cinematography, Art Direction, Sound, Score, Film Editing and Costume Design. OSCAR WIN: *Best Screenplay (Edward Anhalt)*

Dr. Strangelove or: How I Learned to Stop Worrying and Love the Bomb

BLOCKBUSTER CATEGORY: Comedy
STARRING: Peter Sellers, George C. Scott, Peter Bull,
Sterling Hayden, Keenan Wynn, Slim Pickens
DIRECTED BY: Stanley Kubrick

The end of the world was never as funny as this. The hilarious and sometimes terrifying black comedy is about a crazed U.S. general who launches a nuclear attack against an imagined Russian plot to "drain us of our bodily fluids." Sellers handles multiple roles as a British officer, creepy nuclear scientist and U.S. president with aplomb. A deftly directed, clever film with solid acting all around and many memorable scenes. Oscar-nominated for Best Picture, Actor (Sellers), Director (Kubrick) and Screenplay (Terry Southern, Peter George and Kubrick). Registered as a national treasure with the Library of Congress.

Goldfinger

BLOCKBUSTER CATEGORY: Action/Adventure
STARRING: Sean Connery, Honor Blackman, Gert Frobe,
Bernard Lee, Lois Maxwell
DIRECTED BY: Guy Hamilton

Connery, again as British Secret Agent 007, foils the plans of the maniacal Goldfinger, devilishly portrayed by Frobe. The villain is out to destroy Fort Knox in this sinister story, but our hero rescues the world with his usual assortment of gadgets and gimmicks. Goldfinger's henchman, Oddjob - with his deadly bowler hat - is one of the most memorable Bond foes in the entire series and Blackman is appropriately icy as *femme fatale* Pussy Galore. Film debut of the laser as a weapon. OSCAR WIN: *Best Sound Effects*

A Hard Day's Night

BLOCKBUSTER CATEGORY: Music Concerts
STARRING: John Lennon, Paul McCartney, George Harrison,
Ringo Starr
DIRECTED BY: Richard Lester

A day in the life of the Fab Four. This lightly plotted film was intended to introduce the Beatles to moviegoing audiences. It also changed the way popular music would be presented on-screen forever. Director Lester used the Beatles' natural sense of humor and musical talent as a springboard for an inventive string of slapstick jokes, visual puns and elaborate concert presentations that broke through the previous "burst-out-in-song" conventions of movie musicals. A HARD DAY'S NIGHT is frequently cited as the genesis of today's music videos. Oscar-nominated for Best Scoring of Music and Original Screenplay.

Marnie

BLOCKBUSTER CATEGORY: Alfred Hitchcock
STARRING: Tippi Hedren, Sean Connery, Diane Baker,
Louise Latham
DIRECTED BY: Alfred Hitchcock

This intriguing psychological mystery revolves around a frigid, kleptomaniac secretary (Hedren) whose aggressive boss (Connery) is in love with her. When he catches her stealing, he blackmails her into marrying him so that he can discover what makes her tick. Hitchcock's use of carefully controlled color, painted backdrops and stage sets artfully blend reality with fantasy, adding an eerie ambiance while emphasizing Hedren's removed state of mind. One of Hitchcock's most unusual and disturbing films.

Mary Poppins

BLOCKBUSTER CATEGORY: Family
STARRING: Julie Andrews, Dick Van Dyke, David Tomlinson,
Glynis Johns, Ed Wynn
DIRECTED BY: Robert Stevenson

This delightful Disney fantasy tells the tale of a magical nanny who takes two English children on a wonderful journey of exciting adventures. Andrews portrays the spirited title character in her film debut and delivers an outstanding performance. Van Dyke, as the chimney sweep Bert, shines as well. The film reminds us of the human values that outweigh the importance of wealth and money. Oscar-nominated for Best Picture, Director (Stevenson), Screenplay, Cinematography, Art Direction, Sound, Costume Design.
OSCAR WINS: *Best Actress (Andrews), Song ("Chim Chim Cheree"), Score, Film Editing, Special Effects*

My Fair Lady

BLOCKBUSTER CATEGORY: Musicals
STARRING: Rex Harrison, Audrey Hepburn, Wilfrid Hyde-White,
Stanley Holloway, Gladys Cooper
DIRECTED BY: George Cukor

This exuberant musical, based on George Bernard Shaw's *Pygmalion*, is the engaging, wonderful story of a cockney flower girl named Eliza Doolittle. Hepburn is infectiously wonderful as is Harrison in the role of Henry Higgins, the professor that succeeds at turning the peasant into a lady. The Lerner and Loewe music is delightful and the acting charming in this splendid picture. Oscar-nominated for Best Supporting Actor (Holloway), Supporting Actress (Cooper), Screenplay (Alan Jay Lerner) and Film Editing.
OSCAR WINS: *Best Picture, Director (Cukor), Actor (Harrison), Cinematography, Art Direction, Sound, Musical Scoring - adapted, Costume Design*

The Servant
BLOCKBUSTER CATEGORY: Drama
STARRING: Dirk Bogarde, James Fox, Sarah Miles, Wendy Craig
DIRECTED BY: Joseph Losey
This film is about a rich young man who is brutally and gradually tormented and debased by his evil servant. This sinister melodrama has a glossy appeal despite its tone of nastiness. Screenplay by Harold Pinter.

A Shot In The Dark
BLOCKBUSTER CATEGORY: Comedy
STARRING: Peter Sellers, Elke Sommer, George Sanders
DIRECTED BY: Blake Edwards
The second Inspector Clouseau comedy is widely considered the best. The Inspector (Peter Sellers) is absolutely enchanted with the charms of murder suspect Elke Sommer, and steadfastly refuses to believe the mounting evidence that she is guilty. A non-stop avalanche of clever sight gags and chase sequences, this film also introduced the Clouseau foils played by Burt Kwouk (his karate-chopping butler) and Herbert Lom (his exasperated boss). Music by Henry Mancini.

Topkapi
BLOCKBUSTER CATEGORY: Action/Adventure
STARRING: Melina Mercouri, Maximilian Schell, Peter Ustinov, Robert Morley
DIRECTED BY: Jules Dassin
A very funny, unpredictable crime caper about a gang of inept thieves who attempt to steal a priceless dagger from a heavily guarded Turkish museum. The big heist scene is a classic and was modeled after the movie RIFIFI (1954), which Dassin also directed. Unforgettable characters flawlessly portrayed by a superb cast. The soundtrack music is a bonus.
OSCAR WIN: *Best Supporting Actor (Ustinov)*

Zorba the Greek
BLOCKBUSTER CATEGORY: Drama
STARRING: Anthony Quinn, Alan Bates, Lila Kedrova, Irene Papas
DIRECTED BY: Michael Cacoyannis
Freedom and the pursuit of happiness are what it's all about for Zorba, a Greek peasant living on the isle of Crete. Quinn plays free-spirited Zorba with zestful abandon, while Bates is also superb as the uptight Englishman who becomes his friend and learns many valuable life lessons. A visually beautiful, emotionally charged film with memorable theme music. Oscar-nominated for Best Picture, Actor (Quinn), Director (Cacoyannis) and Screenplay (Cacoyannis).
OSCAR WINS: *Best Supporting Actress (Kedrova), Cinematography - b&w, Art Direction - b&w*

Cat Ballou

BLOCKBUSTER CATEGORY: Comedy
STARRING: Lee Marvin, Jane Fonda
DIRECTED BY: Elliot Silverstein

Lee Marvin tackles a dual role in this sendup of the Old West. His off-the-wagon gunfighter must bump off a look-alike desperado. If you like spoofs, you'll love this one. Oscar-nominated for Best Screenplay - adapted (Walter Newman and Frank R. Pierson), Song ("The Ballad of Cat Ballou"), Scoring - adaptation and Film Editing. Fonda fans will enjoy the pre-aerobic Jane as the title character.
OSCAR WIN: *Best Actor (Marvin)*

Darling

BLOCKBUSTER CATEGORY: Drama
STARRING: Julie Christie, Dirk Bogarde, Laurence Harvey
DIRECTED BY: John Schlesinger

Fidelity isn't one of a young model's strong suits in her climb to the top. Christie is radiant in the role that made her a bona fide star. The film's perspective on the free-wheeling 60's is also quite memorable. Oscar-nominated for Best Picture and Director.
OSCAR WINS: *Best Actress (Christie), Story & Screenplay (Frederic Raphael), Costume Design - b&w*

Doctor Zhivago

BLOCKBUSTER CATEGORY: Drama
STARRING: Omar Sharif, Julie Christie, Geraldine Chaplin, Rod Steiger, Alec Guinness, Tom Courtenay
DIRECTED BY: David Lean

A movie of epic proportions. The Russian Revolution is a backdrop for a romantic triangle involving Sharif (in the title role), the prolific Christie (star of 65's DARLING) and Chaplin. This sweeping melodrama is considered a modern day classic. Oscar-nominated for Best Picture, Supporting Actor (Courtenay) and Director (Lean).
OSCAR WINS: *Best Screenplay - adapted (Robert Bolt), Cinematography - color, Art Direction/Set Decoration, Costume Design*

Help!

BLOCKBUSTER CATEGORY: Music Concerts
STARRING: John Lennon, Paul McCartney, George Harrison, Ringo Starr, Leo McKern, Eleanor Bron
DIRECTED BY: Richard Lester

Here's the follow-up to the Beatles' A HARD DAY'S NIGHT (1964). Can Ringo retain his ring? Find out as a cult tries to steal it in this zany farce filled with the songs you grew up on, including a snowbound "Ticket To Ride." The unusual Pop-cartoon quality of the story is a pleasure to behold.

1965

The Ipcress File

BLOCKBUSTER CATEGORY: Action/Adventure
STARRING: Michael Caine, Nigel Green, Guy Doleman
DIRECTED BY: Sidney J. Furie

First in the series of laid-back, Cold War spy thrillers based on Len Deighton's novels about British agent Harry Palmer. Michael Caine's portrayal of the bespectacled Palmer takes him as far from the James Bond concept of the secret agent as possible - cool and detached, rather than sexy and conspicuous. But he's just as deadly when he has to be. Sequel: FUNERAL IN BERLIN.

Juliet of the Spirits

BLOCKBUSTER CATEGORY: Foreign
STARRING: Giulietta Masina, Mario Pisu, Sandra Milo
DIRECTED BY: Federico Fellini

Where Fellini's earlier film, 8 1/2 (1963), explored a film director's fantasies, JULIET is the director's wife's turn. If you're looking for surrealism, symbolism and style characteristic of Fellini's best, your expectations will be pleasantly fulfilled.

The Pawnbroker

BLOCKBUSTER CATEGORY: Drama
STARRING: Rod Steiger, Geraldine Fitzgerald, Brock Peters
DIRECTED BY: Sidney Lumet

A key dramatic film of the 60's. Rod Steiger, in an Oscar-nominated performance, plays a Nazi death camp survivor whose window to the world is the pawnshop he operates in a New York slum. He is also tormented by visions from his nightmarish past. An adult work of mounting terror.

Repulsion

BLOCKBUSTER CATEGORY: Horror
STARRING: Catherine Deneuve, Yvonne Furneaux,
Patrick Wymark
DIRECTED BY: Roman Polanski

Intense psychological horror shocker, not for the squeamish or easily frightened. Catherine Deneuve portrays an emotionally disturbed young woman whose mind unravels when she is left alone in her London apartment for the weekend. We see the disintegration of her world through her eyes. The first major success for writer-director Roman Polanski (CHINATOWN); powerful and unsettling.

Ship of Fools

BLOCKBUSTER CATEGORY: Drama
STARRING: Vivien Leigh, Simone Signoret, Oskar Werner,
Michael Dunn, Lee Marvin
DIRECTED BY: Stanley Kramer

Leigh's final film (the end of an era) is worth watching. It crosscuts between the lives of passengers aboard a ship headed to Germany in the early 30's. Packed with symbolism and fancy camera work, then capped by a *tour de force* finale, this movie was in many ways ahead of its time. Oscar-nominated for Best Picture, Actor (Werner), Supporting Actor (Dunn), Screenplay - adapted (Abby Mann) and Costume Design.
OSCAR WINS: *Best Cinematography - b&w, Art Direction - b&w*

1965

The Sound of Music

BLOCKBUSTER CATEGORY: Musicals
STARRING: Julie Andrews, Christopher Plummer
DIRECTED BY: Robert Wise

A world film favorite for more than two decades! Andrews stars as a nun-turned-governess who wins over her new family - seven kids and their tough father (Plummer) - with charm and Rodgers & Hammerstein's exceptional music. The video version is a keepsake to treasure. Oscar-nominated for Best Actress (Andrews) and Cinematography.
OSCAR SWEEP: *Best Picture, Director (Wise), Sound, Scoring of Music Adaptation or Treatment, Film Editing*

The Spy Who Came in from the Cold

BLOCKBUSTER CATEGORY: Drama
STARRING: Richard Burton, Claire Bloom, Oskar Werner,
Peter Van Eyck
DIRECTED BY: Martin Ritt

A burned-out British spy (Burton) who is ready to retire goes on a painful mission to eliminate an East German enemy (Van Eyck), where he learns he's just a pawn in the big picture. A realistic, in-depth study of the espionage business. Based on the novel by John LeCarre. Burton received a well-deserved Oscar nomination for his brilliant work.

A Thousand Clowns

BLOCKBUSTER CATEGORY: Drama
STARRING: Jason Robards, Barry Gordon, Barbara Harris,
Martin Balsam
DIRECTED BY: Fred Coe

Robards is an unemployed writer for television in this often hilarious comedy-drama adapted from Broadway. While trying to teach his young nephew (Gordon) the ways of the world, he learns a few things himself. The clever dialogue is a must-hear. Oscar-nominated for Best Picture, Adapted Screenplay (Herb Gardner) and Scoring.
OSCAR WIN: *Best Supporting Actor (Balsam)*

Thunderball

BLOCKBUSTER CATEGORY: Action/Adventure
STARRING: Sean Connery, Claudine Auger, Luciana Paluzzi
DIRECTED BY: Terence Young

Fourth James Bond adventure was the longest and costliest to date, and the second and last to date to win an Academy Award. Bond (Connery) tracks a SPECTRE heavy to the tropics, where he has stashed stolen atomic weapons underwater and threatens to use them against the world unless his ransom demands are met.
Adolfo Celi had a tough act to follow after Gert Frobe's Goldfinger, but he turns out to be one of the series' top villains. Climaxed by a spectacular underwater speargun battle and speedboat race-to-the-death.
OSCAR WIN: *Special Effects*

Alfie

BLOCKBUSTER CATEGORY: Comedy
STARRING: Michael Caine, Shelley Winters, Julia Foster
DIRECTED BY: Lewis Gilbert

One of the most popular comedies of the 60's stars Michael Caine in the title role of a cockney womanizer who begins to regret his philandering ways. Memorable supporting cast includes Shirley Anne Field and Denholm Elliott. Caine and director Gilbert re-teamed years later for EDUCATING RITA. Caine, co-star Vivien Merchant, writer Bill Naughton (adapting his own stage play) and the movie itself were nominated for Oscars. The Bacharach-David theme song, also nominated, was performed by Cher.

The Battle Of Algiers

BLOCKBUSTER CATEGORY: Foreign
STARRING: Yacef Saadi, Jean Martin, Brahim Haggiag,
  Tommaso Neri
DIRECTED BY: Gillo Pontecorvo

In this import from Italy, Pontecorvo takes realism to the limit. The battle sequences of the Algerian revolt against the French look like authentic footage. It's hard-hitting drama that earned an Oscar nomination for Best Foreign Language Film, as well as a Story & Screenplay nomination two years later, following its American release.

Blowup

BLOCKBUSTER CATEGORY: Mystery/Suspense
STARRING: David Hemmings, Vanessa Redgrave, Sarah Miles,
  The Yardbirds, Verushka
DIRECTED BY: Michelangelo Antonioni

This controversial and groundbreaking movie, one that employed innovative symbolism throughout, is the portfolio of a photographer's life. As the story develops, we learn that he's captured something sinister with his lens and it may be murder. Redgrave and real-life model Verushka are sultry subjects. Oscar nominations: Best Director (Antonioni), Original Screenplay (Tonio Guerra and Edward Bond). The poignant Herbie Hancock score is a perfect match for the on-screen events.

The Endless Summer

BLOCKBUSTER CATEGORY: Sports/Recreational
STARRING: Mike Hynson, Robert August
DIRECTED BY: Bruce Brown

Where is the perfect wave? This exquisitely filmed look into the world of surfing takes us to Hawaii, Australia, Tahiti and Malibu with a group of the sport's finest. The cinematography will take your breath away. Brown also narrates this rarity in its genre, a surfing documentary which was released at the height of the 60's surf craze. This one held its own with the non-documentary movies of the year, an amazing feat.

Fantastic Voyage

BLOCKBUSTER CATEGORY: Science Fiction
STARRING: Stephen Boyd, Raquel Welch, Edmond O'Brien,
Donald Pleasance
DIRECTED BY: Richard Fleischer

An exploration inside the human body, with Boyd, Welch and company turned into microscopic size and injected within. Their mission: to save a dying dignitary. The dazzling visual effects will mesmerize. Oscar-nominated for its wonderful color cinematography, editing and sound effects.

OSCAR WINS: *Best Art Direction/Set Decoration - color, Special Visual Effects*

The Fortune Cookie

BLOCKBUSTER CATEGORY: Comedy
STARRING: Jack Lemmon, Walter Matthau
DIRECTED BY: Billy Wilder

The ultimate shyster lawyer (Matthau) turns a minor accident into a colossal lawsuit. His client (Lemmon) plays the "victim," a TV cameraman hurt during a football game who is forced to fake serious injury while being observed by suspicious insurance investigators. Billy Wilder and I.A.L. Diamond received an Oscar nomination for their acidic original screenplay.

OSCAR WIN: *Best Supporting Actor (Matthau)*

A Funny Thing Happened on the Way to the Forum

BLOCKBUSTER CATEGORY: Musicals
STARRING: Zero Mostel, Phil Silvers, Buster Keaton,
Jack Gilford, Michael Crawford
DIRECTED BY: Richard Lester

Here's an outrageous musical about a slave (Mostel) in ancient Rome trying to break free. If you like slapstick, you'll love Mostel and Gilford's imaginative pranks as well as the memorable Stephen Sondheim score, adapted from the hit play. The movie is another winning effort from the director of A HARD DAY'S NIGHT (1964) and HELP (1965).

OSCAR WIN: *Best Scoring of Music - adapted*

Georgy Girl

BLOCKBUSTER CATEGORY: Comedy
STARRING: Lynn Redgrave, James Mason, Alan Bates,
Charlotte Rampling
DIRECTED BY: Silvio Narizzano

Redgrave plays the ugly-duckling object of desire for a married man (Mason) in this bittersweet British comedy. Morals and manners - and the lack thereof - were never so funny. It's a gem from Britain's heyday. Oscar-nominated for Best Actress (Redgrave), Supporting Actor (Mason), Cinematography and Song ("Georgy Girl").

1966

A Man and a Woman

BLOCKBUSTER CATEGORY: Foreign
STARRING: Anouck Aimee, Jean-Louis Trintignant, Pierre Barouh
DIRECTED BY: Claude Lelouch

A love story for the 60's. . . and all time. Race car driver (Trintignant) falls for a young, lonely widow (Aimee) in this intelligent, beautiful movie from France. Aimee received a Best Actress nomination for her stirring performance. Twenty years after its release, a sequel was created to recapture the romance, with the tell-all title, A MAN AND A WOMAN, 20 YEARS LATER.

OSCAR WINS: *Best Story & Screenplay (Claude Lelouch and Pierre Uytterhoeven), Foreign Language Film (France)*

A Man for all Seasons

BLOCKBUSTER CATEGORY: Drama
STARRING: Paul Scofield, Wendy Hiller, Leo McKern,
Robert Shaw, Orson Welles, Susannah York,
Vanessa Redgrave
DIRECTED BY: Fred Zinnemann

Religious/political conflict comes into play when Sir Thomas More (Scofield) chooses loyalty to the Catholic church against King Henry VIII's wish. It's a vibrant translation of Robert Bolt's play, and the film brings even more subtle shadings to the richly drawn characters. Shaw received a Best Supporting Actor Oscar nomination for his skilled acting job. Supporting actress Hiller was also cited with a nomination.

OSCAR SWEEP: *Best Picture, Actor (Scofield), Director (Zinnemann), Screenplay - adapted (Robert Bolt), Cinematography - color*

Who's Afraid of Virginia Woolf?

BLOCKBUSTER CATEGORY: Drama
STARRING: Elizabeth Taylor, Richard Burton, George Segal,
Sandy Dennis
DIRECTED BY: Mike Nichols

Burton and Taylor at their best. Edward Albee's provocative drama brings two couples together for their barbed-wire evening of insults and emotional injuries. Don't miss this shattering, groundbreaking film. (Its use of language and theme led to the current Motion Picture Association of America rating system.) Oscar-nominated for Best Picture, Actor (Burton), Supporting Actor (Segal), Director (Nichols), Screenplay - adapted (Ernest Lehman), Sound and Original Music Score.

OSCAR SWEEP: *Best Actress (Taylor), Supporting Actress (Dennis), Cinematography - b&w, Art Direction/Set Decoration - b&w, Costume Design - b&w*

Belle du Jour

BLOCKBUSTER CATEGORY: Not available on video
STARRING: Catherine Deneuve, Jean Sorel, Michael Piccoli
DIRECTED BY: Luis Buñuel

While the newlywed cat is at home, the mouse will punch in at a Parisian brothel. This French-Italian masterpiece from surrealist Buñuel explores a shocking premise in matter-of-fact fashion. Deneuve combines her breathtaking beauty with a skillful performance that is her most stunning work to date.

Bonnie and Clyde

BLOCKBUSTER CATEGORY: Action/Adventure
STARRING: Warren Beatty, Faye Dunaway, Michael J. Pollard, Estelle Parsons, Gene Hackman, Gene Wilder
DIRECTED BY: Arthur Penn

High style marks this landmark film. Bankrobbers are the heroes, with Dunaway and Beatty as the real-life, Depression-era team, Bonnie Parker and Clyde Barrow. The violent, climactic slo-mo scene was a film innovation. Wilder makes his debut here, too. Oscar-nominated for Best Picture, Actor (Beatty), Actress (Dunaway), Supporting Actor (Hackman), Director (Penn), Story & Screenplay (David Newman, Robert Benton).
OSCAR WINS: *Best Supporting Actress (Parsons), Cinematography*

Closely Watched Trains

BLOCKBUSTER CATEGORY: Foreign
STARRING: Vaclav Neckar, Jitka Bendova, Vladimir Valenta
DIRECTED BY: Jiri Menzel

The Nazi Occupation is the unlikely setting for a comedy-drama about a train dispatcher's sexual misadventures.
OSCAR WIN: *Best Foreign Film*

Cool Hand Luke

BLOCKBUSTER CATEGORY: Drama
STARRING: Paul Newman, George Kennedy, J.D. Cannon, Lou Antonio, Strother Martin
DIRECTED BY: Stuart Rosenberg

"What we have here is a failure to communicate." That's what the no-frills warden (Martin) says to a defiant prisoner (Newman), serving hard time for a minor transgression. Rosenberg's film never fails to deliver first-rate, thought-provoking drama. Oscar-nominated for Best Actor (Newman), Screenplay - adapted (Donn Pearce and Frank R. Pierson) and Original Music Score (Lalo Schifrin).
OSCAR WIN: *Best Supporting Actor (Kennedy)*

The Dirty Dozen

BLOCKBUSTER CATEGORY: Action/Adventure
STARRING: Lee Marvin, Ernest Borgnine, Jim Brown, John Cassavetes, Charles Bronson, Donald Sutherland, Telly Savalas, George Kennedy
DIRECTED BY: Robert Aldrich

The lowest of men - murderers, rapists, thieves - are out to redeem themselves at war...World War II to be precise. The action-packed mission - break into and destroy a Nazi command post in a luxurious chalet - makes it more a heist movie than a war picture, part of the reason for its mass appeal in the late 60's. John Cassavetes received an Oscar nomination for Best Supporting Actor.
OSCAR WIN: *Best Sound Effects*

Doctor Dolittle
BLOCKBUSTER CATEGORY: Musicals
STARRING: Rex Harrison, Samantha Eggar, Anthony Newley
DIRECTED BY: Richard Fleischer
Rex Harrison plays the title role in this big-budget, colorful adaptation of Hugh Lofting's delightful stories about a magical doctor and his strange menagerie. Oscar-nominated for Best Picture, Cinematography, Art Direction, Sound, Editing, Musical Score - original score and adaptation.
OSCAR WINS: *Best Song ("Talk to the Animals"), Special Effects*

The Good, The Bad and The Ugly
BLOCKBUSTER CATEGORY: Westerns
STARRING: Clint Eastwood, Eli Wallach, Lee Van Cleef
DIRECTED BY: Sergio Leone
Third and most elaborate of the trio of "spaghetti westerns" that Clint Eastwood made with director Sergio Leone - a European trilogy that changed the western movie for all time. Eastwood and adversaries Eli Wallach and Lee Van Cleef are all after a hidden cache of Confederate gold during the last bloody days of the Civil War. A vivid blend of action, spectacle and wry humor, with an Ennio Morricone score that's hard to get out of your head afterward.

The Graduate
BLOCKBUSTER CATEGORY: Drama
STARRING: Anne Bancroft, Dustin Hoffman, Katharine Ross
DIRECTED BY: Mike Nichols
One of Nichols' finest is both a symbol of the 60's and a modern classic that stands the test of time. Hoffman is a college grad who's seduced by an older woman (Bancroft) before falling in love with her daughter (Ross). This drama mixed with comedy made Hoffman an instant star. Simon and Garfunkel wrote and performed the memorable soundtrack songs. Oscar-nominated for Best Picture, Actor (Hoffman), Actress (Bancroft), Supporting Actress (Ross), Screenplay - adapted (Calder Willingham and Buck Henry) and Cinematography.
OSCAR WIN: *Best Director (Nichols)*

Guess Who's Coming to Dinner
BLOCKBUSTER CATEGORY: Drama
STARRING: Spencer Tracy, Katharine Hepburn, Sidney Poitier, Katharine Houghton, Cecil Kellaway, Beah Richards
DIRECTED BY: Stanley Kramer
Houghton (Hepburn's niece in real life) introduces her fiance to her parents. She's white, he's black, Mom and Dad are confused. In some ways, this film was ahead of its time. It also marks the last teaming of Tracy and Hepburn, and the third of

Hepburn's Best Actress Oscar wins. Oscar-nominated for Best Picture, Actor (Tracy - in his last film), Supporting Actor (Kellaway), Supporting Actress (Richards), Director (Kramer), Art Direction, Scoring and Editing.
OSCAR WINS: *Best Actress (Hepburn), Story & Screenplay (William Rose)*

In Cold Blood
BLOCKBUSTER CATEGORY: Drama
STARRING: Robert Blake, Scott Wilson, John Forsythe, Will Geer
DIRECTED BY: Richard Brooks
This frightening quasi-documentary based on Truman Capote's incisive book reveals the mindset of two brutal murderers (Blake, Wilson) who wreak havoc on an innocent family of farmers. This film has an identical tone to Capote's crime book and influences crime filmmakers to this day. Nominated for four Oscars including Best Director (Brooks), Screenplay (Brooks), Cinematography and Original Score.

In the Heat of the Night
BLOCKBUSTER CATEGORY: Drama
STARRING: Sidney Poitier, Rod Steiger, Warren Oates,
Lee Grant, Scott Wilson
DIRECTED BY: Norman Jewison
Another Poitier portrait for 1967 (see GUESS WHO'S COMING TO DINNER). This time he's a detective sent to help a bigoted Southern sheriff (Steiger) solve a murder mystery. This unique drama is both entertaining and intense. Oscar-nominated for Best Director (Jewison) and Sound Effects.
OSCAR SWEEP: *Best Picture, Actor (Steiger), Screenplay - adapted (Stirling Silliphant), Sound, Film Editing*

King of Hearts
BLOCKBUSTER CATEGORY: Comedy
STARRING: Alan Bates, Genevieve Bujold, Adolfo Celi,
Pierre Brasseur
DIRECTED BY: Philippe de Broca
A friendly Scottish soldier (Bates) travels to a tiny village to defuse a bomb in World War I and finds that a group of escapees from the local insane asylum are the only inhabitants. This movie's deceptively simple charm seems to grow with time and was one of the first substantial cult hits.

Point Blank
BLOCKBUSTER CATEGORY: Action/Adventure
STARRING: Lee Marvin, Angie Dickinson, Keenan Wynn,
Carroll O'Connor, Lloyd Bochner, John Vernon
DIRECTED BY: John Boorman
Marvin plays a San Francisco mobster shot and left for dead on Alcatraz Island by his wife and her boyfriend following a robbery. He lives for sweet revenge...and the loot. This intense and visually innovative thriller from 1967 is an exciting video view more than two decades after its original release.

To Sir, With Love

BLOCKBUSTER CATEGORY: Drama
STARRING: Sidney Poitier, Judy Geeson, Christian Roberts
DIRECTED BY: James Clavell

Sidney Poitier enjoyed his greatest success to date in this unusual film about a black English teacher sent to one of the worst high schools in London. He gradually gets the students to respect him and themselves. Lulu sings the Top 40 title song.

Two for the Road

BLOCKBUSTER CATEGORY: Not available on video
STARRING: Audrey Hepburn, Albert Finney, Eleanor Bron,
         Jacqueline Bisset
DIRECTED BY: Stanley Donen

Another coup for the British. Finney and Hepburn brilliantly portray a couple whose 12-year marriage has become grounds for battling rather than romance. That is, until they look back at the good times and realize it's worth saving. Don't miss this unusual flashback-within-flashbacks screenplay by Frederic Raphael. The poignant Henry Mancini theme is another plus. Double treat: Hepburn also starred in WAIT UNTIL DARK in 1967, offering another stupendous performance for which she received a Best Actress Oscar nomination.

Bullitt
BLOCKBUSTER CATEGORY: Action/Adventure
STARRING: Steve McQueen, Jacqueline Bissett, Robert Vaughn
DIRECTED BY: Peter Yates
The action movie that ushered in the car chase trend for all urban cop films to come. Bullitt (McQueen) is a tough, honest San Francisco police detective who locks horns with an ambitious politician while trying to protect the only surviving witness in a Mafia criminal case. The movie opens with a spectacular killing and from there the action never lets up. Oscar-nominated for Best Sound Recording.
OSCAR WIN: *Film Editing*

Charly
BLOCKBUSTER CATEGORY: Drama
STARRING: Cliff Robertson, Claire Bloom, Lilia Skala, Dick Van Patten
DIRECTED BY: Ralph Nelson
A scientific experiment turns a retarded man (Robertson) into a genius. Caseworker Bloom grows fond of him in the process. Based on Daniel Keyes' book, *Flowers for Algernon*, this poignant story flourishes on the screen. Anyone who watches will be moved by Robertson's rich performance.
OSCAR WIN: *Best Actor (Robertson)*

Funny Girl
BLOCKBUSTER CATEGORY: Musicals
STARRING: Barbra Streisand, Omar Sharif, Kay Medford, Walter Pidgeon
DIRECTED BY: William Wyler
Streisand's Oscar-winning screen debut - she tied with Katharine Hepburn in THE LION IN WINTER for Best Actress, a first - captures the early showbiz life of comedienne Fanny Brice. It's a superstar vehicle filled with the songs that helped make Streisand famous, including "People." Omar Sharif's suave Nicky (Brice's first husband) is the perfect complement to Streisand's dynamic portrayal. The romance, the music, the laughter and the heartbreak all make this a one-of-a-kind treat. Oscar-nominated for Best Picture, Supporting Actress (Medford), Cinematography, Sound, Song ("Funny Girl"), Score of a Musical Picture - adapted and Film Editing.
OSCAR WIN: *Best Actress (Streisand)*

The Lion in Winter
BLOCKBUSTER CATEGORY: Drama
STARRING: Katharine Hepburn, Peter O'Toole, Jane Merrow, Timothy Dalton
DIRECTED BY: Anthony Harvey
Family honor and ambition influence Queen Eleanor (Hepburn) and King Henry (O'Toole) to disagree on which son shall inherit the throne. The result is a powerful drama, with Hepburn inheriting a Best Actress Oscar (tying with Streisand for FUNNY GIRL). Altogether stimulating. Oscar-nominated for Best Picture, Actor (O'Toole), Director (Harvey) and Costume Design.
OSCAR SWEEP: *Best Actress (Hepburn), Screenplay - adapted (James Goldman), Original Score*

The Odd Couple

BLOCKBUSTER CATEGORY: Comedy
STARRING: Jack Lemmon, Walter Matthau, John Fiedler
DIRECTED BY: Gene Saks

Classic Neil Simon comedy about two divorced men - an overbearing slob and a compulsive neatnik - who agree to share an apartment and almost wind up killing each other. Naturally, all of the traits that made them so intolerable as husbands come out in their relationship as roommates. The chemistry between Lemmon and Matthau often recalls Laurel and Hardy at their best. Oscar-nominated for Film Editing, Screenplay Adaptation (Simon).

Oliver!

BLOCKBUSTER CATEGORY: Musicals
STARRING: Ron Moody, Oliver Reed, Shani Wallis, Mark Lester,
Jack Wild
DIRECTED BY: Carol Reed

The musical version of Charles Dickens' *Oliver Twist* is highlighted by colorful settings and high-spirited songs. A young orphan (Lester) becomes entangled with a gang of thieves in 1968's lavish movie. The supporting cast contributes immeasurably to dramatic elements of the story and their musical gifts sing for themselves. Oscar-nominated for Best Actor (Moody), Supporting Actor (Wild), Screenplay - adapted (Vernon Harris), Cinematography, Film Editing and Costume Design.
OSCAR SWEEP: *Best Picture, Director (Reed), Art Direction/Set Decoration, Score of a Musical Picture (John Green), Special Honorary Oscar to Onna White for her outstanding choreography*

Petulia

BLOCKBUSTER CATEGORY: Drama
STARRING: Julie Christie, George C. Scott, Richard Chamberlain,
Shirley Knight
DIRECTED BY: Richard Lester

San Francisco was a favorite 60's film locale. Here, it's the backdrop for a divorced doctor's (Scott) affair with an eccentric woman (Christie) who's not content with her own husband. The arty direction and potent performances make this a must-see, one of the 60's best. Once again, Christie is entrancing.

Romeo and Juliet

BLOCKBUSTER CATEGORY: Drama
STARRING: Leonard Whiting, Olivia Hussey, Milo O'Shea,
Michael York
DIRECTED BY: Franco Zeffirelli

Zeffirelli makes Shakespeare accessible in this romantic and wonderfully acted version of the classic tale of young lovers separated by their families. Hussey and Whiting bring new dimension to the familiar characters and the beautiful theme music has become an entity of its own in the world of romance. With Zeffirelli's images, the combination is piercing. Oscar-nominated for Best Picture and Director (Zeffirelli)..
OSCAR WIN: *Cinematography, Costume*

Rosemary's Baby

BLOCKBUSTER CATEGORY: Horror
STARRING: Mia Farrow, John Cassavetes, Ruth Gordon,
Ralph Bellamy
DIRECTED BY: Roman Polanski

Could the father of a pregnant housewife's baby be...SATAN? You'll have to watch this modern horror classic to figure it out, but it's well worth it. Just be prepared for plenty of scary moments and great acting by Farrow and Gordon, whose oversolicitous neighbor may eerily remind you of someone you know. A unique directorial achievement in filmmaking by Polanski. Oscar-nominated for Best Screenplay - adapted (Roman Polanski).
OSCAR WIN: *Best Supporting Actress (Gordon)*

The Thomas Crown Affair

BLOCKBUSTER CATEGORY: Drama
STARRING: Steve McQueen, Faye Dunaway, Yaphet Kotto
DIRECTED BY: Norman Jewison

Adversaries in love, McQueen and Dunaway plan the perfect crimes, not knowing that romance could muck up the plans. Besides a seductive Dunaway role (playing chess will never be the same) and dynamic multi-screen imagery, you'll love the intricate theme song. Oscar-nominated for Best Original Score (Michel Legrand).
OSCAR WIN: *Best Song ("The Windmills of Your Mind")*

2001: A Space Odyssey

BLOCKBUSTER CATEGORY: Science Fiction
STARRING: Keir Dullea, William Sylvester, Gary Lockwood
DIRECTED BY: Stanley Kubrick

Here's one for the space age, Kubrick's thought-provoking, mind-boggling venture into sci-fi. Humanity battles it out with technology during a trip to Jupiter where untold secrets of mankind's genesis may exist. Dazzling special effects, the dangerous computer, HAL, and Strauss' waltz music are along for the ride. A one-of-a-kind experience by which all sci-fi films are measured. Oscar-nominated for Best Director (Kubrick), Story & Screenplay (Kubrick and Arthur C. Clarke) and Art Direction/Set Decoration.
OSCAR WIN: *Best Special Visual Effects (Stanley Kubrick - How many directors do their own visual effects!)*

Yellow Submarine

BLOCKBUSTER CATEGORY: Music Concerts
DIRECTED BY: George Dunning

It's a cartoon odyssey for anyone who likes Beatles music, surrealistic art, clever puns and unequivocal fun as the Beatles rescue Pepperland from the Blue Meanies. Pop-art inspired animation. The title tune, along with "Lucy in the Sky with Diamonds" and many other favorites, works wonders.

Alice's Restaurant
BLOCKBUSTER CATEGORY: Comedy
STARRING: Arlo Guthrie, Pat Quinn, James Broderick
DIRECTED BY: Arthur Penn
A bit of humor, a bit of rebellion. Relive the 60's with this movie about the counterculture. A wandering musician (Guthrie) and his friends can't stay out of trouble. It's based on the hit record and nicely mixes social commentary with wit and melodrama. Quinn is the perfect Alice and Penn received an Oscar nomination for his swift direction. Don't miss the scene where Guthrie (in his debut movie) is drafted.

Butch Cassidy and the Sundance Kid
BLOCKBUSTER CATEGORY: Westerns
STARRING: Paul Newman, Robert Redford, Katharine Ross,
Strother Martin
DIRECTED BY: George Roy Hill
In the 1890's, two amiable outlaws used the West as their playground for robbing trains and banks. Redford and Newman bring these men back to life in this comedy-tinged western. They just don't make'em like this anymore! Oscar-nominated for Best Picture and Director.
OSCAR WINS: *Best Story & Screenplay (William Goldman), Cinematography, Song ("Raindrops Keep Fallin' On My Head"), Original Score*

Downhill Racer
BLOCKBUSTER CATEGORY: Drama
STARRING: Robert Redford, Gene Hackman, Camilla Sparv
DIRECTED BY: Michael Ritchie
Robert Redford plays an expert amateur skier readying himself for the Olympics in this lean, taciturn film, Redford's first starring role after BUTCH CASSIDY AND THE SUNDANCE KID. Gene Hackman, who would become a star two years later with THE FRENCH CONNECTION, plays Redford's coach. The first of several fascinating movies, all dealing with competition of some type, directed by the talented Michael Ritchie.

Easy Rider
BLOCKBUSTER CATEGORY: Action/Adventure
STARRING: Peter Fonda, Dennis Hopper, Jack Nicholson,
Karen Black
DIRECTED BY: Dennis Hopper
This is the ultimate 60's biker film that started a Hollywood craze. Two drug-dealing cyclists (Fonda and Hopper) high-tail it cross country searching for America and find that they're not welcome in all places. Look for Nicholson's exciting and witty performance, for which he was Oscar-nominated. The Academy also cited the on-target Story & Screenplay by Fonda, Hopper and Terry Southern with a nomination. The film's frequent use of popular music was unique and the cinematography groundbreaking in its use of naturalistic settings.

Hello, Dolly

BLOCKBUSTER CATEGORY: Musicals
STARRING: Barbra Streisand, Walter Matthau, Michael Crawford
DIRECTED BY: Gene Kelly

Barbra Streisand proved her potential as a star by, in only her second movie, taking a role best identified with another actress - Carol Channing, in the stage success - and making it her own. Third-billed Michael Crawford went on to become star of the London and Broadway stage hit, Phantom of the Opera. Oscar-nominated for Best Picture, Cinematography, Editing and Costume Design.
OSCAR WINS: *Best Musical Score Adaptation, Art Direction/Set Decoration, Sound*

if . . .

BLOCKBUSTER CATEGORY: Drama
STARRING: Malcolm McDowell, Christine Noonan, David Wood,
　　　　　　Richard Warwick
DIRECTED BY: Lindsay Anderson

Jarring and surrealistic. Three nonconformists, seniors at a British boarding school, start a revolution where shooting the chaplain is part of the agenda. This unique, anti-establishment film broke ground by its stark handling of subject matter, nudity and violence. Here's a switch: the movie starts out in color and ends in black & white.

The Learning Tree

BLOCKBUSTER CATEGORY: Drama
STARRING: Kyle Johnson, Alex Clarke, Estelle Evans,
　　　　　　Dana Elcar, Mita Waters
DIRECTED BY: Gordon Parks

Famed Life magazine photographer Parks turns to the motion picture medium to convey his autobiographical images. Being black in Kansas during the 1920's is difficult for a young boy (Johnson) who witnesses a murder. The premise is searing and Parks' direction evokes the exact mood necessary to make it a heartfelt experience. Registered as a national treasure with the Library of Congress..

Midnight Cowboy

BLOCKBUSTER CATEGORY: Drama
STARRING: Dustin Hoffman, Jon Voight, Sylvia Miles
DIRECTED BY: John Schlesinger

A good ole boy from Texas (Voight) finds himself in the darker side of New York City where hustling is the name of the game. There he forms an unusual friendship with a seedy street con man (Hoffman). This engrossing film is still a must-see two decades later and stands as a sociological portrait of the 60's. Oscar-nominated for Best Actor (Hoffman), Best Actor (Voight), Supporting Actress (Miles) and Film Editing.
OSCAR WINS: *Best Picture, Director (Schlesinger), Screenplay - adapted (Waldo Salt)*

Once Upon A Time In The West

BLOCKBUSTER CATEGORY: Westerns
STARRING: Henry Fonda, Claudia Cardinale, Charles Bronson
DIRECTED BY: Sergio Leone

When Henry Fonda showed up in Italy to play the villain in this epic western, he shocked the film's director by wearing brown contact lenses and a five-day beard. Director Sergio Leone calmly instructed Fonda to remove the contact lenses - he wanted the handsome, blue-eyed hero of countless American movies to play the homicidal killer in this film. Long, contemplative and often jarringly violent, this revenge saga is both an ode to the westerns of decades past and a full-blooded follow-up to Clint Eastwood's European westerns, by the same director.

The Prime of Miss Jean Brodie

BLOCKBUSTER CATEGORY: Drama
STARRING: Maggie Smith, Robert Stephens, Pamela Franklin
DIRECTED BY: Ronald Neame

Smith sparkles as an eccentric schoolteacher who gains the eventual awe and admiration of her all-girl Edinburgh class. The performance is one of her finest in a career filled with gems and her supporting cast is also wonderful. Oscar-nominated for Best Song ("Jean").
OSCAR WIN: *Best Actress (Smith)*

They Shoot Horses, Don't They?

BLOCKBUSTER CATEGORY: Drama
STARRING: Jane Fonda, Michael Sarrazin, Susannah York,
Gig Young, Bruce Dern, Red Buttons, Bonnie Bedelia
DIRECTED BY: Sydney Pollack

Fonda plays a dancer who enters marathon contests to survive the Depression. Pollack lures us into the lives of the desperate, offset by the cruel emcee (Young), who heartlessly monitors the dances. Oscar-nominated for Best Actress (Fonda, whose performance solidified her reputation as a serious actress), Supporting Actress (York), Director (Pollack), Screenplay - adapted (James Poe and Robert E. Thompson), Art Direction/Set Decoration, Score of a Musical Picture, Film Editing and Costume Design.
OSCAR WIN: *Best Supporting Actor (Young)*

True Grit

BLOCKBUSTER CATEGORY: Westerns
STARRING: John Wayne, Glen Campbell, Kim Darby,
Robert Duvall, Dennis Hopper
DIRECTED BY: Henry Hathaway

An aging marshal (Wayne) aids a 14-year-old girl (Darby) in tracking down the man who murdered her father. There's an arresting shoot'em-up to enhance the pace, as well as Wayne's tremendous performance and the Oscar-nominated title tune. Don't miss the sequel, ROOSTER COGBURN (1975).
OSCAR WIN: *Best Actor (Wayne)*

1969

The Wild Bunch

BLOCKBUSTER CATEGORY: Westerns
STARRING: William Holden, Ernest Borgnine, Robert Ryan,
Bo Hopkins
DIRECTED BY: Sam Peckinpah

Intense action in the Old West. The outlaws and the enforcers have an all-out gang war in the early 1900's. Peckinpah's movie was praised for its dynamic and incisive blend of direction, dialogue, cinematography and, of course, riveting drama. The groundbreaking, slow-motion gunplay set the standard for movie violence to follow. Oscar-nominated for Best Story & Screenplay (Walon Green, Roy N. Sickner and Peckinpah) and Original Score (Jerry Fielding).

Z

BLOCKBUSTER CATEGORY: Foreign
STARRING: Yves Montand, Irene Papas
DIRECTED BY: Costa-Gavras

Political assassination and its aftermath come to light in this French-made thriller from an expert in the genre, the acclaimed Costa-Gavras. The movie boasts an intense performance by Montand as the target of assassination. It's a gripping account based on a true story which received Oscar nominations for Best Picture (aside from the Foreign category nomination and win), Director (Costa-Gavras)and Screenplay - adapted (Jorge Semprun and Costa-Gavras).
OSCAR WINS: *Best Foreign Language Film, Editing*

Airport

BLOCKBUSTER CATEGORY: Drama
STARRING: Burt Lancaster, Dean Martin, George Kennedy, Helen Hayes, Jean Seberg, Jacqueline Bisset, Maureen Stapleton, Van Heflin
DIRECTED BY: George Seaton

Spellbinding entertainment. The first and best of the airplane disaster movies (three sequels and two parodies followed) cuts between the in-air passengers facing a mad bomber and the snowbound loved ones at the airport. Hayes is magnificent as an unexpected little old lady stowaway. Oscar-nominated for Best Picture, Supporting Actress (Stapleton), Screenplay - adapted (George Seaton), Cinematography, Art Direction/Set Decoration, Sound, Original Score, Film Editing and Costume Design.
OSCAR WIN: *Best Supporting Actress (Hayes)*

The Conformist

BLOCKBUSTER CATEGORY: Foreign
STARRING: Jean-Louis Trintignant, Stefania Sandrelli, Dominique Sanda, Pierre Clementi, Pasquale Fortunato
DIRECTED BY: Bernardo Bertolucci

This stark psychological drama mixes the political drive of an Italian fascist with his battle to repress his true sexuality. Trintignant handles the role with aplomb. The striking cinematography and poignant score (by Georges Delerue) further enhance one of Bertolucci's best film achievements. Oscar-nominated for Best Screenplay - adapted (Bertolucci), following its 1971 American release.

Fellini Satyricon

BLOCKBUSTER CATEGORY: Foreign
STARRING: Martin Potter, Hiram Keller, Salvo Randone
DIRECTED BY: Federico Fellini

By the time this movie - shocking in its day but far less so now - came out, the name of director Federico Fellini on a film guaranteed both interest and respect. Here, Italy's leading moviemaker uses Petronius' writings on mythology as a vehicle to explore his own preoccupations. It's all virtually plotless, and though supposedly set in ancient Rome, you'll spot sly references to everything from Nazi partisanship to contemporary morality. Oscar-nominated for Best Director (Fellini).

Five Easy Pieces

BLOCKBUSTER CATEGORY: Drama
STARRING: Jack Nicholson, Karen Black, Billy Green Bush, Fannie Flagg, Susan Anspach, Sally Struthers
DIRECTED BY: Bob Rafelson

This vintage Nicholson piece gives him a chance to eloquently steal scenes. Success as a middle-class musician isn't for his character, who chucks it to work on an oil rig, indulges in one-night stands and plays cards. It's peppered with Nicholson shtick, including his classic rapport with a waitress while trying to get a side order of toast. Oscar-nominated for Best Picture, Actor (Nicholson), Supporting Actress (Black) and Screenplay (Bob Rafelson and Adrien Joyce).

The Honeymoon Killers
BLOCKBUSTER CATEGORY: Horror
STARRING: Shirley Stoler, Tony LoBianco, Mary Jane Higby
DIRECTED BY: Leonard Kastle
Here's a cult classic that weaves the kind of tale you'd find in a crime tabloid and threads Mahler's music into the action quite cleverly. It's a true story of an obese woman (Stoler) and her partner in crime (LoBianco), who rob and kill lonely ladies. Watch it for a unique couple of movie hours.

Little Big Man
BLOCKBUSTER CATEGORY: Westerns
STARRING: Dustin Hoffman, Faye Dunaway, Martin Balsam, Richard Mulligan, Chief Dan George
DIRECTED BY: Arthur Penn
Hoffman is superb as a 121-year-old man who reflects on his life as a pioneer raised by the Indians and a survivor of the historic Custer battle. Hoffman ages well on screen, like the movie itself. The supporting cast is also excellent. Very few movies mix tragedy and comedy with such effectiveness. Here's one that pays off in unmistakable entertainment. Oscar-nominated for Best Supporting Actor (George).

Love Story
BLOCKBUSTER CATEGORY: Drama
STARRING: Ali MacGraw, Ryan O'Neal, Ray Milland, John Marley, Tommy Lee Jones
DIRECTED BY: Arthur Miller
"Love means never having to say you're sorry." If you want to wallow in romance, go to the source. O'Neal and MacGraw beautifully depict a never-ending love interrupted by fatal illness in this popular film adaptation of Erich Segal's best-seller. They were both nominated for Oscars. So was the movie itself (Best Picture nominee), as well as Supporting Actor (Marley), Director (Miller) and Story & Screenplay.
OSCAR WIN: *Best Original Score*

M*A*S*H
BLOCKBUSTER CATEGORY: Comedy
STARRING: Donald Sutherland, Elliot Gould, Tom Skerritt, Sally Kellerman, Robert Duvall
DIRECTED BY: Robert Altman
War is hell...or dark comedy the way Altman sees it. A fine ensemble cast assumes medical garb and gear to show us sides of the Korean War we'd never see otherwise (though you may be curiously reminded of the Vietnam War, happening when this movie was made). Gould and Kellerman stand out, but everyone's great. This movie continued to deliver after its release: a hit TV show was born. Oscar-nominated for Best Picture, Supporting Actress (Kellerman), Director (Altman) and Film Editing.
OSCAR WIN: *Best Screenplay - adapted (Ring Lardner, Jr.)*

1970

Molly Maguires

BLOCKBUSTER CATEGORY: Drama
STARRING: Sean Connery, Richard Harris, Samantha Eggar
DIRECTED BY: Martin Ritt

In the 1870's, a hidden society of Irish mine workers carries on its subversive activities in Pennsylvania. Richard Harris is sent by the authorities to infiltrate it. The chemistry among Harris, Connery and a strong supporting cast is the backbone of this potent, unusual movie. Oscar-nominated for Best Art Direction/Set Decoration.

Patton

BLOCKBUSTER CATEGORY: Action/Adventure
STARRING: George C. Scott, Karl Malden, Stephen Young,
Michael Strong
DIRECTED BY: Franklin Schaffner

Scott gives a *tour de force*, blistering performance as an outspoken World War II general not in sync with the times. Malden is also wonderful as the superior whose only answer to Patton's temper is to terminate his command. Scott made history off-screen by turning down his Oscar honor, denouncing competition. The other eight wins (including Picture, Director and Screenplay) were accepted. Oscar-nominated for Best Original Score.
OSCAR SWEEP: *Best Picture, Actor (Scott), Director (Schaffner) Story & Screenplay (Francis Ford Coppola and Edmund H. North), Art Direction/Set Decoration, Sound, Film Editing*

Ryan's Daughter

BLOCKBUSTER CATEGORY: Drama
STARRING: Robert Mitchum, Sarah Miles, John Mills
DIRECTED BY: David Lean

A simple Irish schoolteacher (Mitchum) marries a beautiful village girl (Miles), whose heart is soon captured by a dashing, young Army officer (Christopher Jones). A deeply moving romance by director David Lean (LAWRENCE OF ARABIA), underappreciated in its time, but now regarded as a classic. Oscar-nominated for Best Actress (Miles), Score and Sound.
OSCAR WINS: *Best Supporting Actor (Mills), Cinematography*

Women in Love

BLOCKBUSTER CATEGORY: Drama
STARRING: Alan Bates, Oliver Reed, Glenda Jackson,
Eleanor Bron
DIRECTED BY: Ken Russell

D.H. Lawrence's novel flourishes on the screen with Russell's vivid direction, which explores two love affairs. Jackson is excellent as one of the title characters in love with one of two close friends. All involved handle the intended eroticism with taste. Oscar-nominated for Best Director (Russell), Screenplay - adapted (Larry Kramer) and Cinematography.
OSCAR WIN: *Best Actress (Jackson)*

Woodstock

BLOCKBUSTER CATEGORY: Music Concerts
STARRING: Joan Baez, Richie Havens, Crosby, Stills and Nash,
Jefferson Airplane, Joe Cocker, The Who,
Arlo Guthrie, Sly and the Family Stone, Jimi Hendrix
DIRECTED BY: Michael Wadleigh

Multi-screens and a half-million communal concertgoers give this powerful
documentary a special appeal, not to mention the highly charged performances by
an all-rock-star cast. Three days of festival in Sullivan County, New York, became
three hours of memorable musical footage and a unique document of the time.
Oscar-nominated for Best Sound and Film Editing.
OSCAR WIN: *Best Documentary Feature*

Carnal Knowledge
BLOCKBUSTER CATEGORY: Drama
STARRING: Jack Nicholson, Candice Bergen, Art Garfunkel,
Ann-Margret, Rita Moreno, Carol Kane
DIRECTED BY: Mike Nichols
A "thirtysomething" for the 70's begins with the college friendship of two men
(Garfunkel and Nicholson) and carries it to their middle age. Their relationships
with women are the primary focus, including respectively, a coed (Bergen) and a
whirling, but sensuous model (Ann-Margret). This was Ann-Margret's first Oscar-
nominated performance (for Best Supporting Actress), the beginning of her serious
status in movies. The incisive script is by cartoonist Jules Feiffer.

A Clockwork Orange
BLOCKBUSTER CATEGORY: Science Fiction
STARRING: Malcolm McDowell, Patrick Magee, Adrienne Corri,
Aubrey Morris
DIRECTED BY: Stanley Kubrick
This Best Picture Academy Award nominee is one of Kubrick's most artistic - and
shocking - movies. McDowell plays a sadistic citizen of the near future who's
indoctrinated, scientifically, into a less threatening citizen and is then tortured by
previous victims. Kubrick's imagery astounds from the first frame, as does Walter
Carlos' synthesized classic score. McDowell is superb. Also Oscar-nominated for
Best Director (Kubrick), Screenplay - adapted (Kubrick) and Film Editing. This
movie predicted the Skinhead movement ten years in advance.

Dirty Harry
BLOCKBUSTER CATEGORY: Action/Adventure
STARRING: Clint Eastwood, Harry Guardino, Reni Santoni,
Andy Robinson
DIRECTED BY: Don Siegel
Eastwood's premier performance in the role he's reprised four times thus far. He's a
no-nonsense cop dedicated to capturing a murderous psychopath (Robinson),
whatever it takes. And it takes action-packed excitement that never lets up. The four
encores: MAGNUM FORCE (1973), THE ENFORCER (1976), SUDDEN IMPACT
(1983), and THE DEAD POOL (1988).

Fiddler on the Roof
BLOCKBUSTER CATEGORY: Musicals
STARRING: Topol, Norma Crane, Leonard Frey, Molly Picon,
Paul Mann, Rosalind Harris, Michele Marsh,
Paul Michael Glaser
DIRECTED BY: Norman Jewison
Topol, as Tevye the milkman, carries this spectacular film version of the hit musical
play. It celebrates the Jewish heritage with a joyous score, including "If I Were A
Rich Man" and "Tradition." There's sadness - Tevye and his family are forced to
leave their home to avoid persecution in Czarist Russia - but also a counterbalance
of uplifting songs and spirit. Oscar-nominated for Best Picture, Actor (Topol),
Supporting Actor (Frey), Director (Jewison) and Art Direction/Set Decoration.
OSCAR WINS: *Best Cinematography, Sound, Scoring*

The French Connection
BLOCKBUSTER CATEGORY: Action/Adventure
STARRING: Gene Hackman, Fernando Rey, Roy Scheider,
Tony LoBianco
DIRECTED BY: William Friedkin

The chase is on. . .one of filmdom's most famous by car. Hackman is brilliant in his role as Popeye Doyle, the N.Y.C. cop whose main goal is to demolish an international drug ring. Oscar-nominated for Best Supporting actor (Scheider), Cinematography and Sound. Hackman returned as Doyle in THE FRENCH CONNECTION II (1975).
OSCAR SWEEP: Best Picture, Actor (Hackman), Director (Friedkin), Screenplay - adapted (Ernest Tidyman), Film Editing

Harold and Maude
BLOCKBUSTER CATEGORY: Comedy
STARRING: Bud Cort, Ruth Gordon, Vivian Pickles, Cyril Cusack,
Charles Tyner
DIRECTED BY: Hal Ashby

December-May romances were never so macabre. A 20-year-old (Cort) with fake suicidal tendencies falls in love with a 79-year-old eccentric (Gordon). This strange movie has a significant cult following. Writer Colin Higgins received critical praise for his unique script.

The Hospital
BLOCKBUSTER CATEGORY: Comedy
STARRING: George C. Scott, Diana Rigg, Barnard Hughes, Nancy
Marchand, Richard Dysart, Stephen Elliott,
Stockard Channing
DIRECTED BY: Arthur Hiller

Paddy Chayefsky received the Oscar for his sardonic script about an urban hospital and its various crises, some funny, some scary, some sad. Scott plays the disillusioned doctor to zany Rigg. Even though he shunned his PATTON Oscar, he received a follow-up nomination for this.
OSCAR WIN: Best Story & Screenplay (Paddy Chayefsky)

Klute
BLOCKBUSTER CATEGORY: Mystery/Suspense
STARRING: Jane Fonda, Donald Sutherland, Charles Cioffi,
Roy Scheider, Jean Stapleton
DIRECTED BY: Alan J. Pakula

Fonda won her first Best Actress Oscar playing a hooker stalked by a psychotic killer. Her multi-layered work is complemented by Sutherland as the devoted detective. When director Pakula wants to make you jump, he gives you an intense denouement. Oscar-nominated for Best Story & Screenplay (Andy and Dave Lewis).
OSCAR WIN: Best Actress (Fonda)

The Last Picture Show
BLOCKBUSTER CATEGORY: Available on video, early 1991
STARRING: Timothy Bottoms, Jeff Bridges, Ben Johnson,
Cloris Leachman, Ellen Burstyn, Cybill Shepherd,
Eileen Brennan, Sam Bottoms, Randy Quaid
DIRECTED BY: Peter Bogdanovich
It's also the *greatest* picture show by Bogdanovich. Small-town Texas in the 50's is resurrected as Bogdanovich weaves in and out of the ensemble's lives for top-notch drama. Supporting actress Leachman as the neglected wife and supporting actor Johnson as the pool hall owner offer stand-out performances. Oscar-nominated for Best Picture, Supporting Actor (Bridges), Supporting Actress (Burstyn), Director (Bogdanovich), Screenplay - adapted (Larry McMurtry and Bogdanovich) and Cinematography.
OSCAR WINS: *Best Supporting Actor (Johnson), Supporting Actress (Leachman)*

McCabe and Mrs. Miller
BLOCKBUSTER CATEGORY: Westerns
STARRING: Warren Beatty, Julie Christie, Rene Auberjonois,
John Schuck, Keith Carradine, William Devane,
Shelly Duvall
DIRECTED BY: Robert Altman
Director Altman is a master with off-beat characters. Here, he debunks notions of a glamorous turn-of-the-century in the Pacific Northwest, centering on a saloon-bordello and its small-time owner (Beatty). Christie is excellent as an ambitious madame. This is vintage Altman. Oscar-nominated for Best Actress (Christie).

Straw Dogs
BLOCKBUSTER CATEGORY: Drama
STARRING: Dustin Hoffman, Susan George, Peter Vaughan,
T.P. McKenna, Peter Arne, David Warner
DIRECTED BY: Sam Peckinpah
Hoffman, in a role unlike any of his others, plays a pacifist from the United States who marries an Englishwoman and moves to a peaceful village. His reaction to their being brutalized by a gang of locals is equally brutal. Don't miss one of the screen's greatest actors in a movie that caused controversy due to its seeming approval of violence. Oscar-nominated for Best Original Dramatic Score.

Cabaret
BLOCKBUSTER CATEGORY: Musicals
STARRING: Liza Minnelli, Michael York, Helmut Griem,
Joel Grey, Fritz Wepper, Marisa Berenson
DIRECTED BY: Bob Fosse
What good is sitting alone in your room when there are movies like this to be seen?
Minnelli is stunning in her Oscar-winning role as an American nightclub singer
living in Nazi Berlin. It's a mixture of dynamic songs and high drama, flash, glitter,
decadence and love. Oscar-nominated for Best Picture and Screenplay - adapted (Jay
Allen).
OSCAR SWEEP: *Best Actress (Minnelli), Supporting Actor (Grey), Director (Fosse),
Cinematography, Art Direction/Set Decoration, Sound, Scoring, Film Editing*

The Candidate
BLOCKBUSTER CATEGORY: Drama
STARRING: Robert Redford, Peter Boyle, Don Porter,
Allen Garfield, Karen Carlson, Melvyn Douglas
DIRECTED BY: Michael Ritchie
This political satire rings all too true these days. It's a must-see for Redford's incisive
performance as a naive politician on the campaign trail who thinks the campaign has
integrity. Ritchie's documentary-style direction is excellent, as is the intelligent
script.
OSCAR WIN: *Best Story & Screenplay (Jeremy Larner)*

Deliverance
BLOCKBUSTER CATEGORY: Drama
STARRING: Jon Voight, Burt Reynolds, Ned Beatty, Ronny Cox,
Billy McKinney, Herbert "Cowboy" Coward
DIRECTED BY: John Boorman
A weekend canoe trip turns into a horrifying nightmare when four Atlanta
businessmen run into backwoods killers. This was Beatty and Cox's first film. Many
consider it the finest acting Reynolds has ever done. Musical relief during this
savage tale comes in the form of "Dueling Banjos." Oscar-nominated for Best
Picture, Director (Boorman) and Film Editing.

Frenzy
BLOCKBUSTER CATEGORY: Alfred Hitchcock
STARRING: Jon Finch, Barry Foster, Barbara Leigh-Hunt,
Anna Massey, Jean Marsh
DIRECTED BY: Alfred Hitchcock
The style and wit that was Hitchcock are both present in his next-to-last film. An
innocent man (Finch) is suspected of a series of rapes and murders in London,
while the real killer (Foster) continues his crimes. Food jokes, precision camera
work, ingenious clues and the trademark glimpse of Hitchcock in front of the lens
make for delicious suspense. Hitchcock's first British film since 1950's STAGE
FRIGHT.

1972

The Godfather

BLOCKBUSTER CATEGORY: Drama
STARRING: Marlon Brando, Al Pacino, James Caan,
Richard Castellano, John Cazale, Diane Keaton,
Talia Shire, Robert Duvall
DIRECTED BY: Francis Ford Coppola
Mario Puzo's pulp novel on Mafia family turf is expertly transferred to the screen.
Brando leads the pack as patriarch in a story of power, abuse, betrayal and
corruption. The rest of the all-star cast are terrific, especially Pacino, Caan and
Duvall, who became stars from this.
OSCAR SWEEP: *Best Picture, Actor (Brando), Screenplay - adapted (Mario Puzo
and Francis Ford Coppola)*

The Heartbreak Kid

BLOCKBUSTER CATEGORY: Comedy
STARRING: Charles Grodin, Cybill Shepherd, Jeannie Berlin,
Eddie Albert, Audra Lindley
DIRECTED BY: Elaine May
A man on his honeymoon couldn't be more in love. . .but not with his wife! Jewish
Grodin falls for WASP Shepherd in this ironic and fully entrancing movie. The pace
is swift thanks to May; the dialogue, crisp and funny thanks to Neil Simon. May's
daughter, Berlin, in her Oscar-nominated supporting stint as the wife is, well,
heartbreaking. Supporting Actor Albert also received a nomination for his skilled
portrayal. Don't miss it.

Jeremiah Johnson

BLOCKBUSTER CATEGORY: Action/Adventure
STARRING: Robert Redford, Will Geer, Stefan Gierasch
DIRECTED BY: Sydney Pollack
Robert Redford stars in one of his most ambitious and exciting movies, portraying a
trapper in the Utah wilderness of the 1850's. The film, directed by frequent Redford
collaborator Pollack (OUT OF AFRICA), chronicles the life of the title character
from wide-eyed greenhorn who nearly perishes in his first, fierce winter to grizzled
old-timer who, by the movie's end, has drifted into legend. Shot on location, the
movie is almost indescribably beautiful to look at. Episodically constructed, its
highlights include Johnson's encounter with a tough-talking bear stalker played by
Geer, and his leading of a party of travelers through the Indian burial ground - and
the dire consequences that follow. Co-scripted by John Milius (MAGNUM FORCE,
APOCALYPSE NOW).

Lady Sings the Blues

BLOCKBUSTER CATEGORY: Drama
STARRING: Diana Ross, Billy Dee Williams, Richard Pryor,
James Callahan
DIRECTED BY: Sidney J. Furie
Ross mesmerizes in her starring debut as real-life jazz legend Billie Holiday. It's a
raw, honest performance which takes the singer from her early days on the road -
where black artists suffered racial injustices - to her growing addiction to drugs.
Williams and Pryor are fine supports, but this is Ross' movie. She received an Oscar

nomination as Best Actress, impressive for a debut. The Story & Screenplay, Art Direction, Scoring and Costumes were also nominated.

Play It Again, Sam

BLOCKBUSTER CATEGORY: Comedy
STARRING: Woody Allen, Diane Keaton, Tony Roberts
DIRECTED BY: Herbert Ross

A movie-obsessed nerd (Allen) cultivates Humphrey Bogart's ghost (Jerry Lacy) as his alter-ego, and begins an affair with his best friend's wife (Keaton). An inspired comic notion - expanded by Allen from his hit play - becomes one of the great comedies of the 70's. Jerry Lacy's impersonation of Bogie is indescribably on-target.

Sleuth

BLOCKBUSTER CATEGORY: Mystery/Suspense
STARRING: Laurence Olivier, Michael Caine
DIRECTED BY: Joseph L. Mankiewicz

Two Oscar-nominated *tour de force* performances comprise this cat-and-mouse thriller of a game of one-upmanship. Olivier is the detective story writer and Caine, his wife's lover. Their vengefulness (trying to incriminate each other) is both deadly and dazzling as is the brisk Anthony Shaffer script and Ken Adam production design. Besides actors Olivier and Caine, director Mankiewicz and music composer John Addison received Oscar nominations.

Sounder

BLOCKBUSTER CATEGORY: Drama
STARRING: Cicely Tyson, Paul Winfield, Kevin Hooks,
              Carmen Matthews, Taj Mahal, James Best
DIRECTED BY: Martin Ritt

Ritt welcomes you into the lives of a black sharecropper's family during the Depression. You'll endure their hardships - an unfair work-camp sentence for Winfield's minor theft to feed the family - and tribulations, such as Hooks' coming of age. Taj Mahal's score is a plus. Tyson, Winfield, the adapted screenplay and the film itself were Oscar nominees. An excellent sequel, PART 2, SOUNDER (1976) followed.

What's Up, Doc?

BLOCKBUSTER CATEGORY: Comedy
STARRING: Barbra Streisand, Ryan O'Neal, Kenneth Mars,
              Austin Pendleton, Madeline Kahn, Sorrell Booke
DIRECTED BY: Peter Bogdanovich

A screwball comedy reminiscent of 30's fare. Zany Streisand keeps bumping in to uptight O'Neal and his nagging fiancee (Kahn). The mix-up of identical flight bags spurs a cavalcade of high jinks, with Streisand at her comic best. The movie's as light as souffle and perhaps the funniest of its year. Listen for O'Neal's send-up of the famous "love means never having to say you're sorry" line from his own movie, LOVE STORY (1970).

American Graffiti
BLOCKBUSTER CATEGORY: Comedy
STARRING: Richard Dreyfuss, Ron Howard, Paul LeMat,
Charlie Martin Smith, Cindy Williams, Candy Clark,
Mackenzie Phillips, Wolfman Jack, Harrison Ford,
Bo Hopkins, Suzanne Somers
DIRECTED BY: George Lucas

The most famous "coming of age" movie is set in the early 60's and features a soon-to-be-all-star cast. Dreyfuss is particularly brilliant in his star-making role. And then there's that irresistible music like "Rock Around the Clock." Lucas followed up this film with STAR WARS (1977). Oscar-nominated for Best Picture, Supporting Actress (Clark), Director (Lucas), Story & Screenplay (Lucas, Gloria Katz and Willard Huyck) and Film Editing.

The Day Of The Jackal
BLOCKBUSTER CATEGORY: Action/Adventure
STARRING: Edward Fox, Delphine Seyrig, Michel Lonsdale
DIRECTED BY: Fred Zinnemann

Based on Frederick Forsyth's non-fiction bestseller. In the 60's, French police learn that a paid assassin - known only as "The Jackal" (Fox) - has been hired to kill President De Gaulle. This meticulously detailed suspense movie alternates between showing The Jackal preparing his crime and the desperate struggle of a determined police inspector (played with unglamorous precision by Lonsdale) to stop the crime. Oscar-nominated for Film Editing.

The Exorcist
BLOCKBUSTER CATEGORY: Horror
STARRING: Ellen Burstyn, Max von Sydow, Linda Blair,
Jason Miller, Lee J. Cobb
DIRECTED BY: William Friedkin

The ultimate horror film. Blair plays a 12-year-old girl who's possessed by the devil and two priests (Miller, Sydow) are needed to rid her body of the evil spirit. Director Friedkin's trademark cold, clinical tone and graphic effects set the standards for subsequent screen horror. The movie received nominations for Best Picture, Actress (Burstyn), Supporting Actress (Blair), Supporting Actor (Miller), Director (Friedkin), Cinematography, Art Direction/Set Decoration and Film Editing.
OSCAR WINS: *Best Screenplay - adapted (William Peter Blatty), Sound*

Last Tango in Paris
BLOCKBUSTER CATEGORY: Drama
STARRING: Marlon Brando, Maria Schneider, Jean-Pierre Leaud
DIRECTED BY: Bernardo Bertolucci

This highly controversial movie features some of Brando's best acting to date. He plays a distraught widower who has an obsessive affair with a stranger (Schneider). Bertolucci's camera finesse shows why he's considered one of the best directors in cinema. Oscar-nominated for Best Director (Bertolucci) and Actor (Brando).

Mean Streets
BLOCKBUSTER CATEGORY: Drama
STARRING: Robert DeNiro, Harvey Keitel, David Proval,
Amy Robinson
DIRECTED BY: Martin Scorsese
This hard-hitting drama was the masterpiece that introduced Scorsese to the ranks of great directors. He explores Little Italy and the friendship between an in-debt DeNiro and a to-the-rescue Keitel, who loses his Mafia status in the process.

The Paper Chase
BLOCKBUSTER CATEGORY: Drama
STARRING: Timothy Bottoms, Lindsay Wagner, John Houseman,
Graham Beckel
DIRECTED BY: James Bridges
The comedic/dramatic dichotomy of Bottoms' freshman year at Harvard Law School is ignited by a high-pressure prof (Houseman) and his daughter (Wagner), who happens to be Bottoms' girlfriend. All parts fit like a glove, making this an entertaining movie. Oscar-nominated for Best Screenplay - adapted (Bridges) and Sound.
OSCAR WIN: *Best Supporting Actor (Houseman)*

Paper Moon
BLOCKBUSTER CATEGORY: Comedy
STARRING: Ryan O'Neal, Tatum O'Neal, Madeline Kahn,
John Hillerman
DIRECTED BY: Peter Bogdanovich
A clever con artist (Ryan) must drive a fiesty young girl (Tatum, Ryan's real-life daughter) to see her "parents." Along the way, they form a like-hate relationship, one that's interrupted by the boisterous Miss Trixie Delight (Kahn). The black and white photography adds to the quaint 1930's charm of it all. Oscar-nominated for Best Supporting Actress (Kahn), Screenplay - adapted (Alvin Sargent) and Sound.
OSCAR WIN: *Best Supporting Actress (Tatum O'Neal, the youngest to ever win - at age 10 - and for her movie debut!)*

Papillon
BLOCKBUSTER CATEGORY: Action/Adventure
STARRING: Steve McQueen, Dustin Hoffman, Don Gordon
DIRECTED BY: Franklin J. Schaffner
Based on the fact-derived account of a cunning thief and murderer, "Papillon" (McQueen) and the embezzler (Hoffman) he befriends on Devil's Island, and their attempts to escape the infamous prison colony. A classic, episodic and suspenseful adventure melodrama, highlighted by location filming and *tour-de-force* acting by the two stars. Oscar-nominated for Best Score.

Save the Tiger
BLOCKBUSTER CATEGORY: Drama
STARRING: Jack Lemmon, Jack Gilford, Laurie Heineman,
Normann Burton
DIRECTED BY: John G. Avildsen

1973

Lemmon turns in an altogether moving portrayal as a middle-aged clothing manufacturer whose rough adult life in the business world can't measure up to the joys of his youth. Avildsen tersely takes us into the story of an American dream that missed the boat. Oscar-nominated for Best Supporting Actor (Gilford) and Story & Screenplay (Steve Shagan).
OSCAR WIN: *Best Actor (Lemmon)*

Serpico
BLOCKBUSTER CATEGORY: Drama
STARRING: Al Pacino, Tony Roberts, John Randolph
DIRECTED BY: Sidney Lumet
Based on Peter Maas' fact-based, best-selling book. Frank Serpico is an honest, New York City cop who finds that standing up to his partners, all of whom are on the take, puts his life in danger. Pacino - who is in almost every scene of this tough, uncompromising movie - was nominated for an Oscar, as was the film's screenplay. Directed by the top New York-based dramatic filmmaker, Sidney Lumet (12 ANGRY MEN, FAMILY BUSINESS). Oscar-nominated for Best Actor (Pacino), Screenplay Adaptation.

Sleeper
BLOCKBUSTER CATEGORY: Comedy
STARRING: Woody Allen, Diane Keaton, John Beck, Mary Gregory
DIRECTED BY: Woody Allen
In this hilarious farce, Allen plays a man who's frozen in the year 1973 and thawed out 200 years later. To avoid ambitious underground scientists and the police, he masquerades as a robot, serving the ever-ditzy Keaton. It's a grab bag of sight gags and energy, egged on by the Preservation Hall Jazz Band instrumentals, featuring Allen on clarinet!

The Sting
BLOCKBUSTER CATEGORY: Comedy
STARRING: Paul Newman, Robert Redford, Robert Shaw, Charles Durning
DIRECTED BY: George Roy Hill
The sparkling feel of Chicago in the 30's makes an elegant backdrop for two cons (Redford and Newman) out to put one over on a murderous hoodlum (Shaw). Scott Joplin's ragtime music is a delightful reminder of an era gone by. Oscar-nominated for Best Actor (Redford), Cinematography and Sound.
OSCAR SWEEP: *Best Picture, Director (Hill), Story & Screenplay (David S. Ward), Art Direction/Set Decoration, Scoring - original song score and/or adaptation (Marvin Hamlisch), Film Editing, Costume Design*

A Touch of Class
BLOCKBUSTER CATEGORY: Comedy
STARRING: George Segal, Glenda Jackson, Paul Sorvino, Hildegard Neil
DIRECTED BY: Melvin Frank
This bubbly comedy intermittently tugs at the heartstrings with its romantic

storyline. A married American (Segal) has a casual fling with a divorced Englishwoman (Jackson). That is, until he really falls in love with her. The screen chemistry between the leads is magical. Jackson gives one of her most appealing and seasoned performances. Oscar-nominated for Best Picture, Story & Screenplay (Melvin Frank and Jack Rose), Song ("All That Love Went To Waste"), and Original Dramatic Score.

OSCAR WIN: *Best Actress (Jackson)*

The Way We Were

BLOCKBUSTER CATEGORY: Drama
STARRING: Barbra Streisand, Robert Redford, Bradford Dillman
DIRECTED BY: Sydney Pollack

Memories. Streisand and Redford unite for one of the most dynamic romances in screen history. It's the story of a handsome writer and an outspoken political activist, the love that binds them and the differences that tear them apart. Pollack's entrancing movie takes us to the past and back again to reveal the characters' beginnings and gradual development of a relationship indelibly stamped in the minds and hearts of all who watch it. Streisand received a Best Actress Oscar nomination for her multi-dimensional portrayal. The movie also received nominations for Best Cinematography, Art Direction/Set Decoration and Costume Design.

OSCAR WINS: *Best Song ("The Way We Were"), Best Original Dramatic Score (Marvin Hamlisch)*

Alice Doesn't Live Here Anymore

BLOCKBUSTER CATEGORY: Drama
STARRING: Ellen Burstyn, Kris Kristofferson, Billy Green Bush,
Alfred Lutter, Diane Ladd, Jodie Foster
DIRECTED BY: Martin Scorsese

Burstyn gives a stunning performance as an over-30 widow with no job, no funds and a 12-year-old son. She tries to resuscitate her childhood dream of singing, but settles for waitressing in the meantime. Director Scorsese's subtle masterpiece takes us through Alice's many moods as she encounters motels, piano bars, boyfriends and a difficult child. Burstyn's extraordinary portrayal is complemented by an excellent supporting cast. Oscar-nominated for Best Supporting Actress (Ladd) and Original Screenplay (Robert Getchell), this profound story inspired the much lighter TV series, "Alice."
OSCAR WIN: *Best Actress (Burstyn)*

Amarcord

BLOCKBUSTER CATEGORY: Foreign
STARRING: Magali Noel, Bruno Zanin, Pupella Maggio,
Armando Brancia
DIRECTED BY: Federico Fellini

"I remember" is how the title translates in this Italian import, one of Fellini's most popular films. He draws largely on his own childhood and plays with his famous illusion-reality devices to cover everything from politics to coming of age. Fellini's obvious love for the 30's and that period of his life in Italy shine through every frame. Oscar-nominated for Best Director (Fellini), Original Screenplay (Fellini and Tonino Guerru) in 1975 for its American release. It won an Oscar a year earlier in the Foreign category for its release abroad.
OSCAR WIN: *Best Foreign Language Film (Italy)*

Chinatown

BLOCKBUSTER CATEGORY: Mystery/Suspense
STARRING: Jack Nicholson, Faye Dunaway, John Huston,
Perry Lopez, John Hillerman, Diane Ladd
DIRECTED BY: Roman Polanski

Nicholson is in splendid form as a detective in the 30's, whose involvement in an infidelity case points him toward a murder mystery and political corruption. Dunaway's allure and the movie's period evocation enhance the mood. Huston, famous for being a director, takes a formidable acting part as the millionaire, and the movie's director, Polanski, does the same as a knife-wielding meanie. Oscar-nominated for Best Picture, Actor (Nicholson), Actress (Dunaway), Director (Polanski), Cinematography, Art Direction, Sound, Original Dramatic Score, Film Editing and Costume Design. The screenplay is considered the model for film writing.
OSCAR WIN: *Best Original Screenplay (Robert Towne)*

The Conversation

BLOCKBUSTER CATEGORY: Drama
STARRING: Gene Hackman, John Cazale, Allen Garfield,
Frederic Forrest, Cindy Williams, Teri Garr,
Harrison Ford, Robert Duvall

DIRECTED BY: Francis Ford Coppola

Something is bugging one of the best wire-tap men in the biz. . .his conscience. He overhears plans for a murder and must choose between professionalism and saving someone's life. The suspense and tension will grip you like a vise. Hackman's work will impress, once again. Look for a young Ford and Duvall as Hackman's employers. The timing of this movie's release - the Watergate scandal - is publicity that couldn't have been bought. Oscar-nominated for Best Picture, Original Screenplay (Coppola) and Sound.

The Godfather, Part II

BLOCKBUSTER CATEGORY: Drama
STARRING: Al Pacino, Robert Duvall, Diane Keaton,
Robert DeNiro, Talia Shire, Lee Strasberg,
Michael V. Gazzo
DIRECTED BY: Francis Ford Coppola

A sequel that measures up to and exceeds its predecessor. With allusions to the Don's youth, this is also a prequel. Organized crime and its effect on marriage are studied on the other one of this film's two spectrums. As was true with the first, the acting is first-rate, especially DeNiro's in the younger version of the role Marlon Brando made famous in the original. Oscar-nominated: Best Actor (Pacino), Supporting Actor (Gazzo), Supporting Actor (Strasberg), Supporting Actress (Shire) and Costume Design.
OSCAR SWEEP: *Best Picture, Supporting Actor (DeNiro), Director (Coppola), Screenplay - adapted (Coppola and Mario Puzo), Art Direction/Set Decoration, Original Dramatic Score*

Harry and Tonto

BLOCKBUSTER CATEGORY: Drama
STARRING: Art Carney, Ellen Burstyn, Chief Dan George,
Geraldine Fitzgerald, Larry Hagman, Melanie Mayron
DIRECTED BY: Paul Mazursky

Man's best friend is a cat in this poignant comedy/drama. Carney is exceptional as the widower who travels cross-country meeting an off-beat sampling of free spirits who are kind by comparison to his own relatives. Relationships and chance encounters, folks in all their finest garb, emotionally and otherwise. . . that's Mazursky's specialty. Oscar-nominated for Best Original Screenplay (Mazursky and Josh Greenfield).
OSCAR WIN: *Best Actor (Carney)*

Lenny

BLOCKBUSTER CATEGORY: Drama
STARRING: Dustin Hoffman, Valerie Perrine, Jan Miner,
Stanley Beck
DIRECTED BY: Bob Fosse

Before Andrew Dice Clay and Eddie Murphy, Lenny Bruce ruled the comedy scene and paved the way for profanity-laden humor. In a stark portrayal, Hoffman peels away all accoutrements of the comic and reveals the self-destructive man. Perrine is at her best as his stripper wife, Honey. Fosse's choice to film in black and white with flashy editing further enhances the raw reality of a star gone astray. Oscar-nominated for Best Picture, Actor (Hoffman), Actress (Perrine), Director (Fosse), Screenplay - adapted (Julian Barry) and Cinematography.

The Parallax View

BLOCKBUSTER CATEGORY: Drama
STARRING: Warren Beatty, Paula Prentiss, William Daniels, Hume Cronyn
DIRECTED BY: Alan J. Pakula

Beatty plays as investigative reporter working on a jigsaw puzzle of political conspiracy. This riveting thriller is unique in that it doesn't have a typical Hollywood ending. Director Pakula proves he's a master of intrigue, and he and Cinematographer Gordon Willis and Production Designer George Jenkins combined forces two years later in ALL THE PRESIDENT'S MEN. Has a growing cult reputation.

The Three Musketeers

BLOCKBUSTER CATEGORY: Action/Adventure
STARRING: Oliver Reed, Raquel Welch, Richard Chamberlain, Michael York, Faye Dunaway, Christopher Lee, Charlton Heston, Frank Finlay
DIRECTED BY: Richard Lester

Guarding the King of France in the 18th century is only a small part of this trio's undertakings. Liquor and ladies figure prominently for Reed, Chamberlain and Finlay, and their new friend, York. The Queen's lady-in-waiting has schemes of her own: to damage her Highness' reputation. This frolicking remake fills the screen with major stars in minor roles, authentic settings and director Lester's penchant for high jinks. A sequel, THE FOUR MUSKETEERS, was shot back-to-back, with the same cast and director.

Young Frankenstein

BLOCKBUSTER CATEGORY: Comedy
STARRING: Gene Wilder, Peter Boyle, Marty Feldman, Teri Garr, Madeline Kahn, Cloris Leachman, Kenneth Mars
DIRECTED BY: Mel Brooks

One of Brooks' funniest movies may be in black and white, but the performances are colorful. While spoofing the horror films of yesteryear, Brooks' ensemble pulls out all the stops, Transylvanian style. Kahn, as Frankenstein's icy fiancee, is uproarious. An unbilled Gene Hackman as the blind forest dweller provides another comedy gem. Oscar-nominated for Best Screenplay (Wilder and Brooks) and Sound. The release earlier in the year of BLAZING SADDLES, his parody of westerns, gave Brooks back-to-back hits.

Barry Lyndon

BLOCKBUSTER CATEGORY: Drama
STARRING: Ryan O'Neal, Marisa Berenson, Patrick Magee,
Hardy Kruger
DIRECTED BY: Stanley Kubrick

Kubrick uses the screen as his canvas, painting a masterful portrait of 18th century Ireland that truly comes to life. O'Neal is the title character - a scandalous hero who sqanders his wife's love as his wealth increases. As the years pass, this deliberately paced Kubrick work of art has received growing acclaim. Oscar-nominated for Best Picture, Director (Kubrick) and Screenplay - adapted (Kubrick).
OSCAR WINS: *Best Cinematography, Art Direction/Set Decoration, Scoring - adapted and Costume Design*

Dog Day Afternoon

BLOCKBUSTER CATEGORY: Drama
STARRING: Al Pacino, John Cazale, Charles Durning,
James Broderick, Chris Sarandon, Carol Kane
DIRECTED BY: Sidney Lumet

The day is August 22, 1972. Another hot, ordinary day in Brooklyn except for the fact that a hoodlum (Pacino) is robbing a bank to pay for his male lover's sex-change operation. Lumet recreates New York and its eccentric residents with a humorous eye, then piles on the gripping suspense. For a true story, this is one of the screen's most unique endeavors and Pacino runs away with his part. Oscar-nominated for Best Picture, Actor (Pacino), Supporting Actor (Sarandon), Director (Lumet) and Film Editing.
OSCAR WIN: *Best Original Screenplay (Frank Pierson)*

Jaws

BLOCKBUSTER CATEGORY: Action/Adventure
STARRING: Roy Scheider, Robert Shaw, Richard Dreyfuss,
Lorraine Gary, Murray Hamilton, Jeffrey Kramer,
Susan Backlinie
DIRECTED BY: Steven Spielberg

This is more than a movie; it's an event where every element is executed to sheer perfection. It's the story of a shark who's hungry for the summer swimmers in New England. The three leads out to stop it are brilliant, as is the heart-pounding music and ingenious direction that put Spielberg on the map. Look quickly for best-selling author, Peter Benchley, who wrote the story, as a reporter talking about "a cloud in the shape of a killer shark!" JAWS was the first of all summer mega-hits to hit the screen. Oscar-nominated for Best Picture.
OSCAR WINS: *Best Sound, Original Score, Film Editing*

The Man Who Would Be King

BLOCKBUSTER CATEGORY: Action/Adventure
STARRING: Sean Connery, Michael Caine, Christopher Plummer,
Saeed Jaffrey
DIRECTED BY: John Huston

Rudyard Kipling's adventure story follows two rogue British Army veterans (Connery and Caine) as they travel from India in the 1880's to a far-off mountain kingdom. There, Connery is mistaken for a god by the superstitious natives. He and Caine play the scam for all it's worth, and watching the two cronies in action is the highlight of Huston's richly entertaining, lighthearted movie. Huston's style recalls the best adventure films of the 1930's, particularly GUNGA DIN. Oscar-nominated for Best Screenplay Adaptation, Art Direction/Set Decoration, Film Editing and Costume Design.

Nashville
BLOCKBUSTER CATEGORY: Drama
STARRING: Henry Gibson, Karen Black, Ronee Blakley,
Keith Carradine, Geraldine Chaplin, Lily Tomlin,
Michael Murphy, Barbara Harris, Shelley Duvall
DIRECTED BY: Robert Altman
It's as if director Altman threw a party for 24 of the most interesting people in Nashville, from the entertainment scene to the wheels of politics. Tomlin is wonderful as the mother of deaf children who has an affair with a country singer (Carradine). Blakley is a delight as a Loretta Lynn-like superstar on the edge. Altman favorites Elliott Gould (M*A*S*H) and Julie Christie make brief appearances as themselves. Oscar-nominated for Best Picture, Supporting Actress (Blakley), Supporting Actress (Tomlin) and Director (Altman).
OSCAR WIN: *Best Original Song ("I'm Easy," Music and Lyrics by Keith Carradine)*

Night Moves
BLOCKBUSTER CATEGORY: Mystery/Suspense
STARRING: Gene Hackman, Jennifer Warren, Susan Clark,
Edward Binns, Melanie Griffith, James Woods
DIRECTED BY: Arthur Penn
A 70's *film noir* that sizzles. Griffith - in her first performance - is a teen on the lam. Hackman plays the L.A. detective who must find her and bring her back. The Florida Keys are a good place to search, where suspense is blended in as a murder mystery takes hold. Penn's direction will weave you into the story until you're caught.

One Flew Over the Cukoo's Nest
BLOCKBUSTER CATEGORY: Drama
STARRING: Jack Nicholson, Louise Fletcher, Brad Dourif,
William Redfield
DIRECTED BY: Milos Forman
If ever two people were each other's Hell on Earth, it's Nicholson's mental hospital patient and Fletcher's cold Nurse Ratched. They're the frontrunners in this engrossing tale of bureaucracy. . . and rebellion. It's the first movie to win all five major Oscars since IT HAPPENED ONE NIGHT (1934). Nicholson is amazing. Oscar-nominated for Best Supporting Actor (Dourif), Cinematography, Original Score and Film Editing. Produced by Michael Douglas.
OSCAR SWEEP: *Best Picture, Actor (Nicholson), Actress (Fletcher), Director (Forman), Screenplay - adapted (Lawrence Hauben and Bo Goldman)*

Shampoo

BLOCKBUSTER CATEGORY: Comedy
STARRING: Warren Beatty, Julie Christie, Goldie Hawn,
Lee Grant, Jack Warden, Carrie Fisher
DIRECTED BY: Hal Ashby

This is a unique film due to its frank depiction of sexual irresponsibility - albeit in a comic light - and is thoroughly engaging to watch. A Beverly Hills hairdresser (Beatty) has affairs with the wife, mistress and daughter of a wealthy politician, as well as his own girlfriend! Christie's famous public display of affection scene is one for the film history books. This is Fisher's debut role. Oscar-nominated for Best Supporting Actor (Warden), Original Screenplay (Robert Towne and Beatty) and Art Direction/Set Decoration.
OSCAR WIN: *Best Supporting Actress (Grant)*

Tommy

BLOCKBUSTER CATEGORY: Musicals
STARRING: Roger Daltrey, Ann-Margret, Oliver Reed, Elton John,
Eric Clapton, Keith Moon, Tina Turner,
Jack Nicholson
DIRECTED BY: Ken Russell

That deaf, dumb and blind kid sure plays a mean pinball. And Director Russell fills the screen with pulsating vignettes, blending vivid imagery and rock music to recreate The Who's popular rock opera. Another stand-out performance by Ann-Margret and magical moments from Daltry, Turner, John and Clapton make this an unforgettable movie experience. Oscar-nominated for Best Actress (Ann-Margret) and Scoring - adaptation (Peter Townsend of "The Who").

The Wind and the Lion

BLOCKBUSTER CATEGORY: Action/Adventure
STARRING: Sean Connery, Candice Bergen, Brian Keith,
John Huston, Geoffrey Lewis
DIRECTED BY: John Milius

It was rare for an old-fashioned romantic adventure movie in the mid-70's to capture an audience's heart and mind, but this one did! Connery (star of two great movies in one year, including THE MAN WHO WOULD BE KING), shines as a Riffian chief who kidnaps a gorgeous American widow and her child. The world watches as President Roosevelt (Keith) intervenes. Oscar-nominated for Best Sound and Original Score.

All the President's Men

BLOCKBUSTER CATEGORY: Drama
STARRING: Robert Redford, Dustin Hoffman, Jason Robards,
Jack Warden, Martin Balsam, Hal Holbrook,
Jane Alexander, Ned Beatty, F. Murray Abraham
DIRECTED BY: Alan J. Pakula

The flood of anguish surrounding the Watergate scandal is channeled into a political journalistic detective thriller which doesn't need to fabricate the story for intrigue. It's all there, with splendid acting by Redford and Hoffman and an equally adept supporting cast. Here's one movie about the media that's as hard-hitting and real as it is entertaining. Oscar-nominated for Best Picture, Supporting Actress (Alexander), Director (Pakula) and Editing. From the same production team that made 1974's political thriller, THE PARALLAX VIEW.
OSCAR SWEEP: *Best Supporting Actor (Robards), Screenplay - adapted (William Goldman), Art Direction/Set Decoration, Sound*

Bound for Glory

BLOCKBUSTER CATEGORY: Drama
STARRING: David Carradine, Ronny Cox, Melinda Dillon,
Gail Strickland, Randy Quaid
DIRECTED BY: Hal Ashby

Carradine offers his most compelling performance to date as folk singer-songwriter Woody Guthrie. His cross-country trek from Texas to California during the Depression era is recreated to capture the beauty of the heartland and one man's voice as a representative for working-class America. This movie is more than a celebration of Guthrie. It's also a celebration of life on the road. Oscar-nominated for Best Picture and Screenplay - adapted (Robert Getchell). Astonishing, then innovative, camerawork by Haskell Wexler.
OSCAR WINS: *Best Cinematography and Score - adapted*

Carrie

BLOCKBUSTER CATEGORY: Horror
STARRING: Sissy Spacek, Piper Laurie, William Katt,
John Travolta, Amy Irving, Nancy Allen,
Betty Buckley, P.J. Soles
DIRECTED BY: Brian DePalma

If only they knew she had the power. Spacek is riveting in the first screen translation of a Stephen King horror novel. She plays a lonely high school waif who uses her telekinetic powers to get even with her prank-playing fellow students. Irving as Carrie's only compassionate schoolmate, Buckley as a sympathetic gym instructor and Soles make their debuts here. DePalma's ultra-stylized direction salutes Hitchcock, DELIVERANCE (1972), THE WILD BUNCH (1969) and even THE POM POM GIRLS (1976) to keep you continuously on the edge of your seat. Oscar-nominated for Best Actress (Spacek) and Supporting Actress (Laurie).

Marathon Man

BLOCKBUSTER CATEGORY: Action/Adventure
STARRING: Dustin Hoffman, Laurence Olivier, Roy Scheider,
William Devane, Marthe Keller, Fritz Weaver
DIRECTED BY: John Schlesinger

Going to the dentist will never be the same after you see Olivier's torturous way with patient Hoffman. Schlesinger's thriller is filmmaking at its best, from the lead story (Hoffman as an innocent student entwined in a Nazi's quest for stolen diamonds) to memorable twists and turns within. When war criminal Olivier is recognized on a busy New York City street by victims from the past, the tension builds to a rousing crescendo. Oscar-nominated for Best Supporting Actor (Olivier). Based on William Goldman's best-selling novel.

Network

BLOCKBUSTER CATEGORY: Drama
STARRING: William Holden, Faye Dunaway, Peter Finch,
Robert Duvall, Ned Beatty, Beatrice Straight
DIRECTED BY: Sidney Lumet

"I'm mad as hell, and I'm not going to take it anymore." Finch's crazed TV personality's words became the most famous line from a movie in 1976 and his performance matched his grand dialogue. The behind-the-scenes view of a television network that will do anything for higher ratings brings together a myriad of sharp performances, including Dunaway as the programmer without a conscience. It's even more appropriate today with Geraldo and tabloid stories on the tube. Oscar-nominated for Best Picture, Actor (Holden), Supporting Actor (Beatty), Director (Lumet), Cinematography and Film Editing.
OSCAR SWEEP: Best Actor (Finch - first actor to win posthumously), Actress (Dunaway), Supporting Actress (Straight), Screenplay (Paddy Chayefsky)

The Outlaw Josey Wales

BLOCKBUSTER CATEGORY: Westerns
STARRING: Clint Eastwood, Sondra Locke, Chief Dan George
DIRECTED BY: Clint Eastwood

Josey Wales is a peaceful Southern farmer who joins the Confederate Army after his wife and young son are killed by renegade Union troops. He spends the rest of the war and several months after it tracking down - and being hunted by - his family's murderers. The most successful western of the 70's, this epic drama helped establish Eastwood as a top movie director, as well as a potent box office star. Oscar-nominated for Best Score.

Robin and Marian

BLOCKBUSTER CATEGORY: Action/Adventure
STARRING: Sean Connery, Audrey Hepburn, Robert Shaw,
Richard Harris, Denholm Elliott
DIRECTED BY: Richard Lester

Medieval melodrama is played beautifully by Connery and Hepburn, who take us into their characters' lives two decades after the adventure began. Connery meets up with Marian as a nun, but changes her mind and reignites their flame. Shaw is the perfect archvillain and the entire production boasts a perfect, lyrical, storybook quality. This movie also marked the return of Hepburn to the screen following a 9 - year hiatus.

Rocky

BLOCKBUSTER CATEGORY: Drama
STARRING: Sylvester Stallone, Talia Shire, Burt Young, Carl Weathers, Burgess Meredith
DIRECTED BY: John G. Avildsen

While boxer Rocky Balboa (Stallone) rearranged his opponent's face in the ring, this movie rearranged the face of cinema. The underdog's victory theme became a staple of many movies to follow. The simple story of a determined young fighter is exquisitely enhanced by top-notch performances from all who appear. Oscar-nominated for Best Actor (Stallone), Actress (Shire), Supporting Actor (Meredith,Young), Screenplay (Stallone), Sound and Original Song ("Gonna Fly Now").
OSCAR WINS: *Best Picture, Best Director (Avildsen), Best Film Editing*

Seven Beauties

BLOCKBUSTER CATEGORY: Foreign
STARRING: Giancarlo Giannini, Fernando Rey, Shirley Stoler, Elena Fiore
DIRECTED BY: Lina Wertmuller

Director Wertmuller's finest cinematic achievement traces a charismatic charmer's (Giannini) plight from insane asylum (punishment for killing his sister's pimp) to army to Nazi prison camp. What he'll do to survive World War II is amazing and Wertmuller makes it seem horrifically real. An explosive and moving picture from Italy. Oscar-nominated for Best Actor (Giannini), Director (Wertmuller), Screenplay (Wertmuller) and Foreign Film.

Small Change

BLOCKBUSTER CATEGORY: Foreign
STARRING: Geory Desmouceaux, Philippe Goldman, Claudio Deluca
DIRECTED BY: Francois Truffaut

Truffaut was a master at calling upon his childhood and weaving the memories into engaging entertainment. This outing is sprinkled with careful observances of youth on all levels and all emotions, including one little boy's rough ordeal. It's another labor of love from one of France's legendary directors. Truffaut defined his own corner of the cinema with such films, this being one of his most precious jewels.

Taxi Driver

BLOCKBUSTER CATEGORY: Drama
STARRING: Robert DeNiro, Cybill Shepherd, Harvey Keitel, Peter Boyle, Jodie Foster, Albert Brooks, Leonard Harris
DIRECTED BY: Martin Scorsese

The harrowing reaction of a psychotic cab driver to the city he serves hits the viewer like a lightning bolt. DeNiro, in the title role, is haunting as the crazed man who wants to help a 12-year-old prostitute (Foster) and alleviate his being rejected by a beautiful woman (Shepherd). His answer: no-holds-barred violence. Scorsese assembles his story and performances with a master director's touch. Oscar-nominated for Best Picture, Actor (DeNiro), Supporting Actress (Foster) and Score.

Annie Hall

BLOCKBUSTER CATEGORY: Comedy
STARRING: Woody Allen, Diane Keaton, Tony Roberts,
Paul Simon, Shelley Duvall, Carol Kane, and many
others
DIRECTED BY: Woody Allen

Like the man who refuses to turn in his crazy brother who thinks he's a chicken
because, "I need the eggs," this funny, intelligent gem of a movie is a unique and
touching treat. Allen is at his best as a comedian having relationship troubles,
psychologically, religiously and culturally. The on-again, off-again love affair he has
with the title character (Keaton) was cherished as much by moviegoers as by
Allen's character and Keaton's fashion statement (baggy pants, vest, hat) started a
national trend. Catch a rising star: Sigourney Weaver and Jeff Goldblum make brief
appearances, nearly a decade before either became household words in their own
starring roles. Oscar-nominated for Best Actor (Allen).
*OSCAR SWEEP: Best Picture, Actress (Keaton), Director (Allen), Screenplay (Allen
and Marshall Brickman). Allen became the first nominee for Actor, Director and
Screenplay since Orson Welles in 1941.*

Close Encounters of the Third Kind

BLOCKBUSTER CATEGORY: Science Fiction
STARRING: Richard Dreyfuss, Francois Truffaut, Teri Garr,
Melinda Dillon
DIRECTED BY: Steven Spielberg

A majestic look at everything that leads up to the first alien's visit to earth.
Spielberg combines poignant performances with dazzling, amorphous visual effects.
Dreyfuss is superb as one of the few who accepts as truth the inevitable, though
he's surrounded by non-believers. John Williams' magical music is woven into the
story as a plot device. The film solidified Spielberg's career (the first movie he made
after JAWS) and aliens and spaceships have never looked the same since. Oscar-
nominated for Best Supporting Actress (Dillon), Director (Spielberg), Art
Direction/Set Decoration, Sound, Original Score, Film Editing and Visual Effects.
*OSCAR WINS: Best Cinematography, Special Achievement Award for Sound Effects
Editing.*

The Goodbye Girl

BLOCKBUSTER CATEGORY: Comedy
STARRING: Richard Dreyfuss, Marsha Mason, Quinn Cummings,
Paul Benedict
DIRECTED BY: Herbert Ross

This quintessential Neil Simon comedy finds a divorced woman (Mason) with a
child (Cummings) becoming the reluctant roommate of a struggling actor
(Dreyfuss) in a New York City apartment not big enough to thwart their budding
mutual attraction. You'll laugh and cry at the romantic and witty story. Oscar-
nominated for Best Picture, Actress (Mason), Supporting Actress (Cummings) and
Screenplay (Simon).
OSCAR WIN: Best Actor (Dreyfuss)

1977

Julia

BLOCKBUSTER CATEGORY: Drama
STARRING: Jane Fonda, Vanessa Redgrave, Jason Robards,
Maximilian Schell, Meryl Streep
DIRECTED BY: Fred Zinnemann

The story of writer Lillian Hellman (Fonda) and the friend she assists in European political resistance in the 1930's. Political activism seems an appropriate subject for Fonda and Redgrave, but they go a step further and handle the friendship storyline, this film's foundation, with expertise and sensitivity. Oscar-nominated for Best Picture, Actress (Fonda), Supporting Actor (Schell), Director (Zinnemann), Cinematography, Original Score, Film Editing and Costume Design.
OSCAR SWEEP: *Best Supporting Actor (Robards), Supporting Actress (Redgrave), Screenplay - adapted (Alvin Sargent)*

New York, New York

BLOCKBUSTER CATEGORY: Musicals
STARRING: Robert DeNiro, Liza Minnelli, Lionel Stander,
May Kay Place
DIRECTED BY: Martin Scorsese

Every major director has a film that, over the years, the critics and public acquire a growing fondness for. This Big Bank era musical melodrama is Scorsese's and it's a nostalgic and carefully realized charmer. DeNiro and Minnelli are saxophonist and singer who play out a stormy relationship as the songs keep flowing. Classic standards are heartfelt here, but none can compare to the title tune under Minnelli's original rendition. The video version features additional production number footage, too!

1900

BLOCKBUSTER CATEGORY: Drama
STARRING: Robert DeNiro, Gerard Depardieu,
Donald Sutherland, Burt Lancaster
DIRECTED BY: Bernardo Bertolucci

A political novel on the screen! Four hours (extracted from six) of the best of Bertolucci cover the story of two friends (Depardieu and DeNiro) born on the same day in 1900 and their socially-shaped relationship over a 45-year time span in Mussolini's Italy. The activity is superb; the episodes throughout are the pure genius that is Bertolucci and the film ranks with the best epics of all time.

The Spy Who Loved Me

BLOCKBUSTER CATEGORY: Action/Adventure
STARRING: Roger Moore, Barbara Bach, Curt Jurgens,
Richard Kiel
DIRECTED BY: Lewis Gilbert

Nobody can possibly do it better than 007. This exciting James Bond thriller is noted for its dazzling visual effects, literally larger-than-life villain named "Jaws" (Kiel), formidable female lead (Bach), who almost shares the movie with Moore,

1977

and top-rate soundtrack featuring a memorable Carly Simon vocal. Oh, the plot: Bond must prevent the enemy (Jurgens) from starting Armageddon! This is the best of the Bond films which starred Roger Moore. Oscar-nominated for Best Art Direction, Song ("Nobody Does It Better") and Score (Marvin Hamlisch).

Star Wars
BLOCKBUSTER CATEGORY: Science Fiction
STARRING: Mark Hamill, Harrison Ford, Carrie Fisher, Alec Guinness, Anthony Daniels, James Earl Jones (voice of Darth Vader)
DIRECTED BY: George Lucas
The force is definitely with this sci-fi extravaganza, the most recently released movie on the National Film Registry's list of 25 landmark films. Exemplary production values mark this celebration of sight and sound in a galactic adventure featuring heros (Ford, Hamill), a princess (Fisher) and friendly robots (R2D2 and C-3PO). Oscar-nominated for Best Picture, Supporting Actor (Guinness), Director (Lucas) and Screenplay (Lucas).
OSCAR WINS: *Best Art Direction/Set Decoration, Sound, Original Score, Film Editing, Costume Design, Visual Effects, Special Achievement Award for Sound Effects*

The Turning Point
BLOCKBUSTER CATEGORY: Drama
STARRING: Anne Bancroft, Shirley MacLaine, Mikhail Baryshnikov, Leslie Brown, Tom Skerritt, Martha Scott
DIRECTED BY: Herbert Ross
This ballet movie features two of the best acting *tour de forces* by women to date! MacLaine and Bancroft play lifelong friends who reunite when MacLaine's daughter (Brown) joins Bancroft's ballet. It is then that MacLaine must come to terms with the career in dancing she gave up to raise a family. The explosive confrontation between the two leads is what memorably entertaining cinema is all about. The authentic dancing is also incredible, spotlighting Baryshnikov in his movie debut. This film received eleven well-deserved Oscar nominations: Best Picture, Actress (Bancroft), Actress (MacLaine), Supporting Actor (Baryshnikov), Supporting Actress (Brown), Director (Ross), Screenplay (Arthur Laurentis), Cinematography, Art Direction/Set Decoration, Sound and Film Editing.

The Buddy Holly Story
BLOCKBUSTER CATEGORY: Drama
STARRING: Gary Busey, Charles Martin Smith, Don Stroud
DIRECTED BY: Steve Rash
Gary Busey received an Oscar nomination for his performance as the legendary 50's rock star, who was killed in a plane crash at the height of his career. The film lovingly recreates such nostalgic vignettes as Holly and his band, The Crickets, making their TV debut on the "Ed Sullivan Show" and encountering resistance from the early crusaders against rock 'n' roll. The stars also perform Holly's songs themselves, rather than simply mouthing the lyrics as the soundtrack plays old records. Oscar-nominated for Best Sound.
OSCAR WIN: Best Musical Score Adaptation

California Suite
BLOCKBUSTER CATEGORY: Comedy
STARRING: Jane Fonda, Alan Alda, Michael Caine, Richard Pryor
DIRECTED BY: Herbert Ross
The setting for this Neil Simon comic romp is the Beverly Hills Hotel, where five separate couples go through marital gyrations. Biggest surprise is finding Jane Fonda (in town for a custody battle with ex-hubby Alan Alda) and Richard Pryor in a decidedly mainstream comedy. Michael Caine has a grand time playing the husband of neurotic British actress Maggie Smith, who's in town to attend the Academy Awards (appropriately, Smith won an Oscar for her performance in this movie!).
OSCAR WIN: Best Supporting Actress (Smith)

Coming Home
BLOCKBUSTER CATEGORY: Drama
STARRING: Jane Fonda, Jon Voight, Bruce Dern,
Robert Carradine, Penelope Milford
DIRECTED BY: Hal Ashby
This is one of the original movies about the Vietnam War, from the perspective of those on the homefront. Fonda plays a woman who finds herself in love with a disabled war veteran (Voight) she meets before her own husband (Dern) has returned. You won't find a more sensitive love story or a more moving look at the living casualties of war. Oscar-nominated for Best Picture, Supporting Actor (Dern), Supporting Actress (Milford), Director (Ashby) and Film Editing.
OSCAR SWEEP: Best Actor (Voight), Actress (Fonda), Screenplay (Nancy Dowd, Waldo Salt and Robert C. Jones)

Days of Heaven
BLOCKBUSTER CATEGORY: Drama
STARRING: Richard Gere, Brooke Adams, Sam Shepard,
Linda Manz, Robert Wilke
DIRECTED BY: Terrence Malick
A love triangle among the farmland is enhanced by the most breathtaking cinematography in years. Director Malick (whose BADLANDS, 1974, was a riveting and violent look at the middle-American slice of life), weaves a calmer, cooler yarn. Added emphasis on a young girl's point of view gives supporting actress Manz one

of the most interesting roles of the year. Oscar-nominated for Best Sound, Original Score and Costume Design.
OSCAR WIN: *Best Cinematography*

The Deer Hunter

BLOCKBUSTER CATEGORY: Drama
STARRING: Robert DeNiro, John Cazale, John Savage,
Meryl Streep, Christopher Walken
DIRECTED BY: Michael Cimino

The year's other Vietnam film (see COMING HOME, above) takes us right onto the battleground besides looking at a group of Pennsylvania soldiers' lives before and after. The gripping challenges they face make for some of the screen's most scalding and emotional moments. Director Cimino's work is awe-inspiring. Oscar-nominated for Best Actor (DeNiro), Supporting Actress (Streep), Screenplay (Cimino, Deric Washburn, Louis Garfinkle and Quinn K. Redeker) and Cinematography.
OSCAR SWEEP: *Best Picture, Supporting Actor (Walken), Director (Cimino), Sound, Film Editing*

Halloween

BLOCKBUSTER CATEGORY: Horror
STARRING: Donald Pleasence, Jamie Lee Curtis, Nancy Loomis,
P.J. Soles
DIRECTED BY: John Carpenter

Scream-queen Curtis heads up an unusual slasher pic in that it was well-made and original at the time. The story is simple: a young murderer escapes from an institution and returns to his old neighborhood. The mood is intense, and Carpenter fills his film with terrifying effects and even a few allusions to past screen scarers. This man of many talents also wrote the musical score! Four, count 'em, sequels and an endless number of copies ensued.

Heaven Can Wait

BLOCKBUSTER CATEGORY: Comedy
STARRING: Warren Beatty, Julie Christie, Jack Warden,
Dyan Cannon, Charles Grodin, James Mason,
Buck Henry
DIRECTED BY: Warren Beatty and Buck Henry

A heavenly rehash of HERE COMES MR. JORDAN (1941) delivers Beatty to the clouds before his time and back down again to earth. The one catch: he's in the body of somebody else. This lighthearted outing has layers of depth, and is capped by an excellent supporting cast, including Cannon at her comic best. Oscar-nominated for Best Picture, Actor (Beatty), Supporting Actor (Warden), Supporting Actress (Cannon), Directors (Beatty and Henry), Screenplay - adapted (Elaine May and Beatty), Cinematography and Original Score. Beatty became the first nominee for Actor, Director, Screenplay and Producer of a Picture since Orson Welles in 1941.
OSCAR WIN: *Best Art Direction*

Interiors

BLOCKBUSTER CATEGORY: Drama
STARRING: Diane Keaton, Geraldine Page, E.G. Marshall, Maureen Stapleton, Kristin Griffith, Mary Beth Hurt, Sam Waterston
DIRECTED BY: Woody Allen

Writer-director Allen doesn't appear in his first all-serious drama, but his innovative vision and Ingmar Bergman-like style make this a masterpiece nonetheless. It's a through-the-keyhole look at the solemn lives of three sisters confronting their parents' divorce. The interiors of buildings, literally and symbolically, play a supporting role. Allen's use of subdued color is offset briefly by dynamic hues that help paint characters. No wonder they call this art! Oscar-nominated for Best Actress (Page), Supporting Actress (Stapleton), Director (Allen), Screenplay (Allen) and Art Direction.

Midnight Express

BLOCKBUSTER CATEGORY: Drama
STARRING: Brad Davis, Irene Miracle, Bo Hopkins, Randy Quaid, John Hurt
DIRECTED BY: Alan Parker

Enthralling. Based on a true story of a young American who tried to smuggle drugs out of Turkey. This man-against-the-system prison picture boasts a dramatic script and pulsating score. Parker's on-target direction has us - the viewers - locked in an unknown hell. Oscar-nominated for Best Picture, Supporting Actor (Hurt), Director (Parker) and Film Editing.
OSCAR WINS: *Best Screenplay - adapted (Oliver Stone), Original Score*

National Lampoon's Animal House

BLOCKBUSTER CATEGORY: Comedy
STARRING: John Belushi, Tim Matheson, John Vernon, Verna Bloom, Thomas Hulce, Donald Sutherland, Karen Allen
DIRECTED BY: John Landis

The late John Belushi set college life on its ear and a nation off its rocker as the crudest, rudest dude on a 60's campus. The toga parties, the beer, the girls. . . nothing was sacred in his screen world, making our world a much funnier place, and this movie one of the most uproarious of its decade.

Superman

BLOCKBUSTER CATEGORY: Action/Adventure
STARRING: Christopher Reeve, Margot Kidder, Marlon Brando, Gene Hackman, Ned Beatty, Jackie Cooper, Valerie Perrine, Trevor Howard
DIRECTED BY: Richard Donner

One of the most expensive - albeit entertaining - movies ever produced. Reeve leaps across the screen as the comic book hero becomes real, with those most special of effects, a fine supporting cast (including Brando in a cameo), bits of sheer humor (literally sheer, induced by the Man of Steel's x-ray vision) and the majestic musical score. Oscar-nominated for Best Sound, Original Score and Film Editing.
OSCAR WIN: *Special Achievement Award for Visual Effects*

1978

An Unmarried Woman

BLOCKBUSTER CATEGORY: Drama
STARRING: Jill Clayburgh, Alan Bates, Michael Murphy,
Cliff Gorman, Pat Quinn
DIRECTED BY: Paul Mazursky

Clayburgh's finest performance to date, as a woman whose husband leaves her for another woman, much to her surprise. She experiences a new relationship as well as the rigors - and a few positive findings - of once-again-single life. The contemporary and honest subject matter hit a chord nationwide. Oscar-nominated for Best Picture, Actress (Clayburgh) and Screenplay (Mazursky).

Alien

BLOCKBUSTER CATEGORY: Science Fiction
STARRING: Sigourney Weaver, Tom Skerritt, John Hurt
DIRECTED BY: Ridley Scott

The crew of the Nostromo, a space trawler on its way back to Earth, is awakened from hibernation prematurely by a distress call from a supposedly dead planet. It turns out to be a ruse by an alien creature that wants to hitch a ride to a planet that it can destroy. Designed as a horrific antidote to the Saturday-matinee heroics of the STAR WARS saga, this much-imitated movie set the standard for a decade of white-knuckle sci-fi shockers. The dark, claustrophobic atmosphere and title creature were designed by European artist H.R. Giger. Oscar-nominated for Art Direction/Set Decoration.
OSCAR WIN: *Special Effects*

All That Jazz

BLOCKBUSTER CATEGORY: Musicals
STARRING: Roy Scheider, Jessica Lange, Ann Reinking,
                     Ben Vereen
DIRECTED BY: Bob Fosse

They say the lights are bright on Broadway. Here, they're electrifying in Director Fosse's largely autobiographical look at the life of a choreographer knocking on death's door. Death, by the way, is played by the intoxicating Lange. She's a diversion, but this happens to be a Scheider *tour de force*. When he lives, he lives. And when he's on the operating table, it's a glitzy musical. That's show biz, folks. Oscar-nominated for Best Picture, Actor (Scheider), Screenplay (Robert Alan Arthur and Fosse) and Cinematography.
OSCAR WINS: *Best Art Direction/Set Decoration, Original Song Score and its Adaptation, Film Editing, Costume Design*

Apocalypse Now

BLOCKBUSTER CATEGORY: Action/Adventure
STARRING: Martin Sheen, Marlon Brando, Robert Duvall,
                     Frederic Forrest
DIRECTED BY: Francis Ford Coppola

Explosive cinema. Coppola's surreal ode to the Vietnam War has inspiration from *Heart of Darkness* by Joseph Conrad. Soldier Sheen's mission is to do away with a U.S. officer (Brando) posing as an idol to the natives in Cambodia. The journey involves a kaleidoscope of war horrors. Coppola's genius comes through on every frame, both aesthetically and emotionally. Oscar-nominated for Best Picture, Supporting Actor (Duvall), Director (Coppola), Screenplay - adapted (John Milius and Coppola), Art Direction/Set Decoration and Film Editing.
OSCAR WINS: *Best Cinematography, Sound*

Being There

BLOCKBUSTER CATEGORY: Comedy
STARRING: Peter Sellers, Shirley MacLaine, Melvyn Douglas,
                     Jack Warden
DIRECTED BY: Hal Ashby

1979

Black comedy at its most subtle and intelligent. The medium is the message in this film about a dimwitted TV buff (Sellers) mistaken for a man of wisdom. Before long, he's a presidential advisor. Sellers is impeccable in the role. Douglas is also brilliant as an ailing politician. The original author, Jerzy Kosinski, translated his own work to the screen with highly successful results. Oscar-nominated for Best Actor (Sellers).
OSCAR WIN: *Best Supporting Actor (Douglas)*

The Black Stallion
BLOCKBUSTER CATEGORY: Family
STARRING: Kelly Reno, Mickey Rooney, Teri Garr, Clarence Muse
DIRECTED BY: Carroll Ballard
This one has universal appeal and crisscrosses all age levels. It's about a young boy's (Reno) adventures with a beautiful horse, from desert island to the racing scene. Rooney appears as the trainer in a loving throwback to his NATIONAL VELVET (1944) days. The sights and sounds will stun. Oscar-nominated for Best Supporting Actor (Rooney) and Film Editing (Robert Dalva).
OSCAR WIN: *Special Achievement Award for Sound Editing*

Breaking Away
BLOCKBUSTER CATEGORY: Drama
STARRING: Dennis Christopher, Dennis Quaid, Paul Dooley,
            Barbara Barrie
DIRECTED BY: Peter Yates
Four Indiana friends spin their wheels after graduation from high school by racing bicycles professionally. You'll also find slices of family life in this funny and moving picture. Dooley, as Christopher's father, turns in a stand-out performance. Oscar-nominated for Best Picture, Supporting Actress (Barrie), Director (Yates) and Original Song Score or Adaptation Score.
OSCAR WIN: *Best Screenplay (Steve Tesich)*

The China Syndrome
BLOCKBUSTER CATEGORY: Drama
STARRING: Jane Fonda, Jack Lemmon, Michael Douglas,
            Scott Brady
DIRECTED BY: James Bridges
This story of a nuclear plant accident and conspiracy to hide the fact was released just days before the real-life Three Mile Island incident occurred, which heightened its power on the screen and its audience-interest level. The direction is swift and the acting is superb. Notable about the soundtrack is the lack of a musical score. It's not needed! Oscar-nominated for Best Actor (Lemmon), Best Actress (Fonda), Best Screenplay (Mike Gray, T.S. Cook and James Bridges), Best Art Direction/Set Decoration.

Kramer vs. Kramer
BLOCKBUSTER CATEGORY: Drama
STARRING: Dustin Hoffman, Meryl Streep, Jane Alexander,
            Justin Henry
DIRECTED BY: Robert Benton

Breaking up isn't hard to do. . . deciding custody of the kid is. Streep flees, leaving her son (Henry) to be raised by dad. Then she comes back, her mind changed. All involved seem made to play their parts. Look quickly for JoBethWilliams as Hoffman's first date, who has an *au naturel* run-in with the boy. Oscar-nominated for Best Supporting Actor (Henry, at age 9, the youngest nominee ever), Supporting Actress (Alexander), Cinematography and Film Editing.
OSCAR SWEEP: *Best Picture, Actor (Hoffman), Supporting Actress (Streep), Director (Benton), Screenplay - adapted (Benton)*

Mad Max
BLOCKBUSTER CATEGORY: Science Fiction
STARRING: Mel Gibson, Joanne Samuel, Steve Bisley
DIRECTED BY: George Miller
In a post-nuclear apocalypse future, marauding gangs of bikers terrorize what's left of humanity. Max (Gibson) is an ex-cop who takes off after one of the gangs after its members kill his wife and child. An extremely violent action picture, packed with impossible-to-describe stunts, that triggered two direct sequels and countless imitations.

Manhattan
BLOCKBUSTER CATEGORY: Comedy
STARRING: Woody Allen, Diane Keaton, Michael Murphy, Mariel Hemingway, Meryl Streep
DIRECTED BY: Woody Allen
Allen's ode to wonderful N.Y.C. He'll make you laugh and cry with top-notch performers, like Hemingway as his underage girlfriend and Streep as his ex-wife who has found a new interest. . .another woman! The black-and-white widescreen photography may make you homesick for the good old days and a finely-tuned Gershwin soundtrack is further testament to Woody's exquisite taste. If you haven't seen this, you're missing one of Allen's very best. Oscar-nominated for Best Supporting Actress (Hemingway) and Screenplay (Allen and Marshall Brickman).

Norma Rae
BLOCKBUSTER CATEGORY: Drama
STARRING: Sally Field, Ron Leibman, Beau Bridges, Pat Hingle, Gail Strickland
DIRECTED BY: Martin Ritt
Field is at her all-time best as a factory worker who ends up leading a rally for a company union to protect her fellow workers' rights. From her wide-eyed sweetness to her tough-as-nails take-charge stance, this is the role that cemented her standing as an actress to be reckoned with. Ritt's direction is also in top shape. Oscar-nominated for Best Picture and Screenplay - adapted (Irving Ravetch and Marriet Frank, Jr.).
OSCAR WINS: *Best Actress (Field), Original Song ("It Goes Like It Goes")*

10
BLOCKBUSTER CATEGORY: Comedy
STARRING: Dudley Moore, Bo Derek, Julie Andrews
DIRECTED BY: Blake Edwards

Dudley Moore is an L.A. songwriter going through a mid-life crisis. When he spots Bo Derek en route to her wedding , he becomes obsessed with her. The quintessential late-70's sex comedy, satirizing everything from hot tubs to encounter groups. Look for Brian Dennehy and Dee Wallace in small roles. Oscar-nominated for Best Song.

The Tin Drum
BLOCKBUSTER CATEGORY: Foreign
STARRING: David Bennent, Mario Adorf, Angela Winkler,
   Daniel Olbrychski
DIRECTED BY: Volker Schlondorff
Gunter Grass' novel translates to the screen in the form of a German masterpiece. The hero is a 12-year-old boy (Bennent) repressed by the surrounding Nazi invasion in World War II, as well as his own stunted growth. His only release: beating a toy drum. The symbolism goes deep, as does Bennent's amazing portrayal.
OSCAR WIN: *Best Foreign Language Film*

The Warriors
BLOCKBUSTER CATEGORY: Action/Adventure
STARRING: Michael Beck, James Remar, Thomas Waites,
   Dorsey Wright
DIRECTED BY: Walter Hill
A ballet of violence. This quickly paced, action-packed movie of conflict in the Bronx still shocks while it entertains. Hill gives his film a one-two punch of shattering images and forceful rock songs. If you're up for some riveting cinema that puts you in the middle of angry, opposing street gangs, go for it.

The Big Red One
BLOCKBUSTER CATEGORY: Action/Adventure
STARRING: Lee Marvin, Mark Hamill, Robert Carradine, Bobby Di Cicco
DIRECTED BY: Samuel Fuller

Cult director Fuller makes a comeback after many years away with this harrowing and hallucinatory vision of World War II based on his own personal experience. There's plenty of action and excellent acting by Marvin as an aging sergeant and his supporting cast of wet-behind-the-ears soldiers.

Coal Miner's Daughter
BLOCKBUSTER CATEGORY: Drama
STARRING: Sissy Spacek, Tommy Lee Jones, Beverly D'Angelo, Levon Helm
DIRECTED BY: Michael Apted

Spacek achieved international stardom with her amazing character study of real-life country singer Loretta Lynn. The vocals are her own, but her acting gifts transform her into Lynn as a 13-year-old child-bride. The music, the down-home charm, an excellent supporting cast and Spacek. . . you will love this movie. Oscar-nominated for Best Picture, Screenplay - adapted (Tom Rickman), Cinematography, Art Direction/Set Decoration, Sound and Film Editing.
OSCAR WIN: *Best Actress (Spacek)*

Dressed to Kill
BLOCKBUSTER CATEGORY: Mystery/Suspense
STARRING: Michael Caine, Angie Dickinson, Nancy Allen, Keith Gordon
DIRECTED BY: Brian DePalma

DePalma owes something to Hitchcock here - the plot is essentially a remake of PSYCHO (1960) - but his clever thriller stands on its own. The hypnotic camera work lures the viewer into a story of two women stalked by a psychotic killer and the son of one who's adept at piecing together clues. The New York City locales are stirring, as are Dickinson's famous shower and cab scenes. Mystery is the name of the game and for visual inventiveness and pure shock treatment, this DePalma film cannot be beat.

The Elephant Man
BLOCKBUSTER CATEGORY: Drama
STARRING: Anthony Hopkins, John Hurt, Anne Bancroft, John Gielgud
DIRECTED BY: David Lynch

Dreamlike black-and-white cinematography carries us into the cruel world's treatment of John Merrick (Hurt), a deformed man whose hell on earth as a circus freak is alleviated by the one doctor (Hopkins) who shows him humanity in Victorian England. Lynch's movie is mesmerizing. Even restrained by heavy make-up, Hurt's brilliance shines through. Oscar-nominated for Best Picture, Actor (Hurt), Director (Lynch), Screenplay - adapted (Christopher Devore, Eric Bergen and Lynch), Art Direction/Set Decoration, Original Score, Film Editing and Costume Design.

The Empire Strikes Back

BLOCKBUSTER CATEGORY: Science Fiction
STARRING: Mark Hamill, Harrison Ford, Carrie Fisher,
Billy Dee Williams, Frank Oz, Alec Guinness,
Anthony Daniels, Voice of James Earl Jones
DIRECTED BY: Irvin Kershner

The sequel to STAR WARS (1977). This film contains the most fully developed character interaction of the series, and spectacular space and land battles. Its double-whammy surprise ending left audiences in eager anticipation of the follow-up, RETURN OF THE JEDI (1983). Everyone's back for more of the intergalactic action and even a newly introduced little guy, Yoda, who's wise beyond all years. Some of the most innovative and imaginative special effects ever. Oscar-nominated for Best Art Direction/Set Decoration and Original Score (John Williams).
OSCAR WINS: *Best Sound, Special Achievement Award for Visual Effects*

The Long Riders

BLOCKBUSTER CATEGORY: Westerns
STARRING: David Carradine, Stacy Keach, Keith Carradine
DIRECTED BY: Walter Hill

Violent, myth-shattering western about the Jesse James-Cole Younger gang and its adventures leading up to the misguided robbery in Northfield, Minnesota, which destroyed them. The first movie to popularize the concept of casting real-life actor brothers as brothers onscreen (this one features Keith, David and Robert Carradine, plus James and Stacy Keach, and Randy and Dennis Quaid). The haunting music is by Ry Cooder.

Melvin and Howard

BLOCKBUSTER CATEGORY: Drama
STARRING: Paul LeMat, Jason Robards, Mary Steenburgen
DIRECTED BY: Jonathan Demme

Watching this movie will make you feel like a million bucks! Nice-guy/gas station fill-'er-upper Melvin Dummar once gave richer-than-rich Howard Hughes a ride in his truck. Melvin's coming forth with a will from Hughes leaving him mega-millions makes for grand entertainment and LeMat and Robards in the respective title roles make it work. Steenbergen plays Melvin's first wife who leaves him to become a professional tap dancer. Look for Dummar himself in a brief appearance. Oscar-nominated for Best Supporting Actor (Robards).
OSCAR WINS: *Best Supporting Actress (Steenburgen), Best Screenplay (Bo Goldman)*

9 To 5

BLOCKBUSTER CATEGORY: Comedy
STARRING: Jane Fonda, Lily Tomlin, Dolly Parton
DIRECTED BY: Colin Higgins

Three women (Fonda, Tomlin, Parton) work for a sexist ogre of a boss (Dabney Coleman) in a large corporation. They kidnap him and, while keeping him locked up in his own home, completely revamp the company to make it both more efficient and socially responsible. A highly popular comedy that benefits from the winning chemistry of its three stars, Coleman's uninhibited nastiness as their boss, and some expertly executed slapstick routines. Sterling Hayden has a memorable cameo as the corporation's chairman in the closing scene. Parton sings the title song, a Top 40 hit nominated for an Oscar.

Ordinary People

BLOCKBUSTER CATEGORY: Drama
STARRING: Donald Sutherland, Mary Tyler Moore, Judd Hirsch, Timothy Hutton, Dinah Manoff, Elizabeth McGovern
DIRECTED BY: Robert Redford

Redford's directorial debut is a winner. A sincere, heartfelt movie about one family's struggle to deal with the older son's accidental death. Moore broke through her "loveable Mary" image as the detached mother who blames the surviving son (Hutton). Redford extracts the highest caliber performances from his stars. Not bad for a first try. Oscar-nominated for Best Actress (Moore) and Supporting Actor (Hirsch).

OSCAR SWEEP: *Best Picture, Supporting Actor (Hutton), Director (Redford), Screenplay - adapted (Alvin Sargent)*

Private Benjamin

BLOCKBUSTER CATEGORY: Comedy
STARRING: Goldie Hawn, Eileen Brennan, Armand Assante
DIRECTED BY: Howard Zieff

After her husband drops dead on their wedding night, spoiled brat Goldie Hawn enlists in the Army, more out of boredom and curiosity than anything else. Naturally, she regrets it immediately. A female version of the classic barracks comedy, with Hawn sparring with Eileen Brennan, the sergeant whose life she makes miserable. Goldie also produced the movie, and Brennan starred in the TV spinoff. Oscar-nominated for Best Actress (Hawn), Supporting Actress (Brennan), Screenplay (Nancy Myers, Charles Shyer, Harvey Miller).

Raging Bull

BLOCKBUSTER CATEGORY: Drama
STARRING: Robert DeNiro, Cathy Moriarty, Joe Pesci, Frank Vincent
DIRECTED BY: Martin Scorsese

The life of a prizefighter - in and out of the ring - is compelling drama when the man is Jake LaMotta and the actor, DeNiro. From his days as a boxer to subsequent endeavors (dabbling in stand-up comedy, being accused of moral indiscretions), LaMotta has inspired one of the starkest glimpses into the human soul. Scorsese has worked black-and-white visual magic in recreating LaMotta's life for the screen. Oscar-nominated for Best Picture, Supporting Actor (Pesci), Supporting Actress (Moriarty), Director (Scorsese), Cinematography and Sound. Voted Best Film of the 80's in a recent critic's poll.

OSCAR WINS: *Best Actor (DeNiro), Film Editing*

The Return of the Secaucus Seven

BLOCKBUSTER CATEGORY: Drama
STARRING: Mark Arnott, Gordon Clapp, Maggie Cousineau, Adam Leferre
DIRECTED BY: John Sayles

Old college friends reunite for a weekend, reflect on their political activism in the 60's and share their current lives with adult responsibilities. This film was made three years before the similarly themed THE BIG CHILL. It was an impressive directorial debut for Sayles, who also wrote the script and took the role of a gas-station attendant.

The Shining

BLOCKBUSTER CATEGORY: Horror
STARRING: Jack Nicholson, Shelly Duvall, Danny Lloyd, Scatman Crothers
DIRECTED BY: Stanley Kubrick

"Heeeere's Johnny!" Nicholson utters one of his most famous lines during a violent rage against his wife (Duvall) and son (Lloyd) in a snow-capped mountain resort in the adaptation of the Stephen King novel. You'll love to hate him as much as he loves to revel in creepy roles like this. The unusual, light-drenched camerawork is a unique achievement in horror.

The Stunt Man

BLOCKBUSTER CATEGORY: Drama
STARRING: Peter O'Toole, Steve Railsback, Barbara Hershey, Chuck Bail
DIRECTED BY: Richard Rush

O'Toole offers a *tour de force* performance as a megalomaniacal film director. He persuades the escaped convict (Railsback) who accidentally bumped off his star stunt man to assume the dangerous role. Surprises await him - and the viewer - at every turn. Oscar-nominated for Best Actor (O'Toole), Director (Rush), Screenplay - adapted (Lawrence B. Marcus and Rush).

1981

Absence Of Malice

BLOCKBUSTER CATEGORY: Drama
STARRING: Paul Newman, Sally Field, Melinda Dillon
DIRECTED BY: Sydney Pollack

An honest Miami businessman (Newman), the son of a deceased mobster, is discredited in a newspaper story written by an ambitious, naive reporter (Field). He sets out to turn the tables on both her and her paper. Newman and Field have two of their best roles in years in this fascinating, topical drama, which makes a valid commentary about media responsibility while still being enormously entertaining. A then-unknown Wilford Brimley has a wonderful, scene-stealing role late in the film, as a federal investigator brought in by the government to unravel the whole mess. Dillon's heartbreaking portrayal of a childhood friend of Newman's earned her an Oscar-nomination.

An American Werewolf in London

BLOCKBUSTER CATEGORY: Horror
STARRING: David Naughton, Jenny Agutter, Griffin Dunne,
John Woodvine
DIRECTED BY: John Landis

Naughton turns in a fine performance as a man who turns into a werewolf after he's been bitten by one on a trek through London. Landis' sense of humor is as potent as his sense of horror, making this an enjoyable piece of entertainment.
OSCAR WIN: Best Make-Up (the first time this category was awarded)

Arthur

BLOCKBUSTER CATEGORY: Comedy
STARRING: Dudley Moore, Liza Minnelli, John Gielgud,
Geraldine Fitzgerald
DIRECTED BY: Steve Gordon

When you get caught between the moon and New York City, the best that you can do is see this movie. Moore plays an often-drunk millionaire who must choose between money and love. Gielgud is equally excellent as the butler with a lifetime supply of quips. This is a comedy worthy of its category in every sense. Oscar-nominated for Best Actor (Moore), Screenplay (Gordon).
OSCAR WINS: Best Supporting Actor (Gielgud), Song ("Arthur's Theme: Best That You Can Do")

Atlantic City

BLOCKBUSTER CATEGORY: Drama
STARRING: Burt Lancaster, Susan Sarandon, Kate Reid,
Robert Joy
DIRECTED BY: Louis Malle

The city of the title is a dealer in dreams. Malle fleshes out his characters to reveal a gangster (Lancaster) and a small-time waitress (Sarandon) who decide to con the mob out of some bucks. The movie pulls you into its world of would-be's and have-been's. The acting is incredible, especially by veteran star Lancaster who's as charismatic as ever. Oscar-nominated for Best Picture, Actor (Lancaster), Actress (Sarandon), Director (Malle), Screenplay (John Guare).

Body Heat

BLOCKBUSTER CATEGORY: Mystery/Suspense
STARRING: William Hurt, Kathleen Turner, Richard Crenna,
Mickey Rourke
DIRECTED BY: Lawrence Kasdan

An inspiring - and perspiring - directorial debut from Kasdan. Turner plays a
cunning bombshell who seduces lawyer Hurt into killing her husband. This begins
like a *film noir* from the 40's, but the theme is updated with high-energy passion
between the two leads.

Chariots of Fire

BLOCKBUSTER CATEGORY: Drama
STARRING: Ben Cross, Ian Charleson, Nigel Havers, Alice Krige,
Ian Holm
DIRECTED BY: Hugh Hudson

The glory of going the distance... two men find it in an Olympic race, circa 1924,
where religious conviction is the motivator. Charleson, a Scottish missionary, and
Cross, a devout Jew, give their all for the victory as well as the exhilarating process.
The breathtaking cinematography and pulsating Vangelis score make this a glorious
movie. Oscar-nominated for Best Supporting Actor (Holm), Director (Hudson) and
Film Editing.
OSCAR WINS: *Best Picture, Screenplay (Colin Welland), Original Score (Vangelis),
Costume*

Diva

BLOCKBUSTER CATEGORY: Foreign
STARRING: Wilhelmenia Wiggins Fernandez, Frederic Andrei,
Richard Bohringer
DIRECTED BY: Jean-Jacques Beineix

Mailman Andrei can't resist recording, illegally, a concert by his opera idol,
Fernandez. When the tape falls into the wrong hands, a thriller ensues. Beineix, in a
mesmerizing directorial debut, gives Paris a new wave makeover. A foreign film that
compares with the best American thrillers.

Excalibur

BLOCKBUSTER CATEGORY: Fantasy
STARRING: Nicol Williamson, Nigel Terry, Helen Mirren,
Nicholas Clay
DIRECTED BY: John Boorman

A medieval epic. Boorman retells the legend of King Arthur (Terry) with a backdrop
of magnificent Ireland locales. He also adds an extra helping of passion and violence
in the story of Camelot's destruction. Oscar-nominated for Best Cinematography.

Gallipoli

BLOCKBUSTER CATEGORY: Drama
STARRING: Mark Lee, Mel Gibson, Bill Kerr
DIRECTED BY: Peter Weir

In the early 1980's, an exciting new wave of films emerged from Australia, bringing with it such stars as Mel Gibson, Rachel Ward and Bryan Brown. Gibson stars in this gripping World War I drama, one of the best films in the Australian cycle. He and co-star Lee play a pair of eager, wide-eyed recruits who soon learn that war is not all heroics and excitement. This first-rate, suspenseful movie is a satisfying blend of action spectacle and thought-provoking historical drama.

On Golden Pond

BLOCKBUSTER CATEGORY: Drama
STARRING: Katherine Hepburn, Henry Fonda, Jane Fonda, Doug McKeon
DIRECTED BY: Mark Rydell

Henry Fonda and Hepburn play husband and wife in their retirement years. When their daughter (Jane Fonda) visits their house on the lake, the emotions pour out. Step-grandson McKeon delights with his now-famous description of kissing: "sucking face". Oscar-nominated for Best Picture, Supporting Actress (Jane Fonda), Director (Rydell), Cinematography, Sound, Original Score and Film Editing.
OSCAR WINS: *Best Actor (Henry Fonda, age 76, oldest Best Actor winner), Actress (Hepburn, age 74, oldest Best Actress winner, her 12th nomination and 4th win. . . three records), Screenplay - adapted (Ernest Thompson)*

Ragtime

BLOCKBUSTER CATEGORY: Drama
STARRING: James Cagney, Elizabeth McGovern, Howard E. Rollins, Jr.
DIRECTED BY: Milos Forman

A period piece based on E.L. Doctorow's book, filled with nostalgia and drama. A black man (Rollins) seeks justice against racial discrimination in turn-of-the-century New York. This is the main storyline in a kaleidoscope of scenarios that weave tales of love, immigration and violence into a memorable exposition. Oscar-nominated for Best Supporting Actor (Rollins), Supporting Actress (McGovern), Screenplay - adapted (Michael Weller), Cinematography, Art Direction, Original Score, Song ("One More Hour", by Randy Newman), and Costume Design. Cagney's final feature after a 20-year hiatus.

Raiders of the Lost Ark

BLOCKBUSTER CATEGORY: Action/Adventure
STARRING: Harrison Ford, Karen Allen, John Rhys-Davies, Paul Freeman
DIRECTED BY: Steven Spielberg

Cliffhanger chills. Romantic thrills. Spielberg packs in the action and adventure in the story of an archaeologist (Ford) racing to beat the Nazis in quest of a valuable religious artifact. This movie brought back the pace of the Saturday matinee cliffhanger and improved upon it. It also solidified Ford as a major star. Oscar-nominated for Best Picture, Director (Spielberg), Cinematography and Original Score (John Williams).
OSCAR WINS: *Best Art Direction, Sound, Visual Effects, Film Editing and Special Achievement Award for Sound Effects Editing*

Reds

BLOCKBUSTER CATEGORY: Drama
STARRING: Warren Beatty, Diane Keaton, Jack Nicholson,
Maureen Stapleton
DIRECTED BY: Warren Beatty

Beatty plays John Reed, the American reporter who becomes involved in the
Russian Revolution amid his relationship with writer Louise Bryant (Keaton). Also
look for a fine turn by Nicholson in a supporting role as the playwright Eugene
O'Neill and by Stapleton as communist Emma Goldman. The political plot is as
intriguing as the love story. Oscar-nominated for Best Picture, Actor (Beatty),
Actress (Keaton), Supporting Actor (Nicholson), Screenplay (Beatty and Trevor
Griffiths), Art Direction, Sound, Film Editing and Costume Design.
OSCAR WINS: *Best Director (Beatty, who was nominated for Director, Actor,
Screenplay and Producer of Best Picture for the second time - the first was HEAVEN
CAN WAIT, 1978), Supporting Actress (Stapleton), Cinematography (Vitorio
Storaro)*

Superman II

BLOCKBUSTER CATEGORY: Action/Adventure
STARRING: Christopher Reeve, Margot Kidder, Gene Hackman
DIRECTED BY: Richard Lester

Three arch-criminals from Krypton, originally exiled to the "Phantom Zone,"escape
and travel to Earth. Equipped with powers identical to Superman's, they cause a
reign of terror. The first sequel to SUPERMAN: THE MOVIE doesn't disappoint;
Terence Stamp, Sarah Douglas and Jack O'Halloran are terrific as the villains, and
the scenes that illustrate their discovery of their new powers are triumphs of special
effects wizardry. Christopher Reeve still makes the perfect Superman, and the
screenwriters have expanded his relationship with Lois Lane (Kidder) to finally
have them fall in love. Hackman's contribution as Lex Luthor is reduced to
accommodate the Krypton villains, but he's a delight whenever he appears.

Blade Runner

BLOCKBUSTER CATEGORY: Science Fiction
STARRING: Harrison Ford, Rutger Hauer, Sean Young,
Edward James Olmos, Daryl Hannah, Joanna Cassidy
DIRECTED BY: Ridley Scott

Adventurous director Scott takes us into the 21st century, where an ex-policeman (Ford) resumes his duties by trying to stop killer Replicants, androids that look exactly like humans. The mammoth production design and heartbreaking Vangelis score make this a sci-fi masterpiece. Oscar-nominated for Best Art Direction/Set Decoration and Visual Effects.

Das Boot (The Boat)

BLOCKBUSTER CATEGORY: Foreign
STARRING: Jurgen Prochnow, Herbert Gronemeyer,
Klaus Wennemann, Hubertus Bengsch,
Martin Semmelrogge
DIRECTED BY: Wolfgang Petersen

An underwater World War II drama from Germany turns the ocean into a battleground with Prochnow guiding his submarine crew through a British obstacle course. In a brilliant turn of events, he sees to it that their sunken ship resurfaces. Riveting action. Oscar-nominated for Best Director (Petersen), Screenplay - adapted (Petersen), Cinematography, Sound, Film Editing and Sound Effects Editing.

Diner

BLOCKBUSTER CATEGORY: Comedy
STARRING: Steve Guttenberg, Daniel Stern, Mickey Rourke,
Kevin Bacon, Ellen Barkin, Paul Reiser
DIRECTED BY: Barry Levinson

Is there life after high school? Yes, and it takes place in a Baltimore diner where friends meet often and help each other cope with the trials and tribulations of the adult world. Writer-director Levinson lets his characters talk their way into our hearts. Late 50's charm and wonderful performances are the key items on the menu. Oscar-nominated for Best Screenplay (Levinson).

E.T. The Extra-Terrestrial

BLOCKBUSTER CATEGORY: Family
STARRING: Dee Wallace, Henry Thomas, Peter Coyote,
Drew Barrymore
DIRECTED BY: Steven Spielberg

Take a ride across the moon in Spielberg's heartwarming masterpiece about the friendship between a 10-year-old boy (Thomas) and a wide-eyed visitor from another planet. Still the most popular movie of all time! The touching climax will make you cry, especially when the beloved creature "phones home" his performance. Oscar-nominated for Best Picture, Director (Spielberg), Screenplay (Melissa Matheson), Cinematography, Sound and Film Editing.
OSCAR WINS: *Best Original Score, Visual Effects, Sound Effects Editing*

48 Hrs.

BLOCKBUSTER CATEGORY: Action/Adventure
STARRING: Nick Nolte, Eddie Murphy, James Remar
DIRECTED BY: Walter Hill

Eddie Murphy and Nick Nolte as a convict and the cop who springs him for two days - to help find a killer - in one of the biggest action/comedy hits of the 1980's. The movie begins with one of the most violent jailbreaks ever filmed (establishing that the bad guys in this movie are real bad), but, once Nolte releases Murphy from jail, begins to rewrite the rules for all "buddy" movies to come. The film's highlight is Murphy's encounter with the rednecks in a country/western saloon.

Gandhi

BLOCKBUSTER CATEGORY: Drama
STARRING: Ben Kingsley, Candice Bergen, Edward Fox,
John Gielgud, Trevor Howard, Martin Sheen
DIRECTED BY: Richard Attenborough

Kingsley expertly becomes the famous charismatic leader Mahatma Gandhi, who led the people of India in the quest for independence from England. Attenborough's epic-size production is a cinematic wonder. Major stars in bit parts pepper the movie with their own special qualities, especially Bergen as photographer Margaret Bourke-White. Oscar-nominated for Best Original Score and Make-Up.
OSCAR SWEEP: *Best Picture, Actor (Kingsley), Director (Attenborough), Screenplay (John Briley), Cinematography, Art Direction/Set Decoration, Sound, Film Editing, Costume Design*

An Officer and a Gentleman

BLOCKBUSTER CATEGORY: Drama
STARRING: Richard Gere, Debra Winger, David Keith,
Louis Gossett, Jr.
DIRECTED BY: Taylor Hackford

A romantic duo that lights up the screen. That's Gere and Winger as a Naval Officer trainee and the factory worker who falls in love with him. Their passion is intense, as are the rigorous drills from a no-nonsense sergeant. It's a Hollywood formula that gets a new coat of paint by the terrific performances. Oscar-nominated for Best Actress (Winger), Screenplay (Douglas Day Stewart), Original Score and Film Editing.
OSCAR WINS: *Best Supporting Actor (Gossett, Jr.), Song ("Up Where We Belong")*

The Road Warrior

BLOCKBUSTER CATEGORY: Science Fiction
STARRING: Mel Gibson, Bruce Spence, Vernon Wells,
Mike Preston, Virginia Hey
DIRECTED BY: George Miller

Gibson returns as a cop gone solo who helps a fuel-injected desert city keep its prized petrol. The futuristic setting and famous chase sequences make this a landmark production, outdoing the renewing interest in the original MAD MAX (1979). THE ROAD WARRIOR is an action-packed remake of SHANE (1953). Gibson reprised the part again for MAD MAX BEYOND THUNDERDOME (1985).

Sophie's Choice

Sophie's Choice

BLOCKBUSTER CATEGORY: Drama
STARRING: Meryl Streep, Kevin Kline, Peter MacNicol
DIRECTED BY: Alan J. Pakula

This movie features the most heart-gripping moment in movies of the 80's! In World War II Poland, a woman must choose between. . . no, you'll have to see it to find out. Streep gives a shattering performance as the Holocaust survivor involved in a romance with Kline and a sincere friendship with a young writer from the south (MacNicol) while living in Brooklyn after the war. The movie is faithful to William Styron's novel and is Streep's finest achievement to date, and is arguably the greatest performance of its decade. Oscar-nominated for Best Screenplay - adapted (Pakula), Cinematography, Original Score and Costume Design.
OSCAR WIN: *Best Actress (Streep)*

Star Trek II: The Wrath of Khan

BLOCKBUSTER CATEGORY: Science Fiction
STARRING: William Shatner, Leonard Nimoy, Ricardo Montalban
DIRECTED BY: Nicholas Meyer

This unexpectedly violent, fast-paced sequel to STAR TREK: THE MOTION PICTURE is actually a followup to a 1967 episode of the TV series, with the sadistic Khan (Montalban), who had been exiled to an asteroid by the crew of the Enterprise, now free and eager for revenge. Montalban has a field day with a dream part, and director Meyer - who made the marvelous H.G. Wells thriller, TIME AFTER TIME (1979) - lends the proceedings a welcome, dangerous edge.

Tootsie

BLOCKBUSTER CATEGORY: Comedy
STARRING: Dustin Hoffman, Jessica Lange, Teri Garr,
Bill Murray, Dabney Coleman, Charles Durning,
Sydney Pollack
DIRECTED BY: Sydney Pollack

One of the funniest movies of all time. When an unemployed actor (Hoffman) puts on a woman's dress and make-up, he finds a job and, more importantly, learns a lot about the other sex. Hoffman is terrific, and Lange's subtle quality is a charmer. Garr is more frenetic, but equally excellent. Director Pollack appears briefly as a theatrical agent who has some interesting encounters with his new star. Oscar-nominated for Best Picture, Actor (Hoffman), Supporting Actress (Garr), Director (Pollack), Screenplay (Don McGuire, Larry Gelbart and Murray Schisgal), Cinematography, Sound, Song and Film Editing.
OSCAR WIN: *Best Supporting Actress (Lange, also nominated for Best Actress for FRANCES in 1982, first time an actress is nominated for both since Teresa Wright in 1942.)*

The Verdict

BLOCKBUSTER CATEGORY: Drama
STARRING: Paul Newman, Charlotte Rampling, Jack Warden,
James Mason
DIRECTED BY: Sidney Lumet

Newman's seasoned finesse at his craft shines as he plays an alcoholic lawyer bent on seeing justice prevail when he takes on a malpractice case against a Catholic hospital. A harsh judge, a prominent attorney and a suspicious woman (whom he falls for) figure prominently in this slick film. Newman is simply great and director Lumet gives his film a sharp edge. Oscar-nominated for Best Picture, Actor (Newman), Supporting Actor (Mason), Director (Lumet) and Screenplay - adapted (David Mamet).

Victor/Victoria

BLOCKBUSTER CATEGORY: Comedy
STARRING: Julie Andrews, James Garner, Robert Preston
DIRECTED BY: Blake Edwards

Hilarious, sophisticated comedy of errors in the best Blake Edwards tradition, with a marvelous 1930's Paris setting. Preston molds destitute singer Andrews into a cabaret sensation, disguising her as a supposedly male crooner. American gangster Garner can't believe he's starting to fall for Andrews. . . who soon wants to drop the whole charade and spill everything to Garner. The comic timing that Edwards honed to perfection on his Inspector Clouseau movies, coupled with superb performances by an inspired cast, make this a comic delight. Oscar-nominated for Best Actress (Andrews), Supporting Actress (Lesley Ann Warren), Costumes and Scoring.

The World According to Garp

BLOCKBUSTER CATEGORY: Drama
STARRING: Robin Williams, Mary Beth Hurt, Glenn Close,
John Lithgow, Hume Cronyn, Jessica Tandy,
Swoozie Kurtz, Amanda Plummer
DIRECTED BY: George Roy Hill

Wrestler/writer Garp (Williams) experiences the spectrum of life in all its joys and hardships. Williams is magnificent in his first serio-comic bid. Close, in her debut movie, plays his eccentric, independent, single mother. There's also a unique turn by Lithgow as a transexual former football player. John Irving's novel gets an engaging screen translation. Oscar-nominated for Supporting Actor (Lithgow) and Supporting Actress (Close).

The Big Chill

BLOCKBUSTER CATEGORY: Drama
STARRING: Tom Berenger, Glenn Close, Jeff Goldblum,
William Hurt, Kevin Kline, Mary Kay Place,
Meg Tilly, JoBeth Williams
DIRECTED BY: Lawrence Kasdan

Nearly two decades have passed when a friend's death reunites a group of college radicals from the 60's. This alternately intelligent and sentimental movie contains a fine ensemble cast of a new breed of actors on the verge of superstardom, including Close, Kline, and Hurt. The Motown-based rock score revived a craze. No Way In: the role of the friend who died was played by Kevin Costner who played in NO WAY OUT (1987). His scenes were entirely edited out for story purposes (Except during the classic opening credit sequence!). Oscar-nominated for Best Picture, Supporting Actress (Close) and Screenplay (Kasdan and Barbara Benedek).

The Dresser

BLOCKBUSTER CATEGORY: Drama
STARRING: Albert Finney, Tom Courtenay, Edward Fox
DIRECTED BY: Peter Yates

A fascinating British movie with two stunning performances: Albert Finney as a bombastic, hammy - yet legendary - Shakespearean actor touring the provinces, and Tom Courtenay as his servant. Despite the abusive relationship on the surface, neither could exist without the other. Adapted from Ronald Harwood's play, and based on the career of Sir Donald Wolfit, this movie proved so mesmerizing to mainstream moviegoers that it lured audiences away from traditional action movies during the hotly competitive Christmas movie season. Oscar-nominated for Best Picture, Actor (Finney, Courtenay), Director (Yates), Screenplay Adaptation (Ronald Harwood).

Fanny and Alexander

BLOCKBUSTER CATEGORY: Foreign
STARRING: Pernilla Allwin, Bertil Guve, Gunn Wallgren,
Allan Edwall, Ewa Froling, Harriet Andersson
DIRECTED BY: Ingmar Bergman

Two siblings face their loving father's death and their mother's new husband, a strict pastor. Much of the tale is told from Alexander's perspective as a child. Sweden at Christmastime in 1907 is quaint and picturesque, the perfect setting for family gatherings and recollections of the emotional rollercoaster that is childhood. This was Bergman's personal masterpiece. Oscar-nominated for Best Director and Screenplay (Bergman).
OSCAR WINS: *Best Foreign Language Film, Cinematography, Art Direction/Set Decoration, Costume Design*

The King of Comedy

BLOCKBUSTER CATEGORY: Drama
STARRING: Robert DeNiro, Jerry Lewis, Diahnne Abbott,
Sandra Bernhard, Shelley Hack, Tony Randall
DIRECTED BY: Martin Scorsese

So you want to be on TV? A showbiz fanatic's (DeNiro) method is to kidnap a Johnny Carson-type late-night host (Lewis) and use air-time as the ransom. This is dark comedy from Scorsese, with winning performances from DeNiro and Lewis and a zippy turn by Bernhard as a crazed "wanna be." Look for a 2-dimensional appearance by Liza Minnelli; she's a cardboard cut-out.

Local Hero

BLOCKBUSTER CATEGORY: Drama
STARRING: Peter Riegert, Burt Lancaster, Fulton MacKay, Denis Lawson, Jenny Seagrove
DIRECTED BY: Bill Forsyth

Everything seems a little out of place in a Scottish seaside village and that's what makes it so appealing to an executive (Riegert) sent to purchase it and build a refinery. One of the most unusual characters, the town biologist (Seagrove) may, in fact, be a mermaid. Riegert reports to an ambitious Lancaster, who turns in a wonderful performance. The movie is a rare treat.

Never Cry Wolf

BLOCKBUSTER CATEGORY: Action/Adventure
STARRING: Charles Martin Smith, Brian Dennehy, Samson Jorah
DIRECTED BY: Carroll Ballard

A haunting try for a different kind of outdoor adventure - and it works every step of the way. Fact-based story has Smith, as author Farley Mowat, living in virtual seclusion in the Arctic to study wolves in their natural habitat. Powerful, hypnotically watchable, and breathtakingly shot on location. One of the major, early ventures of the "new" Disney Studios. Oscar-nominated for Sound Recording.

Return Of The Jedi

BLOCKBUSTER CATEGORY: Science Fiction
STARRING: Mark Hamill, Harrison Ford, Carrie Fisher
DIRECTED BY: Richard Marquand

Third and final (to date) entry in the STAR WARS saga. As Luke Skywalker, Han Solo and Princess Leia re-team to combat the dreaded Deathstar, producer George Lucas and his Oscar-winning effects team introduce the series' most hideous villain, the monstrous Jabba the Hut, and the furry, lovable Ewoks, who proved so popular that they earned their own TV series. Lightning paced, it's constructed like a FLASH GORDON matinee serial - which was, in fact, the inspiration for the STAR WARS opus in the first place. Oscar-nominated for Art Direction/Set Decoration, Sound, Sound Effects Editing, Score.
OSCAR WIN: *Special Effects*

The Right Stuff

BLOCKBUSTER CATEGORY: Action/Adventure
STARRING: Sam Shepard, Scott Glenn, Ed Harris, Dennis Quaid, Fred Ward, Barbara Hershey, Kim Stanley
DIRECTED BY: Philip Kaufman

When President John F. Kennedy called upon the nation to awaken its fledgling space program, seven pioneering astronauts responded. This semi-documentary, but wholly entertaining account of the Mercury program features heroic

performances by Shepard as pilot Chuck Yeager, Harris as John Glenn and Quaid as a devil-may-care Gordon Cooper. The blend of space flights with on-the-ground action is magical. Look for the real Yeager in a cameo. Oscar-nominated for Best Picture, Supporting Actor (Shepard), Cinematography and Art Direction/Set Decoration.
OSCAR WINS: *Best Sound, Score, Film Editing, Sound Effects Editing*

Risky Business

BLOCKBUSTER CATEGORY: Comedy
STARRING: Tom Cruise, Rebecca DeMornay, Curtis Armstrong, Bronson Pinchot
DIRECTED BY: Paul Brickman

"Take those old records off the shelf," is what the song says and Cruise lip-syncs to it in a star-making turn. He plays a high school senior who transforms his house into a brothel when Mom and Dad leave town. There's also a memorable subway scene with Cruise and a charming callgirl (DeMornay). Director Brickman's script may paint a darker, rebellious side of adolescence, but Cruise's charisma offsets this and keeps everything funny.

Silkwood

BLOCKBUSTER CATEGORY: Drama
STARRING: Meryl Streep, Kurt Russell, Cher, Craig T. Nelson
DIRECTED BY: Mike Nichols

In another character transformation, Streep becomes the real-life Karen Silkwood, a nuclear-parts factory employee who joins a union to protect herself and fellow workers from safety hazards. This turns out to be quite dangerous. Cher plays the gay roommate and Russell plays Silkwood's usually devoted boyfriend. Both are exceptional, but this is still Streep's movie. Oscar-nominated for Best Actress (Streep), Supporting Actress (Cher), Director (Nichols), Screenplay (Nora Ephron and Alice Arlen) and Film Editing.

Tender Mercies

BLOCKBUSTER CATEGORY: Drama
STARRING: Robert Duvall, Tess Harper, Betty Buckley, Ellen Barkin
DIRECTED BY: Bruce Beresford

Duvall offers his most compelling performance as an alcoholic former country star putting the pieces of his life back together. This film is a subtle gem, spotlighting Duvall, but also showing some fine support, namely Harper as the widow he falls for and Buckley as his ex-wife. Screenwriter Horton Foote created this exclusively for Duvall, who even penned the songs he sings within. Oscar-nominated for Best Picture, Director (Beresford) and Song ("Over You").
OSCAR WINS: *Best Actor (Duvall), Best Screenplay (Horton Foote)*

Terms of Endearment

BLOCKBUSTER CATEGORY: Drama
STARRING: Shirley MacLaine, Debra Winger, Jack Nicholson, Jeff Daniels, John Lithgow
DIRECTED BY: James L. Brooks

Every slice-of-life movie released after this one has been compared to it. MacLaine and Winger brilliantly play out an evolving mother-daughter relationship over three decades. Nicholson appears as MacLaine's boisterous next-door neighbor in a wonderful comic turn. The entire cast is perfect, but this movie belongs to MacLaine, an emotional whirlwind as she confronts her daughter's new family, a new man in her mid-life and a tragic turn of events. Laugh, cry, think and feel with her in writer/director/producer Brooks' directorial debut. Oscar-nominated for Best Actress (Winger), Art Direction, Sound, Original Score and Film Editing.
OSCAR SWEEP: *Best Picture, Actress (MacLaine), Supporting Actor (Nicholson), Director (Brooks), Screenplay - adapted (Brooks)*

The Year of Living Dangerously
BLOCKBUSTER CATEGORY: Action/Adventure
STARRING: Mel Gibson, Sigourney Weaver, Linda Hunt,
              Michael Murphy
DIRECTED BY: Peter Weir
Another great Weir-Gibson teaming (they did GALLIPOLI in 1981) from Australia. Gibson garnered serious-actor status as an Australian journalist in Indonesia, 1965, right before its civil war. His sidekick/photographer is a fiesty gent with integrity (played by actress Hunt, masquerading as a man). Weaver plays a British embassy worker who catches his eye. She's also got a nose for news which has positive and negative effects on their romance.
OSCAR WIN: *Best Supporting Actress (Hunt, first to win for playing the opposite sex)*

Yentl
BLOCKBUSTER CATEGORY: Musicals
STARRING: Barbra Streisand, Mandy Patinkin, Amy Irving,
              Nehemiah Persoff
DIRECTED BY: Barbra Streisand
This is the first hit film produced by, written by, directed by and starring a woman (Streisand). She plays a girl disguised as a boy to get a religious education in Eastern Europe, early 1900's. The pastoral settings and heartfelt music by composer Michel Legrand and lyricists Alan and Marilyn Bergman help make this an important directorial debut. It's also the first film with music to use interior monologues to express the character's thoughts as opposed to the conventional breaking-out-in-song mode of other musicals. The supporting stars are excellent, too. Oscar-nominated for Best Supporting Actress (Irving), Art Direction and Songs ("Papa, Can You Hear Me" and "The Way He Makes Me Feel"). Based on the short story by Isaac Bashevis Singer.
OSCAR WIN: *Best Original Score*

Zelig
BLOCKBUSTER CATEGORY: Comedy
STARRING: Woody Allen, Mia Farrow, Garrett Brown
DIRECTED BY: Woody Allen
The chameleon man stars in this witty fake-documentary about a man who fits into the 1920's celebrity hall of fame by changing appearances. Allen plays the title role in a carefully constructed mosaic, a celebration in editing and camera technique as well as costume changes! The newsreel feel is impeccable. Oscar-nominated for Best Cinematography and Costume Design.

Amadeus

BLOCKBUSTER CATEGORY: Drama
STARRING: F. Murray Abraham, Tom Hulce, Elizabeth Berridge, Simon Callow, Jeffrey Jones
DIRECTED BY: Milos Forman

One is genius; the other is jealous. Mozart (Hulce) composes musical masterpieces with ease, while court composer Salieri (Abraham) can't transcend the ordinary in his writing, but it's nothing a little poison can't cure. The two leads give powerhouse performances while Forman supplies sharp direction against an elaborate Prague backdrop. Sheer excellence! Oscar-nominated for Best Actor (Hulce), Cinematography and Film Editing.
OSCAR SWEEP: *Best Picture, Actor (Abraham), Director (Forman), Screenplay - adapted (Peter Shaffer), Art Direction/Set Decoration, Sound, Costume Design, Make-Up*

Choose Me

BLOCKBUSTER CATEGORY: Drama
STARRING: Genevieve Bujold, Keith Carradine, Lesley Ann Warren, Rae Dawn Chong
DIRECTED BY: Alan Rudolph

A younger version of Dr. Ruth on the radio (Bujold), a mental Romeo (Carradine) and a bar owner (Warren) are the subject of a dusk-to-dawn relationship study. There's a nice amalgamation of downbeat comedy and drama in this engaging and original movie. Teddy Pendergrass' music brings the soundtrack to life.

The Gods Must Be Crazy

BLOCKBUSTER CATEGORY: Comedy
STARRING: Marius Weyers, Sandra Prinsloo, N!xau
DIRECTED BY: Jamie Uys

In Africa, a Coke bottle drops out of the sky and lands among a tribe of Botswana natives, who attach mystical significance to the event. This sets into motion a chain reaction of hilarious comic - and cosmic - misadventures, in the cleverest, most original comedy in years. Made on a small budget, with a cast of unknowns, this consistently inventive movie played U.S. theaters for months, and demonstrated that you don't always need a lot of money, just a great idea and the skill to carry it out, to create a movie that people will embrace.

The Karate Kid

BLOCKBUSTER CATEGORY: Drama
STARRING: Ralph Macchio, Noriyuki (Pat) Morita, Elizabeth Shue
DIRECTED BY: John G. Avildsen

The triumph of the underdog is the theme of this highly successful movie, which has so far triggered two sequels. Macchio is a kid from New Jersey who feels like a fish out of water when he and his mom move to Southern California. Morita is the Asian neighbor who teaches the boy karate - and, more importantly, that the martial arts are a discipline that must be used with skill and judgement. An early highlight is a scene in which Morita turns on the high school bullies who are taunting Macchio. The movie has a real emotional pull - which should be no surprise, since it was made by the man who directed ROCKY. Oscar-nominated for Best Supporting Actor (Morita).

The Killing Fields

BLOCKBUSTER CATEGORY: Drama
STARRING: Sam Waterson, Haing S. Ngor, John Malkovich,
Julian Sands, Craig T. Nelson
DIRECTED BY: Roland Joffe

Art imitates life when real-life Cambodian refugee Ngor replays that torturous part of his life as Dith Pran, who faces the terror of war, left behind in his country while the New York Times journalist and friend he assisted, Schanberg (Waterston), makes it back to America. Waterston and Ngor are riveting as Pran's quest for freedom becomes the focal point of a harrowing movie. John Lennon's song "Imagine" figures prominently in one of the most touching denouements ever to grace the screen. Oscar-nominated for Best Picture, Actor (Waterston), Director (Joffe) and Screenplay - adapted (Bruce Robinson).
OSCAR WINS: *Best Supporting Actor (Ngor), Cinematography, Film Editing*

The Natural

BLOCKBUSTER CATEGORY: Drama
STARRING: Robert Redford, Glenn Close, Robert Duvall
DIRECTED BY: Barry Levinson

The first entry in the current wave of baseball movies, but with a difference: its hero, played by Robert Redford, is almost supernaturally gifted. He turns up, middle-aged and with a shadowy past, and singlehandedly reverses the fortunes of a troubled New York ball club. An adaptation of Bernard Malamud's richly symbolic novel about a baseball hero of mythical proportions - and who else but Redford would you cast in a part like that? The powerhouse supporting cast includes Kim Basinger as a femme fatale and an unbilled Darren McGavin in a marvelous cameo as a sinister agent with a glass eye!

Once Upon a Time in America

BLOCKBUSTER CATEGORY: Drama
STARRING: Robert DeNiro, James Woods, Elizabeth McGovern,
Tuesday Weld, Larry Rapp, Jennifer Connelly
DIRECTED BY: Sergio Leone

A Jewish GODFATHER set in Brooklyn that traces two friends' lives for five decades, spanning theft, murder and rape. DeNiro and Woods are tremendous in this, the uncut version of master director Leone's sprawling epic. The complete, restored version runs 227 minutes.

A Passage to India

BLOCKBUSTER CATEGORY: Drama
STARRING: Judy Davis, Victor Banerjee, Peggy Ashcroft,
Alec Guinness
DIRECTED BY: David Lean

Director Lean (LAWRENCE OF ARABIA, 1962) helms a grandiose epic based on E.M. Forster's novel depicting a culture gap between the English and the Indians in the 1920's. Davis plays a stubborn Englishwoman en route to India with her fiance's mother (Ashcroft). Both are marvelous in their respective roles. Tension mounts as anti-Indian prejudice underlies Davis' radical accusation that an Indian friend attempted rape! Oscar-nominated for Best Picture, Actress (Davis), Director

鵬鵬鵬鵬鵬鵬鵬鵬鵬鵬鵬鵬鵬鵬鵬鵬鵬鵬鵬鵬鵬鵬鵬鵬鵬鵬鵬鵬鵬鵬鵬鵬鵬鵬鵬鵬鵬鵬鵬

(Lean), Screenplay - adapted (Lean), Cinematography, Art Direction, Sound, Film
Editing and Costume Design.
OSCAR WINS: *Best Supporting Actress (Ashcroft), Original Score*

Places in the Heart
BLOCKBUSTER CATEGORY: Drama
STARRING: Sally Field, Lindsay Crouse, Ed Harris, Amy Madigan,
John Malkovich, Danny Glover
DIRECTED BY: Robert Benton
One of the best in the save-the-farm genre. Field plays a widow on a Texas cotton
farm in the Depression era fighting storms, plummeting prices and the KKK.
Farmhand Glover and blind occupant Malkovich support her in her brave quest to
make harvest. It's some of Field's best work ever and her Oscar speech for this role
is perhaps the most famous ever: "You like me. . . you really like me!" Oscar-
nominated for Best Picture, Supporting Actor (Malkovich), Supporting Actress
(Crouse) and Director (Benton).
OSCAR WINS: *Best Actress (Field), Screenplay (Robert Benton)*

Romancing the Stone
BLOCKBUSTER CATEGORY: Action/Adventure
STARRING: Kathleen Turner, Michael Douglas, Danny DeVito
DIRECTED BY: Robert Zemeckis
A romance novelist (Turner) finds herself in a cliff-hanger-style adventure when she
comes to Colombia to find her sister. Alone in the wilds, she meets a rough-around-
the-edges soldier of fortune (Douglas). Together, they battle the thieves and cons
out to get their hands on the treasure map she doesn't even know she holds.
DeVito is hilarious as one of the bandits. Turner, once again, steals the show. She,
Douglas and DeVito reteamed for a sequel, JEWEL OF THE NILE (1985) and a non-
related gem, THE WAR OF THE ROSES (1989).   Oscar-nominated for Best Film
Editing.

A Soldier's Story
BLOCKBUSTER CATEGORY: Drama
STARRING: Howard E. Rollins, Jr., Adolph Caesar, Dennis
Lipscomb, Denzel Washington, Patti LaBelle
DIRECTED BY: Norman Jewison
An explosive account of racism and murder among a black military unit. Attorney
Rollins finds (as we do, through flashback) how a tough sergeant (Caesar) was
bumped off. As the puzzle is assembled, the performances ripen to perfection.
LaBelle has a memorable cameo as a dynamic saloon singer who's "been there."
Oscar-nominated for Best Picture, Supporting Actor (Caesar), Screenplay - adapted
(Charles Fuller).

Splash
BLOCKBUSTER CATEGORY: Comedy
STARRING: Tom Hanks, Daryl Hannah, John Candy
DIRECTED BY: Ron Howard
One of the most joyous, infectiously upbeat love stories of recent years, this is also
an extremely funny slapstick comedy. Tom Hanks is a harried yuppie so wrapped up

in the family produce business that he can't find time for a lasting romantic relationship. Then he meets Daryl Hannah, a shy, beautiful young woman who makes him happier than he's ever been. What Hannah doesn't tell Hanks is she's a mermaid, who must submerge herself in water from time to time - temporarily sprouting tail, fins and all! - or she will perish. There are some great comic interludes, mostly supplied by Hanks' slovenly brother (Candy) and Eugene Levy as a scientist tracking Hannah, but the film's lasting charm is in its sweetness, and its faith in unconditional love.

Stop Making Sense
BLOCKBUSTER CATEGORY: Music Concerts
STARRING: Talking Heads
DIRECTED BY: Jonathan Demme
Here is an electrifying rock concert movie starring David Byrne and his band. The subtle light show, rear screen projections and spare stage setting lift this from the ranks of other concert outings. And, unlike other concert films, audience reaction shots are virtually absent, the emphasis is on the performance. What's more, the video version contains three extra numbers!

The Terminator
BLOCKBUSTER CATEGORY: Science Fiction
STARRING: Arnold Schwarzenegger, Michael Biehn,
 Linda Hamilton
DIRECTED BY: James Cameron
Non-stop, action-packed, no-holds-barred adventure. Schwarzenegger is a cyborg from the 21st century sent back in time to eliminate the future mother (Hamilton) of the man who will save the human race. Besides the swift pace and high-tech gloss, there are tinges of humor and surprisingly top-notch performances. It's guaranteed entertainment. Director Cameron is the modern-day master of sci-fi/adventure, with ALIENS (1986) and THE ABYSS (1989) to his credit.

Back to the Future

BLOCKBUSTER CATEGORY: Comedy
STARRING: Michael J. Fox, Christopher Lloyd, Crispin Glover,
Lea Thompson
DIRECTED BY: Robert Zemeckis

This movie grows on you, with its infectious charm blending science fiction and fantasy with comedy. Fox plays a teenager of the 80's sent back to the 50's via time machine to encourage his future parents' union, thus, his own existence. Lloyd plays the "mad" scientist who helps Fox go back and forth in time. Steven Spielberg had a hand in producing this, ensuring top quality production values. Huey Lewis sings on the soundtrack besides making a brief appearance. Oscar-nominated for Best Screenplay (Zemeckis and Bob Gale), Sound and Song ("The Power of Love").
OSCAR WIN: *Best Sound Effects Editing*

Brazil

BLOCKBUSTER CATEGORY: Comedy
STARRING: Jonathan Pryce, Kim Greist, Robert DeNiro,
Katherine Helmond, Bob Hoskins, Ian Holm
DIRECTED BY: Terry Gilliam

Star cameos (Hoskins, DeNiro) brighten this black comedy about a bureaucrat (Pryce) who finds himself in an Orwell-inspired nightmare due to a computer malfunction. It's a compelling forecast for a bleak future society. Director Gilliam, Monty Python member, applies English wit to his elaborate visions. The settings and production design are spectacular. Helmond's visually surreal appearance is a lot of fun. Oscar-nominated for Best Screenplay (Gilliam, Tom Stoppard and Charles McKeown) and Art Direction.

The Breakfast Club

BLOCKBUSTER CATEGORY: Drama
STARRING: Emilio Estevez, Judd Nelson, Molly Ringwald,
Ally Sheedy
DIRECTED BY: John Hughes

An ambitious departure from the rash of mid-80's "brat pack" movies, this is a drama with flashes of humor, rather than the other way around. Five kids who have been exiled to a day of high school detention confront their feelings about school, their families and each other. Rather than turn into a hokey talkfest, the movie showed that its bright stable of stars could really act, and that director-writer Hughes - maker of SIXTEEN CANDLES and other comedies - had something to say.

Cocoon

BLOCKBUSTER CATEGORY: Science Fiction
STARRING: Don Ameche, Wilford Brimley, Hume Cronyn,
Brian Dennehy, Steve Guttenberg,
Maureen Stapleton, Jessica Tandy, Tahnee Welch
DIRECTED BY: Ron Howard

Fantasy maven Howard brings kind aliens to earth. Their pods turn a swimming pool into a fountain of youth, giving new life to the inhabitants of a retirement home

as well as an out-of-this-world choice for eternal life! Welch - yes, Raquel's daughter - is one of the aliens. Ameche is invigorating in his breakdance scene.
OSCAR WINS: *Best Supporting Actor (Ameche)*, *Visual Effects*

The Color Purple

BLOCKBUSTER CATEGORY: Drama
STARRING: Whoopi Goldberg, Danny Glover, Margaret Avery, Oprah Winfrey, Adolph Caesar, Rae Dawn Chong
DIRECTED BY: Steven Spielberg

Alice Walker's Pulitzer Prize-honored book is translated into a sweeping screen melodrama by Spielberg. Goldberg in her movie debut is awe-inspiring as a poor black woman suppressed by her cruel husband (Glover) over a 40-year time span. Winfrey (her debut, too) is excellent. Keep the Kleenex handy. Oscar-nominated for Best Picture, Actress (Goldberg), Supporting Actress (Avery), Supporting Actress (Winfrey), Screenplay - adapted (Menno Meyjes), Cinematography, Art Direction/Set Decoration, Song ("Miss Celie's Blues"), Score, Costume Design, Make-up.

Desperately Seeking Susan

BLOCKBUSTER CATEGORY: Comedy
STARRING: Rosanna Arquette, Madonna, Aidan Quinn, Steven Wright
DIRECTED BY: Susan Seidelman

Get into the groove with this offbeat comedy set in frenetic New York City. Arquette plays a bored housewife who, after fantasizing about the personal columns and getting amnesia, mistakes her own identity in this urban-based caper. This film was released when Madonna was entering the height of superstardom as a singer, making it all the more interesting. Quinn is terrific as Arquette's love interest.

Kiss of the Spider Woman

BLOCKBUSTER CATEGORY: Drama
STARRING: William Hurt, Raul Julia, Sonia Braga
DIRECTED BY: Hector Babenco

An electrifying performance by Hurt is the centerpiece of this movie. He plays a gay prisoner who shares a cell with a straight political activist (Julia). They form a meaningful friendship, with each using his own perspective to cope. Hurt fantasizes about old Hollywood movies. Director Babenco brilliantly meshes illusion and reality to take us through the story. Oscar-nominated for Best Picture, Director (Babenco) and Screenplay - adapted (Leonard Schrader).
OSCAR WIN: *Best Actor (Hurt)*

Out of Africa

BLOCKBUSTER CATEGORY: Drama
STARRING: Meryl Streep, Robert Redford, Klaus Maria Brandauer
DIRECTED BY: Sydney Pollack

A hypnotic orange sunset or a ride through the clouds turns the screen into a magnificent display of color and magic. This epic drama retells the life of Karen Blixen (a.k.a. author Isak Dinessen), and Streep handles the role with her usual finesse. Her marriage of convenience to an apathetic Brandauer is offset by romance with a handsome English adventurer (Redford). Brandauer is terrific and Streep, once again, enthralling. Oscar-nominated for Best Actress (Streep), Film Editing and Costume Design.

OSCAR SWEEP: *Best Picture, Director (Pollack), Screenplay - adapted (Kurt Luedtke), Cinematography, Art Direction/Set Decoration, Sound, Original Score*

Prizzi's Honor

BLOCKBUSTER CATEGORY: Drama
STARRING: Jack Nicholson, Kathleen Turner, Angelica Huston, Robert Loggia, William Hickey, John Randolph
DIRECTED BY: John Huston

A dark dramatic comedy about the mob. Nicholson plays a hit man who falls in love with a hit woman (Turner). The only problem is, according to family code, he should "ice" her instead of getting married. An extremely unusual story which works due to the on-screen and behind-the-scenes talent across the board. Oscar-nominated for Best Picture, Actor (Nicholson), Supporting Actor (Hickey), Director (Huston), Screenplay - adapted (Richard Condon and Janet Roach), Film Editing and Costume Design.

OSCAR WIN: *Best Supporting Actress (Huston)*

Ran

BLOCKBUSTER CATEGORY: Foreign
STARRING: Tatsuya Nakadai, Satoshi Terao, Jinpachi Nezu, Mieko Harada
DIRECTED BY: Akira Kurosawa

This Japanese-French epic is a powerful adaptation of Shakespeare's King Lear, with a Samurai lord giving his oldest son the right to succeed him. The younger sons are angry, especially knowing that the eldest's wife has evil intentions. Besides the intriguing plot, the elaborately choreographed battle scenes add to the thrill of grand scale drama. Oscar-nominated for Best Director (Kurosawa), Cinematography and Art Direction.

OSCAR WIN: *Costume Design*

The Trip to Bountiful

BLOCKBUSTER CATEGORY: Drama
STARRING: Geraldine Page, John Heard, Carlin Glynn, Rebecca DeMornay
DIRECTED BY: Peter Masterson

Horton Foote's quaint touch runs through his screenplay about an old widow (Page) living unhappily with her son and his wife, but yearning to return to her hometown, Bountiful, Texas. Her determination plus the memory lane travel upon arrival make this a sincere, sentimental and amusing portrait. DeMornay is appealing as another passenger on the bus trip. This was Page's last starring role (she had a supporting part in NATIVE SON, 1986). Oscar-nominated for Best Screenplay - adapted (Foote).

OSCAR WIN: *Best Actress (Page)*

1985

Witness

BLOCKBUSTER CATEGORY: Drama
STARRING: Harrison Ford, Kelly McGillis, Alexander Godunov,
Lukas Haas, Danny Glover, Patti LuPone
DIRECTED BY: Peter Weir

Weir's incisive direction enhances this entertaining drama about a city policeman who must protect the son of a widowed Amish woman (McGillis) because he witnessed a murder tied to police corruption. Weir handles the change from melodrama to action with supreme skill. The scene where the killer is hunting down Haas in a men's room is highly suspenseful. Oscar-nominated for Best Picture, Actor (Ford), Director (Weir), Cinematography, Art Direction and Original Score. OSCAR WINS: *Best Screenplay (Earl W. Wallace, William Kelley and Pamela Wallace), Film Editing*

Aliens
BLOCKBUSTER CATEGORY: Science Fiction
STARRING: Sigourney Weaver, Michael Biehn, Paul Reiser,
Carrie Henn
DIRECTED BY: James Cameron

This sequel to ALIEN (1979) outdoes its predecessor in acting, set design, special effects, and non-stop chills 'n thrills. Weaver is like a female Rambo taking on an army of the slimy killer creatures. Her range is demonstrated in more tender scenes with a little girl lost (Henn). Cameron (THE TERMINATOR, 1984) proves, once again, he's a gifted action director. Oscar-nominated for Best Actress (Weaver), Art Direction, Sound, Original Score and Film Editing.
OSCAR WIN: *Best Visual Effects*

Blue Velvet
BLOCKBUSTER CATEGORY: Mystery/Suspense
STARRING: Kyle MacLachlan, Isabella Rossellini, Dennis Hopper,
Laura Dern, Hope Lange, Dean Stockwell
DIRECTED BY: David Lynch

A highly unusual film that breaks convention in plot and execution. Writer/director Lynch weaves a mysterious web of murder, torture, sex and small-town values. College kid MacLachlan has intense relationships with sultry songstress (Rossellini) and wholesome teen (Dern) within this framework. Hopper is riveting as a deadly psycho. Oscar-nominated for Best Director (Lynch).

Children of a Lesser God
BLOCKBUSTER CATEGORY: Drama
STARRING: William Hurt, Marlee Matlin, Piper Laurie,
Philip Bosco
DIRECTED BY: Randa Haines

This moving drama takes us into the deaf world with care and grace. Hurt plays a teacher of the deaf who falls in love with a hearing impaired janitor (Matlin) who has withdrawn into her own world. Both offer sincere portraits in Haines' heartfelt, but never-mushy directorial debut. Laurie plays Matlin's frustrated, but understanding mother in a superb supporting effort. Oscar-nominated for Best Picture, Actor (Hurt), Supporting Actress (Laurie) and Screenplay - adapted (Hesper Anderson and Mark Medoff).
OSCAR WIN: *Best Actress (Matlin, in her debut is the first deaf actress to win)*

The Color of Money
BLOCKBUSTER CATEGORY: Drama
STARRING: Paul Newman, Tom Cruise,
Mary Elizabeth Mastrantonio, Helen Shaver
DIRECTED BY: Martin Scorsese

In the sequel to THE HUSTLER (1961), Newman turns in a gritty performance as an aging pool shark who mentors a haughty, up-and-coming pool hustler (Cruise). Co-star Mastrantonio is compelling as Cruise's street-smart girlfriend and Newman is expectedly terrific. The surprise is Cruise, a recent graduate of Advanced Scene Stealing. Oscar-nominated for Best Supporting Actress (Mastrantonio), Screenplay - adapted (Richard Price) and Art Direction.

OSCAR WIN: *Best Actor (Newman, his first win after 6 other competitive nominations. He received an Honorary Oscar in 1985).*

The Fly

BLOCKBUSTER CATEGORY: Horror
STARRING: Jeff Goldblum, Geena Davis, John Getz, Joy Boushel
DIRECTED BY: David Cronenberg

This chilling remake is not for the squeamish. Goldblum plays an adventurous scientist perfecting a matter-transporting machine. All's well until a fly lands inside of it and the result is part Goldblum, part fly, which keeps growing into something sticky and gooey and quite dangerous. Davis has a provocative role as the compassionate and pregnant girlfriend. Look for her baby in THE FLY II (1989).
OSCAR WIN: *Best Make-Up*

Hannah and Her Sisters

BLOCKBUSTER CATEGORY: Comedy
STARRING: Woody Allen, Michael Caine, Mia Farrow, Carrie Fisher, Barbara Hershey, Dianne Wiest, Tony Roberts, Julie Kavner
DIRECTED BY: Woody Allen

Allen returns to his favorite setting, New York, to spin a tale of three sisters (Farrow, Wiest and Hershey) and their involvements with him and life in general. Allen is in rare form as the complaining ex-husband of Farrow; Wiest is hilarious as a self-involved sister and the rest of the cast matches them all the way. It's a cornucopia of wit and wisdom from one of America's most cherished writers/directors. Oscar-nominated for Best Picture, Director (Allen), Art Direction and Film Editing.
OSCAR WINS: *Best Supporting Actress (Wiest), Supporting Actor (Caine), Original Screenplay (Allen)*

Jean De Florette/Manon of the Spring

BLOCKBUSTER CATEGORY: Foreign
STARRING: Yves Montand, Gerard Depardieu, Emmanuelle Beart
DIRECTED BY: Claude Berri

Breathtaking cinema from France. A hunchback farmer (Depardieu) tills his new land as a ruthless neighbor (Montand) sees to it that a much-needed, hidden spring stays hidden. Director Berri's use of pastoral backdrops and first-rate performances from his stars make folklore seem real. He weaves greed and sin into the story, then lets revenge and retribution respond in a mesmerizing sequel, MANON OF THE SPRING (1986). Both are must-sees.

Mona Lisa

BLOCKBUSTER CATEGORY: Drama
STARRING: Bob Hoskins, Cathy Tyson, Michael Caine
DIRECTED BY: Neil Jordan

Genesis' song "In Too Deep" underlies one of the recent cinema's most piercing moments: Hoskins, as an ex-con, searching the seedier side of London for the friend of a young callgirl (Tyson) he loves. Director Jordan blends the harsh cruelties of the underworld with an unusual love story. Hoskins is magnificent, Tyson elicits a special grown-up charm, and Caine is in top shape as a criminal low-life. Oscar-nominated for Best Actor (Hoskins).

My Beautiful Laundrette
BLOCKBUSTER CATEGORY: Drama
STARRING: Saeed Jaffrey, Roshan Seth, Daniel Day Lewis, Gordon Warnecke
DIRECTED BY: Stephen Frears
This unique drama laced with comedy is a stirring slice-of-life tale about a Pakistani man (Warnecke) managing a laundromat in London with his British lover (Day Lewis). Racism, bigotry and economics are issues melded into the relationships and handled with honesty and intelligence thanks to Hanif Kureishi's Oscar-nominated script.

Platoon
BLOCKBUSTER CATEGORY: Action/Adventure
STARRING: Tom Berenger, Willem Dafoe, Charlie Sheen, Forest Whitaker, Kevin Dillon
DIRECTED BY: Oliver Stone
Writer/Director Stone's shattering account of the Vietnam War is seen through the eyes of a young soldier (Sheen) who enlisted by choice. Dafoe and Berenger play sergeants on opposite ends of the sanity spectrum. The other star of this film is the explosive battle footage which will shake all who see it. This movie led a late 80's Vietnam movie craze: many subsequent war films were released soon after. Stone directed another masterful war pic in 1986, SALVADOR. Oscar-nominated for Best Supporting Actor (both Berenger and Dafoe), Screenplay (Stone) and Cinematography.
OSCAR SWEEP: *Best Picture, Director (Stone), Film Editing, Sound*

A Room With a View
BLOCKBUSTER CATEGORY: Drama
STARRING: Maggie Smith, Helena Bonham Carter, Denholm Elliot, Julian Sands, Daniel Day Lewis
DIRECTED BY: James Ivory
E.M. Forster's delightful novel of manners flourishes on screen. A socially-prominent young Englishwoman (Carter) falls in love with an unsuitable suitor (Sands), the son of a working class man (Elliot), but agrees to marry someone else who's well-off, but boring (Day Lewis). The gorgeous settings and top-notch performances make this a sight to behold. Smith is deliciously uptight as the chaperone. Oscar-nominated for Best Picture, Supporting Actor (Elliot), Supporting Actress (Smith), Director (Ivory) and Cinematography.
OSCAR SWEEP: *Best Screenplay - adapted (Ruth Prawer Jhabvala), Art Direction, Costume Design*

Ruthless People
BLOCKBUSTER CATEGORY: Comedy
STARRING: Bette Milder, Danny DeVito, Judge Reinhold, Helen Slater, Anita Morris
DIRECTED BY: Jim Abrahams, David Zucker, Jerry Zucker

"I've been kidnapped by K-Mart!" cries a distressed Midler, whose nasty husband (DeVito) won't pay her kidnappers' ransom fees, forcing them to mark down the price. Friendship, weight loss and getting even are mixed into the high jinks of this laugh-a-minute comedy. Midler's telephone retort - where the expletives fly - is a riot! The other stars are also hilarious in their madcap moments.

Salvador

BLOCKBUSTER CATEGORY: Drama
STARRING: James Woods, Jim Belushi, John Savage
DIRECTED BY: Oliver Stone

An absolute knockout of a movie, the powerhouse political melodrama that would make a star out of James Woods and send director Oliver Stone on the road leading to PLATOON and his Oscar-winning BORN ON THE FOURTH OF JULY. Woods plays journalist Richard Boyle, who goes to El Salvador in 1980 looking for a story, finds corruption, bloodshed and life-threatening danger around every corner, and is nearly killed himself. Belushi is memorable as his unwitting travelling companion - a perpetually stoned disc jockey - and Savage contributes a magnificent performance as a committed photojournalist who takes his camera to the front lines and has cause to regret it. Amazingly, despite the suspense and terror that moves the film along, there are also moments of considerable humor, such as a hilarious scene in which Woods, at the urging of his Latin American fiancee, attends confession for the first time in over 10 years. Oscar-nominations for Woods and Stone. The haunting score is by French composer Georges Delerue.

Something Wild

BLOCKBUSTER CATEGORY: Comedy
STARRING: Jeff Daniels, Melanie Griffith, Ray Liotta,
Margaret Colin
DIRECTED BY: Jonathan Demme

This Demme gem never misses a beat, even when the comedy turns to suspense. Griffith is intoxicating as a carefree woman who "kidnaps" a conservative businessman (Daniels) for a lost weekend. Later on, her dangerous husband (Liotta) shows up and he's not too happy with what he sees. "Off-beat" is an understatement for this movie, but it's always entertaining and well-acted. Look for two of Demme's favorite directors in cameo bits: John Waters and John Sayles.

Stand By Me

BLOCKBUSTER CATEGORY: Drama
STARRING: Wil Wheaton, River Phoenix, Corey Feldman,
Kiefer Sutherland, John Cusack, Richard Dreyfuss
DIRECTED BY: Rob Reiner

Dreyfuss narrates a flashback recalling his childhood adventure with three buddies looking for a classmate's corpse. On their thrilling and scary two-day-trek, they smoke, cuss, dodge trains, face hoodlums and learn about friendship and growing up. Director Reiner's careful attention to detail - right down to the Nehi poster in a general store - and his skill at getting maximum impact from child actors make this movie a fascinating enterprise. Based on a novella by Stephen King. Oscar-nominated for Best Screenplay - adapted (Raynold Gideon and Bruce A. Evans).

1987

Au Revoir Les Enfants
BLOCKBUSTER CATEGORY: Foreign
STARRING: Gaspard Manesse, Raphael Fejto, Francine Racette
DIRECTED BY: Louis Malle

At the height of World War II, a French schoolmaster puts his life in danger by deciding to hide several Jewish children from the Nazi onslaught. Based on an incident from director Malle's youth, this gripping French film works because its potentially melodramatic theme is kept small and intimate. We get to know the children, their families, the schoolteacher and townspeople in terms of their relationships with each other, not as figures in the larger landscape of war. When the climax finally arrives, it does so with overwhelming power.

Babette's Feast
BLOCKBUSTER CATEGORY: Foreign
STARRING: Stephane Audran, Jean-Philippe Lafont,
Gudmar Wivesson, Bibi Anderson, Bodil Kjer,
Birgitte Federspiel
DIRECTED BY: Gabriel Axel

Denmark's finest import from 1987 is a rare gem. In the 19th century, two sisters (Kjer and Federspiel) choose to lead austere lives despite their beauty and chance for more. One day, after many years of service, their housekeeper (Audran) uses her lottery winnings to prepare a lavish banquet which sets off a change in attitudes. Director Axel also wrote the script based on an Isak Dinessen (author of *Out of Africa*) tale. The movie is a cinematic feast of wonderful performances and profound thoughts.
OSCAR WIN: *Best Foreign Language Film (Denmark)*

The Big Easy
BLOCKBUSTER CATEGORY: Mystery/Suspense
STARRING: Dennis Quaid, Ellen Barkin, John Goodman,
Ned Beatty
DIRECTED BY: Jim McBride

A sparkling thriller set in New Orleans. The intriguing atmosphere plus the uncontainable chemistry between Quaid (a confident cop) and Barkin (a nervous D.A.) light up the screen in a suspenseful tale of police corruption. This is pure entertainment with star-solidifying performances by the dynamic leads. The Cajun-based soundtrack is also a spicy treat!

Broadcast News
BLOCKBUSTER CATEGORY: Comedy
STARRING: William Hurt, Holly Hunter, Albert Brooks,
Joan Cusack, Lois Chiles
DIRECTED BY: James L. Brooks

Writer/Director Brooks (TERMS OF ENDEARMENT, 1983) gives us another masterpiece. It's a triangle romance played out against the network TV news industry. A charismatic anchorman (Hurt) turns the head of a no-nonsense producer (Hunter), while her friend, a reporter of substance (Brooks) is falling in love with her. The three leads are simply brilliant. There's also a wonderful performance by Cusack as a frenetic production assistant and an unbilled cameo by

Jack Nicholson as a star anchor. You won't find a more absorbing, intelligent, funny and touching movie. Oscar-nominated for Best Picture, Actress (Hunter), Actor (Hurt), Supporting Actor (Brooks), Original Screenplay (Brooks), Film Editing and Cinematography.

Empire Of The Sun

BLOCKBUSTER CATEGORY: Drama
STARRING: Christian Bale, John Malkovich, Miranda Richardson
DIRECTED BY: Steven Spielberg

A wealthy British lad, cut off from his parents in Shanghai at the start of World War II, learns to survive amid the squalor and terror of the Japanese invasion. A powerful movie that blends the awesome scope we expect from a Steven Spielberg production with the human drama of J.G. Ballard's autobiography, on which it is based. Oscar-nominated for Cinematography, Art Direction, Sound, Score, Editing, Costumes.

Fatal Attraction

BLOCKBUSTER CATEGORY: Mystery/Suspense
STARRING: Michael Douglas, Glenn Close, Anne Archer
DIRECTED BY: Adrian Lyne

When Close, as a discarded casual fling, said, "I will not be ignored!" a national nerve was hit and every married man was affected. This is one of the most popular thrillers ever, with riveting performances by Close, Douglas as the married lawyer and Archer as his sincere wife. Director Lyne fills his intriguing probe of crazed woman with edge-of-your-seat shockers. Combined with designer lighting and a surprise ending, this is a can't miss movie all the way around. Oscar-nominated for Best Picture, Actress (Close), Supporting Actress (Archer), Director (Lyne), Screenplay - adapted (James Dearden) and Film Editing.

Full Metal Jacket

BLOCKBUSTER CATEGORY: Action/Adventure
STARRING: Matthew Modine, Adam Baldwin, Vincent D'Onofrio, Lee Ermey
DIRECTED BY: Stanley Kubrick

Kubrick's anti-Vietnam effort is really two movies in one: boot camp training for Marines and the battlefield showdown. In the first half, former real-life D.I. Ermey plays a mean-spirited sergeant who pushes one of his recruits over the edge. The next half is equally explosive, focusing on the dehumanizing effects of cold, cruel killing. Modine leads the troop of top-notch performances and Kubrick's sense of pacing and careful camera work is as mesmerizing as ever. Oscar-nominated for Best Screenplay - adapted (Kubrick, Michael Herr and Gustav Hasford).

Hope and Glory

BLOCKBUSTER CATEGORY: Comedy
STARRING: Sarah Miles, David Hayman, Derrick O'Connor, Sammi Davis, Ian Bannen, Sebastian Rice Edwards
DIRECTED BY: John Boorman

The process of coming of age is a comedy/drama in itself. When it's set against World War II, it's even more unusual. Director Boorman lived it; now he retells it through a boy's (Edwards) perspective. Highlighting the nostalgic atmosphere in a London household and the intermittent fireworks of war is a very funny script. Edwards is wonderful, as is mom Miles and rebellious sister Davis. Boorman's film rings as true emotionally as it shines visually. Oscar-nominated for Best Picture, Director (Boorman), Screenplay (Boorman), Cinematography and Art Direction.

The Last Emperor

BLOCKBUSTER CATEGORY: Drama
STARRING: John Lone, Joan Chen, Peter O'Toole, Ying Ruocheng
DIRECTED BY: Bernardo Bertolucci

This Italian/British/Chinese co-production is an epic masterpiece inviting us to behold the splendor of China's Forbidden City, where scenes were filmed. It's the true story of Pu Yi (Lone), made emperor of China when he was three years old. Revolution changed his life by taking away his title and pushing him into the real world. Bertolucci spared no expense in creating an elaborately designed, costumed, scored - and of course, acted - event!

OSCAR SWEEP: Best Picture, Director (Bertolucci), Screenplay - adapted (Mark Peploe and Bertolucci), Art Direction, Cinematography, Sound, Film Editing, Original Score, Costume Design

Moonstruck

BLOCKBUSTER CATEGORY: Comedy
STARRING: Cher, Nicolas Cage, Vincent Gardenia,
Olympia Dukakis, Danny Aiello
DIRECTED BY: Norman Jewison

Here's a wonderful comedy/love story with Cher in command of the screen as an Italian-American widow who agrees to marry a passionless suitor (Aiello), before meeting and falling in love with his younger brother (Cage). Cher is magnificent, whether she's going to confession, getting a makeover, or telling a lovesick Cage to "snap out of it!" Dukakis is also great as her opinionated mother. Oscar-nominated for Best Picture, Supporting Actor (Gardenia) and Director (Jewison).

OSCAR SWEEP: Best Actress (Cher), Supporting Actress (Dukakis), Original Screenplay (John Patrick Shanley)

Nuts

BLOCKBUSTER CATEGORY: Drama
STARRING: Barbra Streisand, Richard Dreyfuss,
Maureen Stapleton, Karl Malden, Eli Wallach,
Robert Webber, James Whitmore, Leslie Nielsen
DIRECTED BY: Martin Ritt

A hard-hitting courtroom drama. Streisand, in her most provocative role to date, plays a prostitute fighting to prove she's not insane after killing a client in self-defense. Hers is an emotional *tour de force*, complemented by Dreyfuss' incisive performance as her sympathetic attorney. Wonderful supporting turns by an all-star cast highlight a powerful movie. Streisand also produced this one and wrote the stirring theme music.

Radio Days

BLOCKBUSTER CATEGORY: Comedy
STARRING: Mia Farrow, Seth Green, Julie Kavner
DIRECTED BY: Woody Allen

Great, nostalgic throwback to the Woody Allen comedies of old and a simpler time in America. Reverent look at the 40's heydey of radio - and the way the public was glued to the radio set each night - is mixed with a character study of radio personalities and one particularly quirky family of listeners. Lots of memorable comic caricatures: the radio stars who are all sweetness and light on the air but bicker constantly away from the mike; the older sister who's desperate to settle down but only dates married men; the prim schoolteacher who is also the neighborhood exhibitionist. Allen narrates so exuberantly that it almost seems afterward that he also appeared in the movie. Oscar-nominated for Screenplay and Art Direction.

Raising Arizona

BLOCKBUSTER CATEGORY: Comedy
STARRING: Nicolas Cage, Holly Hunter, Trey Wilson,
John Goodman
DIRECTED BY: Joel Coen

A riotous romp about a petty robber (Cage) and the police officer (Hunter) who signs him into prison on a recurring basis. They fall in love and decide to steal a baby from a set of quintuplets because they can't have their own, and that's only the first ten minutes! There's lots of action/chase sequences and lots of laughs, many of which are bizarre. Cage and Hunter play terrifically off each other. Coen's sense of humor is daring, especially where babies are involved. This one promises plenty of fun...and delivers.

Robocop

BLOCKBUSTER CATEGORY: Action/Adventure
STARRING: Peter Weller, Nancy Allen, Daniel O'Herlihy,
Ronny Cox
DIRECTED BY: Paul Verhoeven

Continuous action that just doesn't let up. It's Detroit in the future and a cop (Weller) killed on the beat is transformed into a forceful anti-crime robot. Afterwards, he goes on a mission of revenge. The stop-motion animation, slick production design and electrifying visual effects will take your breath away. Oscar-nominated for Best Sound and Film Editing.
OSCAR WIN: *Sound Effects Editing*

Roxanne

BLOCKBUSTER CATEGORY: Comedy
STARRING: Steve Martin, Daryl Hannah, Rick Rossovich,
Shelley Duvall
DIRECTED BY: Fred Schepisi

A modernized *Cyrano De Bergerac* with tinges of *Pinocchio*. That is, fire chief Martin's nose is bigger than life, as is his love for Hannah who's hung up on Martin's co-worker Rossovich. It sounds complex, but it's all quite simple and charming with a standout bid by Martin. His self-deprecating comic flair shines, especially in his nose joke call-out scene. Hannah has never looked more ravishing on screen. Martin also wrote the script.

Tin Men
BLOCKBUSTER CATEGORY: Comedy
STARRING: Richard Dreyfuss, Danny DeVito, Barbara Hershey, John Mahoney
DIRECTED BY: Barry Levinson
Two aluminum salesmen (Dreyfuss, DeVito) crash cars and their rivalry escalates to war. Director Levinson, who also wrote, returns to his DINER (1982) roots in early 60's Baltimore for an altogether engaging comedy that explores small-town style and ever-so-sweet revenge. His acute feel for dialogue and performances makes this a hands-down winner.

The Untouchables
BLOCKBUSTER CATEGORY: Action/Adventure
STARRING: Kevin Costner, Sean Connery, Robert DeNiro, Charles Martin Smith, Andy Garcia, Patricia Clarkson
DIRECTED BY: Brian DePalma
DePalma's film buff allusions play exquisitely here, especially his tribute to the Odessa Steps sequence from POTEMKIN (1925). This crime drama/adventure pours on the thrills as fed Eliot Ness (Costner) does his best to stop the brutal Al Capone (DeNiro) and company in the age of Prohibition. Connery is superb as the street wise cop who helps Ness, and Costner's star quality here (along with his performance in NO WAY OUT in 1987) elevated him to heart-throb status. This is one of DePalma's best. Oscar-nominated for Best Art Direction, Original Score and Costume Design.
OSCAR WIN: *Best Supporting Actor (Connery)*

Wall Street
BLOCKBUSTER CATEGORY: Drama
STARRING: Michael Douglas, Charlie Sheen, Daryl Hannah, Martin Sheen, Sean Young, Sylvia Miles
DIRECTED BY: Oliver Stone
Stone's mark for hard-hitting drama is all over this no-nonsense "business thriller." Charlie Sheen is an ambitious stock broker who gets entangled in the greed for power and wealth, his role model being a star financier (Douglas) with his own set of rules. For once, Douglas plays the bad guy and he's extremely good at it! Charlie Sheen's real-life dad, Martin, appears as the father he deceives. Look quickly for director/co-writer Stone in a split-screen brokerage deal.
OSCAR WIN: *Best Actor (Douglas)*

Wings of Desire
BLOCKBUSTER CATEGORY: Foreign
STARRING: Bruno Ganz, Solveig Dommartin, Otto Sander, Curt Bois, Peter Falk
DIRECTED BY: Wim Wenders

This German/French movie offers a dreamy tale about an angel (Ganz) guarding human life in West Berlin, who longs to become human himself. Falk is extraordinary as a movie star from America. Director Wenders weaves profound fantasy into cinema magic, and Henri Alekan's black & white and color cinematography shimmers. In German and English.

The Witches of Eastwick
BLOCKBUSTER CATEGORY: Comedy
STARRING: Jack Nicholson, Cher, Susan Sarandon,
Michelle Pfeiffer, Veronica Cartwright
DIRECTED BY: George Miller

"Women. A mistake? Or did He do it to us on purpose?" Nicholson is perfectly cast as the reveling devil who turns the lives of three unwitting witches upside down. John Updike's novel makes for a unique movie experience that blends dark comedy, fantasy and fright with charismatic performances. The dialogue is crisp and these actors know how to extract maximum impact from it. John Willams' music and the superb set are marvelous embellishments. Oscar-nominated for Best Sound and Original Score.

The Accidental Tourist

BLOCKBUSTER CATEGORY: Drama
STARRING: William Hurt, Kathleen Turner, Geena Davis
DIRECTED BY: Lawrence Kasdan

Ann Tyler's best-selling novel comes to the screen in all its subtle brilliance with Hurt as a travel writer trying to cope with the loss of his 12-year-old son. His estranged wife (Turner) and a quirky pet-shop owner (Davis) do their best to break through his somber state with differing results. Oscar-nominated for Best Picture, Screenplay - adapted and Original Score. Hurt, Turner and Kasdan reunited for the first time since BODY HEAT (1981).
OSCAR WIN: *Best Supporting Actress (Davis)*

The Accused

BLOCKBUSTER CATEGORY: Drama
STARRING: Jodie Foster, Kelly McGillis
DIRECTED BY: Jonathan Kaplan

Foster has enough emotional range to last a lifetime as a gang-rape victim in this movie inspired by a true story. McGillis, as the initially cool prosecutor, provides the perfect counterpoint to her client's rage. Once Foster reveals the trauma that lingers, McGillis forfeits her plea-bargaining ways to find justice.
OSCAR WIN: *Best Actress (Foster)*

Beaches

BLOCKBUSTER CATEGORY: Drama
STARRING: Bette Midler, Barbara Hershey, John Heard
DIRECTED BY: Garry Marshall

Two girls meet on a beach and form a friendship which survives their different backgrounds and changing lives over a 30-year period. Through separate career successes (one's a singer; the other, a lawyer) and personal heartbreaks, they share laughter and tears. You will, too. The soundtrack features Midler's best singing to date, including the hit songs, "Wind Beneath My Wings" and "Under The Boardwalk." Her rendition of "The Glory of Love" is heartrending. The gorgeous art direction/set decoration received an Academy Award nomination.

Big

BLOCKBUSTER CATEGORY: Comedy
STARRING: Tom Hanks, Elizabeth Perkins, Robert Loggia
DIRECTED BY: Penny Marshall

Hanks is wonderful as a 13-year-old boy who "wishes" he were an adult. When he wakes up one morning with a 35-year-old's body, his adventure in the grown-up world begins. Here we have the 1980's "body switch" genre's most heartfelt movie. Hanks received a Best Actor nomination for his excellent acting. The screenplay was also nominated.

Bull Durham

BLOCKBUSTER CATEGORY: Comedy
STARRING: Kevin Costner, Susan Sarandon, Tim Robbins
DIRECTED BY: Ron Shelton

An intelligent and very funny movie about baseball and love. Costner hits a home run as the aging minor leaguer who must coach an often reluctant young star (Robbins). Sarandon plays the eccentric team groupie with her own bizarre set of rules off the field. This is an altogether absorbing motion picture experience. Shelton's original screenplay received an Oscar nomination.

A Cry in the Dark
BLOCKBUSTER CATEGORY: Drama
STARRING: Meryl Streep, Sam Neill
DIRECTED BY: Fred Schepisi
Streep received a Best Actress nomination for her latest dramatic feat. She plays the real-life Lindy Chamberlain, an Australian woman who loses her baby to a wild dog, only to be accused of the murder herself in a headline-making trial influenced by the media instead of the facts. With Australian accent in place and all the right character ornaments, Streep, once again, earns the "best actress of her generation" status.

Dangerous Liaisons
BLOCKBUSTER CATEGORY: Drama
STARRING: Glenn Close, John Malkovich, Michelle Pfeiffer,
Uma Thurman
DIRECTED BY: Stephen Frears
If you thought Close was a terror in FATAL ATTRACTION (1987), wait 'til you see her in this period piece about lust, greed and manipulation in 18th century France. Her motto: "Win or die!" Oscar-nominated for Best Picture, Actress (Close), Supporting Actress (Pfeiffer) and Director (Frears).
OSCAR WINS: *Best Screenplay - adaptation (Christopher Hampton), Art Direction, Costume Design*

Die Hard
BLOCKBUSTER CATEGORY: Action/Adventure
STARRING: Bruce Willis, Alan Rickman, Bonnie Bedelia,
Alexander Godunov
DIRECTED BY: John McTiernan
When a gang of thieves posing as terrorists dominate an L.A. skyscraper, only one man (Willis) can save the day. It's an edge-of-your-seat, action-packed thriller. Rickman, as the cruel leader, mixes charisma with murder. The suspense is capped by a plethora of top-notch special effects, which received an Oscar nomination, and Willis provides an "everyman" believability to a character that could have just been a Rambo. Other Oscar nominations were for Best Sound, Sound Effects Editing and Film Editing.

A Fish Called Wanda
BLOCKBUSTER CATEGORY: Comedy
STARRING: John Cleese, Jamie Lee Curtis, Kevin Kline,
Michael Palin
DIRECTED BY: Charles Crichton
Crime pays in dividends of laughter for this English caper spotlighting one of the best ensemble casts ever assembled. Curtis tries to seduce an uptight Cleese in order to recover stolen jewels (not hers). Kline demonstrates comic genius as her

insipid boyfriend. From the director of THE LAVENDER HILL MOB (1951). Oscar-nominated for Best Director (Crichton) and Original Screenplay (Cleese).
OSCAR WIN: *Best Supporting Actor (Kline)*

Gorillas in the Mist

BLOCKBUSTER CATEGORY: Drama
STARRING: Sigourney Weaver, Bryan Brown
DIRECTED BY: Michael Apted
Anthropologist Diane Fossey traveled to Africa in 1967 to study - and save - a breed of mountain gorillas facing extinction. Weaver becomes Fossey in her most compelling role to date, luring us into one woman's dream-turned-obsession. Oscar-nominated for Best Actress (Weaver, who also received a Supporting Actress nomination for WORKING GIRL in 1988), Screenplay - adapted, Film Editing, Original Score and Sound.

Mississippi Burning

BLOCKBUSTER CATEGORY: Mystery/Suspense
STARRING: Gene Hackman, Willem Dafoe, Frances McDormand
DIRECTED BY: Alan Parker
Hackman turns in a riveting performance as a forceful FBI agent investigating the disappearance of three civil rights workers in the South, circa 1964. His calm and collected partner (Dafoe) has a different approach, until the stakes get too high. This controversial film was Oscar-nominated for Best Picture, Actor (Hackman), Supporting Actress (McDormand), Director (Parker), Film Editing and Sound.
OSCAR WIN: *Cinematography*

Rain Man

BLOCKBUSTER CATEGORY: Drama
STARRING: Dustin Hoffman, Tom Cruise, Valeria Golino
DIRECTED BY: Barry Levinson
After his father's funeral, an over-confident salesman (Cruise) meets the brother (Hoffman) he never knew he had, who happens to be an autistic savant. The two strangers travel cross-country and find their brotherhood along the way. This is by far 1988's most poignant movie. Hoffman (in an astonishing *tour de force*) amazes and Cruise holds his own. Together they're great. Oscar-nominated for Film Editing, Cinematography and Art Direction.
OSCAR SWEEP: *Best Picture, Actor (Hoffman), Director (Levinson), Original Screenplay (Ronald Bass and Barry Morrow)*

Stand And Deliver

BLOCKBUSTER CATEGORY: Drama
STARRING: Edward James Olmos, Lou Diamond Phillips,
　　　　　　　Rosana de Soto
DIRECTED BY: Ramon Menendez
A BLACKBOARD JUNGLE for the late 80's and beyond. Miami Vice's Edward James Olmos gives an Oscar-nominated performance as Jaime Escalante, a teacher sent to the worst high school in the Los Angeles barrio, who convinces his minority students they'll be stuck in poverty, crime and dead-end jobs the rest of their lives unless they graduate high school and go on to college. How he reaches them makes

for an inspiring film that is first-rate drama without ever preaching. Some top-flight young actors, notably Phillips and, as a shady administrator, Andy Garcia (GODFATHER III), worked in the movie for very little money because they believed in the project. The across-the-board devotion shows onscreen.

The Thin Blue Line

BLOCKBUSTER CATEGORY: Documentary
STARRING: Randall Adams, David Harris, Edith James, Dennis White
DIRECTED BY: Errol Morris

The power of film is demonstrated by this groundbreaking documentary about a man (Adams) wrongfully accused of murdering a policeman. The movie helped reverse his conviction and death sentence by influencing a reopening of the case. Director Morris blends live interviews with a dramatization of the crime. An eerie score by Philip Glass adds to the intrigue of this landmark motion picture.

Who Framed Roger Rabbit

BLOCKBUSTER CATEGORY: Comedy
STARRING: Bob Hoskins, Christopher Lloyd, Joanna Cassidy
DIRECTED BY: Robert Zemeckis

The movie beautifully blends animation with live action. Hoskins shares the screen with a wisecracking rabbit who lands in the middle of a murder mystery. In a stellar achievement, the cartoon characters of yesterday - Bugs Bunny, Droopy, Mickey Mouse, Dumbo, Tweety and a host of others - reunite on screen! And wait 'til you hear the voices behind the sultry Jessica Rabbit: Kathleen Turner is Jessica's speaking voice and Amy Irving, her singing voice. What a combo. No wonder ROGER hopped off with three Oscars.
OSCAR WINS: *Best Film Editing, Sound Effects Editing, Visual Effects, Special Oscar for Animation*

Women on the Verge of a Nervous Breakdown

BLOCKBUSTER CATEGORY: Foreign
STARRING: Carmen Maura, Fernando Guillen, Antonio Banderas
DIRECTED BY: Pedro Almodovar

The wife is upset because of the mistress. The mistress is upset because of a new mistress who's taking her place. It's 1988's most popular foreign film and anything is possible. One thing that's definite is an entertaining, riotous romp through life, with Pepa (Maura) as the jilted mistress stealing the show. In Spanish with English subtitles, but the colorful images speak for themselves. For a foreign comedy, it sure had a lot of Americans seriously relating to it. Oscar-nominated as Best Foreign Language Film (Spain). Scheduled to be remade in English starring Jane Fonda.

Working Girl

BLOCKBUSTER CATEGORY: Comedy
STARRING: Melanie Griffith, Harrison Ford, Sigourney Weaver, Joan Cusack, Alec Baldwin
DIRECTED BY: Mike Nichols

The boss from Hell (Weaver) meets her match in the secretary (Griffith) determined to beat the odds and become an executive herself! Griffith's sincere quality and deft timing highlight her star-making role. Ford is excellent in a comic turn as her new boyfriend/business partner. Co-star Cusack as the brash, but loyal friend is hilarious. Carly Simon's theme, "Let The River Run," enhances the magical blend of performances. You won't be able to resist its jungle beat. Oscar-nominated for Best Picture, Actress (Griffith), Director (Nichols), Supporting Actress (Weaver) and Supporting Actress (Cusack).

OSCAR WIN: *Best Song ("Let The River Run")*

The Adventures Of Baron Munchausen
BLOCKBUSTER CATEGORY: Action/Adventure
STARRING: John Neville, Eric Idle, Oliver Reed, Sarah Polley
DIRECTED BY: Terry Gilliam

Baron Munchausen was the Middle Ages' most notorious liar, and his yarns - which few believed but everyone loved to hear - were so fantastic that three movies have been based on the Baron's life. The latest and most audacious of them is by former Monty Python member (and accomplished filmmaker) Terry Gilliam (who also made the dazzling 1985 fantasy, BRAZIL). The movie runs just over two hours, yet never lags for a second, as Gilliam and his star-studded cast (including, in marvelous bits, Sting and Robin Williams) spread out a visual smorgasbord that takes the Baron around the globe, into distant space, and back again. John Neville, who played a dagger-sharp Sherlock Holmes in 1965's A STUDY IN TERROR, is Munchausen. Oscar-nominated for Costumes, Art Direction, Special Effects and Makeup.

Batman
BLOCKBUSTER CATEGORY: Family
STARRING: Jack Nicholson, Michael Keaton, Kim Basinger,
Billy Dee Williams
DIRECTED BY: Tim Burton

"Ever danced with the devil in the pale moonlight?" Nicholson, as the Joker, plays it to the hilt. Michael Keaton in the title role and Kim Basinger as the sumptuous Vicki Vale also shine in this mesmerizing adaptation in the spirit of the original comic books. The elaborate production design is amazing.
OSCAR WIN: *Art Direction*

The Bear
BLOCKBUSTER CATEGORY: Family
STARRING: Bart, Douce, Jack Wallace, Andre Lacombe
DIRECTED BY: Jean-Jacques Annaud

A haunting outdoor adventure that tries something different and pulls it off. When a bear cub's mother is killed by hunters, the young animal must learn to survive on its own. Taking advantage of state-of-the-art resources and equipment available to modern filmmakers, director Annaud eavesdrops on the bear in its habitat - the spectacular wilds of Vancouver - with such skill that the movie's few staged sequences are undetectable. Oscar-nominated editing adds to the bear's "performance."

Born on the Fourth of July
BLOCKBUSTER CATEGORY: Drama
STARRING: Tom Cruise, Kyra Sedgwick, Carolyn Kova,
Willem Dafoe, Tom Berenger
DIRECTED BY: Oliver Stone

Cruise, in his most powerful role to date, plays real-life Vietnam veteran Ron Kovic, whose views on fighting for his country radically changed after going overseas and experiencing the unforgettable horrors of battle. It's a *tour de force* where Cruise remarkably conveys one man's conviction and rage. Dafoe is also magnificent in a supporting role as a suffering fellow veteran. Director Stone, whose PLATOON

(1986) focused on the 'Nam battlefields, expands his visions of life before and after in this explosive, graphic and moving masterpiece. Oscar-nominated for Best Actor (Cruise), Cinematography, Sound, Screenplay - adapted (Stone, Kovic).
OSCAR WINS: *Director (Stone), Film Editing*

Casualties of War

BLOCKBUSTER CATEGORY: Drama
STARRING: Michael J. Fox, Sean Penn, Don Harvey, Thuy Thu Le
DIRECTED BY: Brian De Palma

Gut-wrenching drama...literally. The rules were different in Vietnam, but a young soldier (Fox) can't forgive or forget his sergeant's (Penn) most inhumane crime, kidnapping and brutalizing an innocent Vietnamese girl (Thu Le). Fox conveys an emotional depth new to his screen characterizations and Penn has "hateful" down pat. Cheers to DePalma's slick, stylized direction as well.
A true story of 1966.

Cinema Paradiso

BLOCKBUSTER CATEGORY: Foreign
STARRING: Phillippe Noiret, Jacques Perrin, Salvatore Cascio
DIRECTED BY: Giuseppe Tornatore

The local movie palace is the hub of activity in a small Italian town in the years just after World War II. This Oscar-winner for Best Foreign Film (and many other awards internationally) views several years of small-town life through the eyes of a little boy, who is obsessed with movies, hangs around the village projectionist, and eventually takes over his job when the man is blinded in a fire. The notion of a movie about a character whose point of reference for everything in life - from girlfriends to war - is movies, hadn't been used since the earliest movies of France's "New Wave" directors of the 60's.
OSCAR WIN: *Best Foreign-Language Film*

Crimes and Misdemeanors

BLOCKBUSTER CATEGORY: Drama
STARRING: Woody Allen, Martin Landau, Anjelica Huston,
Alan Alda, Mia Farrow, Sam Waterston, Claire Bloom
DIRECTED BY: Woody Allen

Writer/director Allen's best work in years weaves the lives of two men in moral and personal dilemmas into a piercing, but funny movie. Allen's the neurotic nebbish in love with his untouchable dream (Farrow). Landau is the blackmailed philanderer pushed to the limits by his mistress (Huston). It's everything you'd expect from Woody and a little of the unexpected, too. Oscar-nominated for Best Director (Allen), Screenplay - original, Supporting Actor (Landau).

Dead Poets Society

BLOCKBUSTER CATEGORY: Drama
STARRING: Robin Williams, Robert Sean Leonard, Ethan Hawke,
Josh Charles
DIRECTED BY: Peter Weir

Rare is the serious flick released in summer, but this movie became a major hit. Williams, in his most subdued role, plays a prep school teacher, circa 1959, who teaches his students to "seize the moment" in life and to appreciate good poetry.

Weir is adept at applying faces to the screen with an artist's touch, then developing his characters into entirely interesting entities. Oscar-nominated for Best Picture, Actor (Williams) and Director (Weir).
OSCAR WIN: *Screenplay (Tom Shulman)*

Do the Right Thing
BLOCKBUSTER CATEGORY: Drama
STARRING: Danny Aiello, Ossie Davis, Ruby Dee, Spike Lee
DIRECTED BY: Spike Lee
Racial hostility boils over between blacks and Italians in Brooklyn. Aiello's pizza restaurant owner finds himself on one side of a neighborhood war in this tense drama. Lee (who wrote, produced, directed and co-stars) succeeded in delivering a stylistic and stirring movie that refuses to take sides - right to the very end. Oscar-nominated for Supporting Actor (Aiello), Screenplay.

Driving Miss Daisy
BLOCKBUSTER CATEGORY: Drama
STARRING: Morgan Freeman, Jessica Tandy, Dan Aykroyd
DIRECTED BY: Bruce Beresford
The character study of a 25-year relationship between a stubborn Jewish widow (Tandy) and her black chauffeur (Freeman). Race differences and social levels are submerged as their long-term friendship develops. A moving experience with dazzling work by the two leads and director Beresford. Oscar-nominated for Supporting Actor (Aykroyd), Cinematography.
OSCAR WINS: *Best Picture, Actor (Freeman), Actress (Tandy), Screenplay - adapted (Albert Uhry), Makeup*

Drugstore Cowboy
BLOCKBUSTER CATEGORY: Drama
STARRING: Matt Dillon, Kelly Lynch, James Le Gros,
          Heather Graham
DIRECTED BY: Gus Van Sant, Jr.
This gritty movie looks at a group of rebels from 1971. They're drug addicts who steal from pharmacies to feed their addictions. Dillon makes his character vividly real, amid director/co-writer Van Sant, Jr.'s carefully orchestrated scenarios. Lynch is also compelling as his devoted wife, as is William S. Burroughs, in a cameo, as an ex-priest-turned-junkie. Van Sant, Jr. never judges his characters; he lets them live by their own set of rules. They're somewhat sympathetic and in the age of "just say no," that's incredible. A true story.

Enemies, A Love Story
BLOCKBUSTER CATEGORY: Drama
STARRING: Angelica Huston, Ron Silver, Lena Olin
DIRECTED BY: Paul Mazursky
A haunting and original drama with a fascinating premise: In 1949, a New Yorker (Silver) who narrowly escaped the Nazi Holocaust leads a dual life with the devoted woman (Margaret Sophie Stein) who shielded him during the war and the free-spirited married woman (Olin) with whom he is having an affair. Then, unexpectedly, his first wife (Huston), who was presumed dead, shows up! Rather than turn this material into a murky soap opera, director and co-writer Paul

Mazursky (AN UNMARRIED WOMAN) delivers a movie of passion, drama and humor. Silver, who plays lawyer Alan Dershowitz in the recent REVERSAL OF FORTUNE, is perfect as a man struggling with his conscience. Oscar-nominated for Best Supporting Actress (Huston and Olin), Screenplay Adaptation (Mazursky and Roger L. Simon from the Isaac B. Singer novel).

The Fabulous Baker Boys

BLOCKBUSTER CATEGORY: Drama
STARRING: Jeff Bridges, Michelle Pfeiffer, Beau Bridges
DIRECTED BY: Steve Kloves

The Bridges are at their all-time best as piano-playing lounge lizards. Pfeiffer, however, steals the show as a reformed bad girl who joins the nightclub duo and lights up the screen. Her "Makin' Whoopee" solo is a sizzler in this drama of family bonds meant to be broken. Michael Ballhaus' moody cinematography enhances the marvelous performances. Oscar-nominated for Best Actress (Pfeiffer), Cinematography, Sound, Editing.

Field of Dreams

BLOCKBUSTER CATEGORY: Drama
STARRING: Kevin Costner, Ray Liotta, Amy Madigan,
James Earl Jones, Burt Lancaster
DIRECTED BY: Phil Alden Robinson

Costner hears a voice telling him to build a baseball field - a diamond in the rough - which allows him to recreate an historical World Series before coming to terms with his father, who passed away. The movie is full of heartfelt performances and gorgeous Iowa settings. A Frank Capra-esque film for the 80's that proved audiences can enjoy an "old-fashioned" movie. Oscar-nominated for Best Picture, Screenplay - adapted (Alden), Score (James Horner).

Glory

BLOCKBUSTER CATEGORY: Drama
STARRING: Matthew Broderick, Denzel Washington,
Morgan Freeman
DIRECTED BY: Edward Zwick

One of the top movies of its year, this is both an exciting Civil War battle adventure and a potent character study. Broderick plays a young Union officer placed in command of a company of black infantrymen. From the start, it's clear that the cast and director (Edward Zwick, co-creator of TV's *thirtysomething*) aren't simply going to rehash the cliches of blacks and whites struggling to get along together. The movie is based on a factual, little-known episode from the Civil War, and derives a portion of its structure from the Broderick character's letters home to his family. The closing battle is one of the most gripping ever dramatized in a movie.
OSCAR WINS: *Best Supporting Actor (Washington), Cinematography, Sound*

Henry V

BLOCKBUSTER CATEGORY: Drama
STARRING: Kenneth Branagh, Derek Jacobi, Brian Blessed,
Ian Holm
DIRECTED BY: Kenneth Branagh

More than just another screen version of Shakespeare's Henry V, this movie became an international must-see event because of the approach taken by its Oscar-nominated star and director(Branagh). Branagh transforms the familiar saga of the warrior king into a furiously exciting, blood-and-thunder battle spectacle that takes full advantage of the technical resources of modern moviemaking. A mesmerizing experience, with superb performances.
OSCAR WIN: *Costumes*

Indiana Jones and the Last Crusade
BLOCKBUSTER CATEGORY: Action/Adventure
STARRING: Harrison Ford, Sean Connery, Denholm Elliott, River Phoenix
DIRECTED BY: Steven Spielberg
A guaranteed thrill-a-minute, as Spielberg and producer George Lucas' trademark action extravaganza leaps from the screen. For this second sequel to RAIDERS OF THE LOST ARK (1981), Indiana (Ford) is joined by his father (Connery) in a courageous search for the Holy Grail. River Phoenix plays Indy as a boy in the exciting opening scene. Oscar-nominated for Score.
OSCAR WIN: *Sound Effects Editing*

The Little Mermaid
BLOCKBUSTER CATEGORY: Kids
STARRING: Voices of Jodi Benson, Pat Carroll, Samuel E. Wright, Buddy Hackett
DIRECTED BY: John Musker and Ron Clements
Hans Christian Andersen's classic becomes a palette of stunning color and song. Ariel (the title cutie) is a heroine who falls in love with a ship-wrecked prince. Possibly the best Disney-animated feature since 101 DALMATIONS (1961). The clever song score was written by the same team that penned the music for LITTLE SHOP OF HORRORS (1986).

The Little Thief
BLOCKBUSTER CATEGORY: Not available on video
STARRING: Charlotte Gainesbourg, Didier Bezace, Simon de la Brosse, Raoul Billery, Chantal Banlier
DIRECTED BY: Claude Miller
Based on a character conceived by the late Francois Truffaut, one of France's best moviemakers. A gamin named Janine (Gainsbourg) steals things regardless of the consequences; she's usually caught. She is also the victim - of stolen youth. Much of it is self-induced coming of age, especially her relationship with a married man in his 40's. A younger biker/rebel turns out to be more than a diversion. It's a masterful scrapbook of a larcenous young girl who doesn't seem to mind paying the price. Gainsbourg is excellent and director Miller has created a moving portrait that would do Truffaut proud.

My Left Foot
BLOCKBUSTER CATEGORY: Drama
STARRING: Daniel Day-Lewis, Brenda Fricker, Ray McAnally
DIRECTED BY: Jim Sheridan

An upbeat, warm and often funny movie based on the real-life story of a man whose biography, in the hands of lesser filmmakers, could have been bleak and depressing. Daniel Day-Lewis won an Oscar as Best Actor for his unforgettable portrayal of Christy Brown, cerebral palsy-afflicted son of a large Irish coal mining family, who overcomes his handicap to become a renowned painter. Heartfelt without being sentimental, tough without resorting to melodrama, this fresh and inspiring movie is consistently entertaining. Oscar-nominated for Best Picture, Director (Sheridan), Screenplay - adapted - (Sheridan and Shane Connoughton). OSCAR WINS: *Best Actor (Day-Lewis), Supporting Actress (Fricker)*

Parenthood

BLOCKBUSTER CATEGORY: Comedy
STARRING: Steve Martin, Mary Steenburgen, Dianne Wiest,
Jason Robards
DIRECTED BY: Ron Howard

Imagine a comedy in which every conceivable pitfall of being part of a large family is depicted in the setting of a weekend family reunion. There's the ne'er-do-well brother who always shows up in need of money; the overachiever yuppie who has his kids studying advanced math before they're out of diapers; the good-time slob who's just a big kid himself. Those characters are played by, in order, Tom Hulce, Rick Moranis and Steve Martin. Jason Robards is the family patriarch. The long-suffering wives are represented chiefly by Mary Steenburgen and Dianne Wiest. It's called PARENTHOOD because that's the stage of their lives that's obviously giving all of the characters the most trouble. Oscar-nominated for Screenplay.

Roger and Me

BLOCKBUSTER CATEGORY: Documentary
STARRING: Michael Moore, Roger Smith, Pat Boone,
Anita Bryant, Bob Eubanks
DIRECTED BY: Michael Moore

You wouldn't think anybody could make a funny movie whose springboard is the layoff of 40,000 Michigan auto workers. But that's just what Michael Moore has done with this masterpiece. Moore grew up in Flint, Mich., the birthplace of General Motors, and his amazement when GM, during one of its most profitable years, laid off its entire work force was matched only by the devastating effect on Flint itself. Moore decided to track down GM chairman Roger Smith, who successfully dodges Moore for most of the movie, as the hapless moviemaker and his crew are tossed out of office buildings, exclusive clubs, posh parties and so on. A must-see, with several priceless scenes you'll be talking about for days afterward.

Scandal

BLOCKBUSTER CATEGORY: Drama
STARRING: John Hurt, Joanne Whalley-Kilmer, Bridget Fonda
DIRECTED BY: Michael Caton-Jones

Compulsively watchable movie about one of the most notorious real-life sex scandals of modern times. The most amazing thing is that it took this long to get to the screen - but it was worth the wait. Ian McKellen plays British Cabinet Minister John Profumo, who is enjoying an affair with call girl Christine Keeler without realizing that she is simultaneously seeing a Soviet agent. John Hurt plays the social-climbing society hanger-on who introduces them all. This adult film, full of crisp, intelligent dialogue and its share of controversial scenes, gives a feel for the period and particularly the panic that resulted when the whole nasty story was leaked to the press.

sex, lies and videotape

BLOCKBUSTER CATEGORY: Drama
STARRING: James Spader, Andie MacDowell, Peter Gallagher, Laura San Giacomo
DIRECTED BY: Steven Soderbergh

A yuppie-lawyer (Gallagher) cheats on his beautiful wife (MacDowell) with her carefree sister (San Giacomo). His double standard shows, however, when a school chum (Spader) shows up with a camcorder and an affinity for MacDowell. Soderbergh won the Cannes Film Festival's highest honor for his first feature! Spader was also honored for his strong performance. Oscar-nominated for Best Screenplay - original (Soderbergh)

Steel Magnolias

BLOCKBUSTER CATEGORY: Drama
STARRING: Sally Field, Dolly Parton, Shirley MacLaine, Daryl Hannah, Olympia Dukakis, Julia Roberts, Tom Skerritt
DIRECTED BY: Herbert Ross

Six of today's top actresses star in a warm, deeply felt comedy-drama that compares favorably to TERMS OF ENDEARMENT (1983). The local beauty parlor in a tiny Louisiana town provides a comfortable setting for them to share their lives and loves, dreams and disappointments with each other. . . and with us. Hannah is especially touching as the town's ugly duckling, and Roberts is excellent in one of her last supporting roles before the smash hit, PRETTY WOMAN (1990). More than just a glossy tearjerker, this fine film also allows room for some leading male stars - including Sam Shepard and Tom Skerritt - to shine. Oscar-nominated for Best Supporting Actress (Roberts).

The War of the Roses

BLOCKBUSTER CATEGORY: Comedy
STARRING: Kathleen Turner, Michael Douglas, Danny DeVito
DIRECTED BY: Danny DeVito

This dark comedy delves into the other side of marriage: divorce. Love is only a faint memory and the spouses are, literally, at each other's throats. Douglas and Turner act out this ultimate battle of the sexes with expertise and DeVito turns in an uncharacteristically friendly performance. DeVito solidified his standing as an innovative director with this one. The ending is an unexpected stunner.

When Harry Met Sally . . .

BLOCKBUSTER CATEGORY: Comedy
STARRING: Billy Crystal, Meg Ryan, Carrie Fisher, Bruno Kirby
DIRECTED BY: Rob Reiner

Can a man and a woman just be friends? Ryan and Crystal try to sustain friendship, but there's one problem: they're falling in love. Both are extraordinary and Ryan has one of the funniest scenes in cinema history simulating ecstasy in a deli. Director Reiner delivers another heart-tugging gem. Oscar-nomination for Original Screenplay (Nora Ephron).

Avalon

BLOCKBUSTER CATEGORY: Drama
STARRING: Aidan Quinn, Elizabeth Perkins, Armin Mueller-Stahl,
　　　　　Joan Plowright
DIRECTED BY: Barry Levinson

A richly absorbing and entertaining movie about the lives of several generations of an Eastern European family who migrate to America shortly before the 1920's. They settle in Baltimore, and the movie follows the tumultuous events in their lives over the next several decades. Director/writer Barry Levinson, who gave us RAIN MAN and GOOD MORNING, VIETNAM, based this film - like his earlier DINER and TIN MEN - on his own recollections of his family, as he grew up in Baltimore. At the films center is the relationship between Aidan Quinn (portraying the character modeled upon Levinson's real-life father) and Armin Mueller-Stahl, as powerful a father-son relationship as the movies have depicted in many years. The entire movie is beautifully acted - Lou Jacobi is a comic delight as a cantankerous uncle who arrives late for every family event - and Levinson captures the period setting with meticulous detail.

Dances With Wolves

BLOCKBUSTER CATEGORY: Westerns
STARRING: Kevin Costner, Mary McDonnell, Graham Greene,
　　　　　Rodney A. Grant
DIRECTED BY: Kevin Costner

Box office superstar Kevin Costner turned director with this magnificent adventure, in which he plays a cavalry soldier who takes up with the Sioux Indians in their struggle for survival. The movie opens with Costner an inexperienced recruit who asks to be sent on a mission to the far west, "to see the frontier, before it's gone". Instead of a pioneer settlement, he finds only the majestic, western plains - and a nation of Sioux, who eventually accept him as one of them, even allowing him to marry one of their women (Mary McDonnell). Trouble results when Costner must confront his identity as a member of the U.S. Army, which has embarked on a ruthless push west. Stunningly photographed and enormously moving, this film places Costner in the top ranks of actors-turned-director.

The Godfather Part III

BLOCKBUSTER CATEGORY: Drama
STARRING: Al Pacino, Diane Keaton, Talia Shire, Andy Garcia,
　　　　　Bridget Fonda, Eli Wallach, Joe Mantegna
DIRECTED BY: Francis Coppola

"Just when I think I'm out, they pull me back in", shouts a furious Michael Corleone (Pacino) midway through this spectacular, long-awaited follow-up to the first two GODFATHER classics. As Michael struggles to make peace with the Catholic Church and what remains of his family - pulling himself out of gambling, drug and vice interests - the "new" Mafia rushes in with bloodthirsty vigor to take over. Just as Robert DeNiro shot to stardom in GODFATHER II, this time Andy Garcia has the movie's key supporting role as the illegitimate son of hot-tempered Sonny Corleone, who turns out to be a feisty chip-off-the-old-block. Pacino and Garcia lock horns in the movie's most potent scenes. Packed with gangland assassinations, gunfights and acts of vengeance, the movie also weaves a love story into the brew (between Michael's daughter, played by Sofia Coppola, and Garcia) and restores director-writer Francis Coppola to vintage form.

Goodfellas

BLOCKBUSTER CATEGORY: Drama
STARRING: Robert DeNiro, Ray Liotta, Joe Pesci,
Lorraine Bracco
DIRECTED BY: Martin Scorsese

A searing, contemporary crime thriller - incredibly, almost as funny as it is unpredictably violent - with Oscar-worthy performances by DeNiro, Liotta and Pesci as small-time New York gangsters. Based on Nicholas Pileggi's book, "*Wiseguy*" (the title was changed to avoid confusion with the TV series), the movie follows the Liotta character from childhood as a runner for a local hoodlum (Paul Sorvino) to young adulthood in the early 70's, to his downfall in the 80's, as his cronies begin to drop like flies in a mob war. DeNiro is superb as always, and Pesci - who made his first screen impact as Jake LaMotta's brother in Scorsese's RAGING BULL - contributes a powerhouse performance as an out-of-control, over-age punk with a terrifying violent streak. Another directorial *tour de force* from Scorsese, the distinctive talent behind MEAN STREETS, RAGING BULL and TAXI DRIVER.

The Grifters

BLOCKBUSTER CATEGORY: Drama
STARRING: Anjelica Huston, John Cusack,
Annette Bening
DIRECTED BY: Stephen Frears

Here is a tough, no-nonsense, brass-knuckled crime movie - the kind they supposedly don't make anymore. A "grifter" is a con artist, and the experts at that trade in this furious little movie are a mother (Huston), her estranged son (Cusack), and the young man's floozy of a girlfriend (Bening), who spend the movie variously working together and outfoxing each other. It's based on a book by legendary pulp-crime novelist Jim Thompson (*The Getaway*), and the screenplay was written by contemporary author Donald E. Westlake, who also scripted the cult hit, THE STEPFATHER.

Men Don't Leave

BLOCKBUSTER CATEGORY: Drama
STARRING: Jessica Lange, Arliss Howard, Joan Cusack,
Chris O'Donnell
DIRECTED BY: Paul Brickman

Jessica Lange stars as a widowed mom with two sons in this second movie by the director of the Tom Cruise comedy, RISKY BUSINESS. Lange delivers another of her assured, realistic performances as a woman trying to deal with having no husband, no money and two sons to raise. Director Brickman opts for humor instead of soap opera and introduces a nurse, played by *Saturday Night Live* veteran Joan Cusack, who seduces the older of the boys. If the younger son looks familiar, that's because he's Charlie Korso, who plays "The Kid" in Warren Beatty's DICK TRACY.

Miller's Crossing

BLOCKBUSTER CATEGORY: Drama
STARRING: Albert Finney, Gabriel Byrne, John Turturro
DIRECTED BY: Joel and Ethan Coen

In the year that most people will remember for giving us GODFATHER III and GOODFELLAS - two movies about the traditional Mafia - the makers of BLOOD SIMPLE and RAISING ARIZONA came up with this wild thriller about Irish-American gangsters. Albert Finney delivers a bravura performance as an Irish mob lord whose violent ways, and his control of his organization, die hard. Although the movie contains plenty of gunplay and killing, it also recognizes the gallows humor inherent in the high-stakes world of organized crime. The film was featured as an American entry in the New York Film Festival.

Misery

BLOCKBUSTER CATEGORY: Mystery/Suspense
STARRING: James Caan, Kathy Bates, Richard Farnsworth
DIRECTED BY: Rob Reiner

A knockout of a suspense movie, with two bravura performances by James Caan and Kathy Bates. Caan plays a bestselling novelist who's en route to deliver his latest manuscript to a publisher when his car veers of the road during a snowstorm and he is injured. Bates, an ex-nurse, rescues Caan and takes him to her isolated mountain cabin to treat his wounds. There, she proclaims herself his "number one fan,"and Caan realizes to his mounting terror, that she has no intention of letting him leave. Although it's based on a novel by shock author Stephen King, this is far more than a conventional horror film. The claustrophobic setting is used to maximum advantage by director Reiner (who also made STAND BY ME, one of the best of the earlier King movies), and there are flashes of dark humor along with the expected chills. Oscar-winning screenwriter William Goldman (ALL THE PRESIDENT'S MEN) wrote the script. Richard Farnsworth, as a rural sheriff, and Lauren Bacall, as Caan's agent, contribute memorable support.

INDEX

INDEX

INDEX

INDEX

INDEX

INDEX

INDEX

INDEX